TWO KOREAS IN DEVELOPMENT

TWO KOREAS IN DEVELOPMENT

A Comparative Study of Principles and Strategies of Capitalist and Communist Third World Development

Byoung-Lo Philo Kim

Transaction Publishers
New Brunswick (U.S.A.) and London (U.K.)

Library of Congress Catalog Number: 91-8160
ISBN: 0–88738–437–4
Printed in the United States of America

Library of Congress Cataloging-in-Publication Data

Kim, Byoung-Lo Philo.
    Two Koreas in development: a comparative study of principles and
strategies of capitalist and communist Third World development /
Byoung-Lo Philo Kim.
      p. cm.
    Includes bibliographical references and index.
    ISBN 0–88738–437–4
    1. Korea (North)—Economic conditions. 2. Korea (North)—
Social conditions. 3. Korea (South)—Economic conditions.
4. Korea (South)—Social conditions. 5. Economic development.
6. Capitalism. 7. Communism. I. Title.
HC467.K45   1991   91–8160
338.9519—dc20   CIP

This book is dedicated
to my parents

Contents

Tables and Figures

Tables

ix

Figures

Preface

The year 1990 was a monumental moment in postwar Korean history as well as in the modern world. Gorbachev's *perestroika* had no less significant an impact on Northeast Asia than on Eastern Europe. It has radically changed the old order in the Korean peninsula. The Soviet Union, which had been its original sponsor and operator, withdrew its support from North Korea. The Soviet Union's revolutionary "betrayal" cast North Korea adrift as it held on to its old system. Soon after consolidating its relationship with China, North Korea found another dependable friend, Japan, negotiating colonial reparation of $8 billion. And with the United States, North Korea has had diplomatic contact more than fourteen times. At the same time, South Korea normalized relations with the Soviet Union. At the Moscow Summit in December 1990, South Korea received a pledge of peace and security in the Korean peninsula from the old enemy who had been involved in the Korean War and in the shooting of KAL Flight 007. For this promise, South Korea had to grace her new ally with $3 billion.

Gorbachev's Asian drama appears to have created a new research agenda showing how communism and capitalism in Northeast Asia could be successfully restructured or redirected in a new world order. It is evident, however, that communism has so far fared poorly with respect to capitalism in Northeast Asia. The systemic inadequacies of communism have led to a general feeling of relative deprivation rooted in the disparity between "material production" and private consumption. In comparative terms, private consumption has deteriorated despite an increase in means of production.

The relative merits of capitalism and communism in national development have long been argued in the sociology of development. Dependency theory has suggested that Third World development should be cut off from the world capitalist system, and that self-reliant economies should be established for development to occur. Modernization theory has, for its part, suggested that capitalism is the fulfillment of developmental impulses. To test these claims, "dependent" capitalist South Korea has been compared with "self-reliant" communist North Korea. Their artificial division, imposed in 1945 upon a homogeneous nation, provides a unique laboratory for comparing divergent development processes undertaken by conflicting social systems, using different principles and strategies.

This book is a modest attempt to illuminate the possibilities and limitations of capitalist and communist development in the Third World. The experience of the two Koreas' development reveals a reverse of the phenomenon dependency theory posits: "Dependent" capitalist South Korea has outperformed "self-reliant" communist North Korea by three times in per capita GNP output; exceeding it in per capita GNP since 1976, in per capita NMP since 1980, and in standard of living since 1971. The North Korean self-reliance model achieved far more successful growth during its first fifteen years through radical transformation of political institutions and through mass mobilization techniques. However, it has since been faced with numerous structural limitations on sustained development: the unavailability of foreign capital and technology, inefficient allocation of labor force and capital, low motivation from the exhaustion of moral incentive, serious military defense burdens in both personnel and fiscal terms, low aspiration from strict income equality at low income levels, and social rigidity from strict controls on political freedom and civil liberties. All of these structural characteristics contrast strikingly with South Korea's selective imitation principle and export-oriented strategy.

The experience of the two Koreas suggests that the solution to underdevelopment may not be a simple withdrawal from the world capitalist system, nor the oppressive mobilization of economic and sociopolitical forces. Rather, there is a growing realization that exclusionary theories need modification in the light of special historical and sociological circumstances such as those found in the Korean experiences. In this way, the special circumstance of one nation may help put in perspective current sociological theories about development.

The new world order has reactivated the inter-Korean dialogue in the peninsula. There is no doubt that the dialogue fosters inter-Korean reconciliation. So far, however, both Koreas have not met to look at each other's treasure. Rather, they have met to look for the outside vanity. The dialogue has been necessary for North Korea to secure favorable economic assistance from Japan and other capitalist countries. For South Korea, it has been necessary to have its political legitimacy confirmed by the South Korean people. My feeling is that, while more political exchanges than ever are expected, protracted competition between the two Koreas for economic development, legitimacy, and recognition, will likely continue in this newly emerging world order. My hope is that this book offers a helpful understanding of modern capitalism and communism through the experiences of the two Koreas, and that it generates a greater research interest in the comparative study of capitalism and communism as well.

Acknowledgments

I would like to express my sincere appreciation to those who helped make this publication possible. To Professor Irving Louis Horowitz, I owe the greatest debt of gratitude for his guidance and advice. I am grateful to him for his knowledge of social science, hard-working integrity, and shepherding, which have helped my crude ideas develop into a well-manicured book. I heartily appreciate his recommendation and encouragement of this book to be published. I also thank Professor Anne Foner for her intellectual stimulation, continuing guidance in the sociological realm, and detailed correction of my English. Her careful concern, criticism, comments, and advice were immensely valuable in completing this book. I am thankful to Professor Young C. Kim at George Washington University for his early guidance, valuable comments, and helpful advice including methodological assistance. I heartily appreciate his enormous encouragement. And my thanks also to Professors Peter Li, Jonghoe Yang, and Roy U.T. Kim for their comments, suggestions, and thoughtful concern.

I am greatly indebted to Transaction Publishers for awarding me a chance to be a Fellow during my research. Their help, both academic and financial, were indispensable in completing and publishing this book. The encouragement, concern, and help of each member of the Transaction staff will not be forgotten. I am also grateful to the Department of Sociology at Rutgers University and Professor Allan Horwitz, chair of the Department, for financial assistance during the research.

Finally, I am grateful to my family in South Korea for their support and encouragement. They have prayed for this moment for more than a decade. This is the fruits of their prayers. I thank my wife, Helen, for reading the manuscript and her advice and counsel. I am also grateful for her endurance in taking care of our two children, Grace and James, while I neglected family work when writing this book. And, for all of the foregoing, I thank God.

Abbreviations and Acronyms

ACDA	Arms Control and Disarmament Agency
ACE	Advanced Capitalist Economies
AGIL	Adaptation-Goal Attainment-Integration-Latent Pattern Maintenance
AID	Agency for International Development
AMG	American Military Government
BA	Bureaucratic Authoritarianism
CDU	Christian Democratic Union
CIA	Central Intelligence Agency
CMEA	Council for Mutual Economic Assistance
COMECON	Council for Mutual Economic Assistance
CPEs	Central Planned Economies
CSU	Christian Socialist Union
DCRK	Democratic Confederal Republic of Koryo
DJP	Democratic Justice Party
DLP	Democratic Liberal Party
DMZ	Demilitarized Zone
DNP	Democratic Nationalist Party
DP	Democratic Party
DPRK	Democratic People's Republic of Korea
DRP	Democratic Republican Party
DRV	Democratic Republic of Vietnam
EC	European Community
EG	East Germany
EIU	Economic Intelligence Unit
EPB	Economic Planning Board
FAO	Food and Agriculture Organization
FDI	Foreign Direct Investment
FDP	Free Democratic Party
FEER	Far Eastern Economic Review
FEZ	Free Economic Zone

FLPH	Foreign Language Publishing House
FPAB	Five Provinces Administration Bureau
FRG	Federal Republic of Germany
GDP	Gross Domestic Product
GDR	German Democratic Republic
GNP	Gross National Product
GSP	Gross Social Product
IISS	International Institute for Strategic Studies
JETRO	Japanese Economic and Trade Research Organization
JMG	Japanese Military Government
KAL	Korean Air Lines
KCIA	Korea Central Intelligence Agency
KCP	Korean Communist Party
KDI	Korea Development Institute
KDP	Korea Democratic Party
KMT	Kuomintang
KPA	Korean People's Republic
KPG	Korean Provisional Government
KPPC	Korean Provisional People's Committee
KWP	Korean Workers Party
LP	Liberal Party
MNCs	Multinational Corporations
NCU	National Conference for Unification
NDP	New Democratic Party
NDRP	New Democratic Republican Party
NES	New Economic System
NI	National Income
NICs	Newly Industrializing Countries
NK	North Korea
NKP	New Korea Party
NKWP	North Korean Workers Party
NMP	Net Material Product
NNP	Net National Product
NPP	New People's Party
NS	National Society
NUB	National Unification Board
PDP	Peace Democratic Party
PP	People's Party

PPP	Purchasing Power Parity
RDP	Reunification Democratic Party
ROK	Republic of Korea
SCNR	Supreme Council for National Reconstruction
SED	Socialist Unity Party of Germany
SIPRI	Stockholm International Peace Research Institute
SK	South Korea
SKLP	South Korean Labor Party
SMI	Small- and Medium-sized Industry
SMRC	South Manchurian Railway Company
SOC	Social Overhead Capital
SPA	Supreme People's Assembly
SPC	State Planning Commission
SPD	Socialist Democratic Party
STE	Soviet-Type Economies
STR	Scientific Technological Revolution
UN	United Nations
UNKRA	United Nations Korean Reconstruction Agency
US	United States
USSR	Union of Soviet Socialist Republics
WG	West Germany

1

Introduction

Forty-six years have passed since the division of Korea was imposed by the United States and the Soviet Union at the conclusion of the Second World War in 1945. The Soviet forces occupied the area north of the 38th parallel, and the American forces the region south of it. The occupation was initially made as a temporary measure for the purpose of receiving the Japanese surrender in the Korean peninsula as it had been defined by the Yalta and Potsdam Conferences. Although the occupation ended Japanese colonialism in Korea, like many temporary measures, it led to the emergence of two separate political systems in one land. This, in turn, led to the adoption of two entirely divergent and competing developmental systems. The South followed an American capitalist economic model, and the North a Soviet communist economic model under the conditions of Stalinism. Separate development and extraordinary reconstruction were begun by both sides. The two Koreas have grown apart as their developmental systems followed strikingly different models, not only of American capitalism and Soviet communism, but of democracy and authoritarianism under Cold War conditions.

The unusual division of Korea in 1945 created a laboratory of the political economies of capitalism and socialism in smaller, independent nations. The wide disparity in the developmental patterns and outcomes between South and North Korea offers an unusual opportunity for a comparative study of Third World national development. Their development experiences over the past four and half decades highlights the possibilities and limitations of capitalist and Communist development in the Third World.

1

The purpose of this book is to analyze and compare North and South Korea's development experience from the postwar period until the present in order to elucidate the strengths and weaknesses of capitalism and communism in Third World national development. Holding as a constant the "take-off" period (1945), it seeks to compare the two models of economic development employed in the South (political pluralism and capitalism) vis-à-vis the North (political monism and communism). Specifically, this study first seeks to analyze and compare the socioeconomic performances of South and North Korea. The former has outpaced the latter since the mid-1960s; and surpassed it since the mid-1970s. Second, it also aims to locate the underlying economic and structural reasons and sources for the uneven development in the two Koreas, which revolve around the South's outward-looking, imitative strategies vs. the North's self-reliant stance. Third, it seeks to examine political, military, and social causes of the uneven development and to assess their impact upon the possibilities of integration of the two states. Finally, my work will discuss the theoretical and empirical implications of the two Korean developments for confirming and/or modifying extant theories of Third World development.

This book attempts to show that the reasons for the South's overall success vis-à-vis the North's failure are multiple: (1) the state's disciplined guidance including the maximum use of the large proletariat and competent bourgeois class; (2) the maximum utilization of Western capital and technology; (3) success in expanding foreign markets and foreign exchange; (4) careful allocation of industrial investment (both capital and labor); (5) a policy of incentives based on a moral/material combination rather than moral exhortation; (6) a lower military defense burden; and (7) higher income level. Similar social performance in education, urbanization, and health care disguise the quality and results. The social developments exclusive to South Korea, such as the growth of a new middle class, multiple political parties, Christian religion, and a large service sector have also contributed to South Korea's economic success.

The success of North Korea vis-à-vis South Korea during the very early period of 1945–65 is credited to (1) political consolidation in the North; (2) early equalization through the socialization of all industries and the collectivization of land; (3) mass mobilization strategies; and (4) moral incentive policies. However, the measures that North Korea pursued in its early years do not work for economic development in the long run because, although they prove advantageous at the early stage of development where the development can be achieved by expanded utilization of natural resources and unemployed labor, they fall behind in productivity and efficiency at the later stage of intensive development where productivity must be raised through more advanced technology. Moreover, mass mobilization exhausts the motivation to increase productivity; the strict equalization of rewards brings about low expectations. North Korea's persistence in self-reliant strategies had its roots in the ideology of Stalinist communism, the revival of the traditional "Korean exclusionism," and the xenophobic consequences of Japanese colonialism and the Korean War.

Background

The relative merits of capitalist-open versus Communist-closed development have long been debated in the classical literature of the sociology of development from Marx to Weber. The debate became particularly acute over the problem of Third World development. In criticizing capitalist development in the Third World, dependency theorists have argued that for various reasons little or no further development is possible for Third World countries within the constraints of the world capitalist system (Wallerstein 1989, 1984; Amin et al. 1982; Frank 1981; Chirot 1977). Economic underdevelopment leads to an internally uneven development in the production system, class structure, and political processes. They have suggested, implicitly or explicitly, that the presently capitalist Third World must therefore "close off" and establish "self-reliance" in order to be developed. "Except for a few odd cases in the early stages of industrialization," Chirot wrote, "it is better for an economy to close itself off from the world (capitalist) system in order to nurture its infant industries" (Chirot, 1977:204).

The experiences of the two Koreas' development reveal the reverse phenomenon of what such forms of dependency theory assert. The nondependent socialist alternative of North Korea does not seem very promising. Autarkic development of North Korea appears to have been associated with stagnation and more or less complete dependency on the Soviet Union. The rapid development of South Korea has shown that successful development can be achieved through openness to the capitalist world economy. This book tests basic theorems in the sociology of development in general in the light of Korean development. It is a test of modernization, developmental, and dependency theories, and attempts to answer which is more adequate under what conditions and why.

The Korean case has been widely touched upon as a key test case for the dependency argument. The artificial division created a laboratory of political economies. South Korea has taken a more dependent path than the North: it went all out to increase export production for the global market and thoroughly integrated itself into international capitalism. South Korea today, despite a late awakening, is emerging as a major industrial country in the Pacific region—preempting world markets for steel and shipbuilding and making important inroads into the semiconductor and auto industries. This achievement has given rise to admiration for "the (South) Korean model." Development theorists point to South Korea as living proof that capitalism works; that integration into the world market, on the basis of comparative advantage, is the only way forward. Sometimes, however, the model is criticized by dependency theorists as "a house built on sand," involving an enormous foreign debt burden, the longest average work week in the industrial capitalist world, vulnerability to the international economic crisis, and rule by military dictatorship.

North Korea has taken *juche*, or "self-reliance," as its motto and boasts of having built an industrial economy on the basis of its own raw materials, oriented to, and powered by, its domestic market. Not content with withdrawing from the world capitalist system, it has only joined CMEA (Council for Mutual Economic Assistance, or COMECON) selectively. North Korea, which started with vigor and surpassed the South in the early period, is now suffering from international "default" and "moratorium." No country in the world lives with such a wide gap between its own self-image as a socialist "paradise on earth" and the view of most of the outside world that North Korea is a bleak workhouse ruled by a megalomaniac, Kim Il Sung. Despite the fact that its political system is one of the most dreadful ever constructed in the name of socialism, North Korea has been praised by some socialist-oriented countries such as Tanzania, Congo, Libya, Cuba, Iran, and Zimbabwe, as the model of agricultural self-sufficiency and rapid, self-reliant industrialization with virtually no linkage with the world capitalist economy. Both claims and counter-claims of the two Koreas are examined in this book.

Before the division, the two Koreas had been a homogeneous nation that shared the same race and ethnicity. They share, in addition, the same language, and similar historical and cultural backgrounds. How is it that there should have been such amazingly diverse outcomes given a common postwar starting point? What are the similarities and differences of the two developments? What kind of strategies have the two Koreas pursued for their development? What are the factors which have brought about the results? And what have been the costs and benefits of pursuing each model?

Considering the amount of interest in both Koreas, it is surprising that little has been written on the comparative development of South Korea and North Korea. The prevailing mode of scholarly inquiry into Korean development is largely monosystemic and exclusive rather than comparative and structural. The majority of studies in the literature tends to focus on one of the two systems, particularly on the South. There are many valuable works done on South Korean development: Michell (1988), Petri (1988), H. Koo (1987), H.C. Lim (1985), Jones and Sakong (1980), Kuznets (1977), Cole and Lyman (1971). There are some valuable studies on North Korean development: P.S. Lee (1982, 1972), Bunge (1981), Halliday (1981), C. S. Lee (1978), Brun and Hersh (1976), I.J. Kim (1975), J. S. Chung (1974), J. K. Lee (1974), Scalapino and Lee (1972), D.S. Suh (1970), Scalapino (1960). But the comparative perspective has lagged.

The comparative study of two Koreas' development has expanded recently. It was initially stimulated by the CIA report on the economic race between the North and the South (CIA, 1978). Before the report, the comparative study of Korea had been dominated by the overflow-ing research on political issues, in particular, on the political unifica-tion policies. J.A. Kim (1975), Y.C. Kim and Halpern (1977), and H. J. Kim (1977) provided valuable political comparisons. Nevertheless, many political studies were often obsessed by zeal for political unifi-cation abstracted from social and economic development on the two sides. The political study of the two Koreas was sometimes restricted by the control of government of vital information.

After the CIA report was released, some specialists on North Korean development began to turn their focus to the comparison with the South. Chung (1980), B.Y. Lee (1980), Cumings (1984, 1981), Kihl (1984), Foster-Carter (1985), Clough (1987), Halliday (1987), and Gregor (1990) are the most knowledgeable scholars on the comparative development in South and North Korea. Their studies are valuable for their own purposes, but they seem to be inconclusive with respect to the analysis and comparison of the two developmental systems. The focus that the studies dealt with in regard to the development is somewhat narrow: Cumings discusses it before the Korean War; B.Y. Lee compares economic sectoral performances; and Foster-Carter covers the dependency issue. Chung, Kihl, and Halliday provide valuable comparisons of economic performance, but they lack the analytic framework necessary for a full-scale comparision of capitalism and communism as operating economic systems. Keynote principles of rapid industrialization, effects of war, patterns of socialization and land reform, and the roles of foreign capital, trade, income equality, social class, democracy, and so forth, in development have not been discussed or adequately compared in previous studies. This book seeks to remedy this deficit.

Sociology of Development and Comparative Study

The sociology of development as an academic enterprise came into its own with the emergence of new Third World nations (Horowitz, 1972). As nationalist and revolutionary movements in the Third World gathered force, a master paradigm for promoting a specific kind of development through state intervention and international assistance, mostly from the advanced capitalist countries, was adopted in this new world from ideas later conceptualized as modernization theory. Modernization theory assumes that all countries must develop along a single upward slope of the tradition-modern continuum to become roughly like the United States—the idealized model and ultimate goal of development. In this theory development was identified with capitalism. To be developed, nations had to identify and remove social and ideological obstacles. Underdevelopment was regarded as the result of a country's deficient value system and economic structure. Such transformation was, in essence, the transfer of Western technology and rationality in order to increase production without radical change of class structure. Modernization produces a more highly motivated population and better satisfies the demands of a literate, skilled population, which would not tolerate the kinds of inequality typical of older, traditional monarchies and empires.

Many newly created countries in Asia, Africa, and Latin America have tried to achieve modernization with great vigor. Their experience to date has often revealed the disparity between the myth of development and democracy and the reality of uneven development and authoritarianism. Underdevelopment in the Third World, in particular, seemed to lead to the emergence of communism in several states. The way in which socialist societies have been developed fit the Parsons' AGIL system in which Marxism-Leninism performs the function of pattern maintenance at the apex of the hierarchy (Lane 1976). Although the failure of modernization led to communist development, the idea of modernization certainly influenced the communist developmental processes, particularly in the area of military build-up.

Since the sixties, the widespread emergence of authoritarian, totalitarian, and military regimes in the Third World has led to an academic reconsideration of modernization theory. The long-cherished dream of modernization was fading. Oppressive regimes were established not only in the underdeveloped countries, but in highly industrialized countries as well. For an explanation of this, attention turned to Marxist perspectives. The revival and renewal of Marxist theories placed a new emphasis upon political economy, class structure, and the dynamics of capital accumulation within a global matrix. The dependency perspective challenged the modernization perspective as a dominant paradigm in the study of Third World development. Dependency theorists have argued that Third World development is not simply a matter of removing internal obstacles by introducing advanced values, institutions, capital, and technology. Rather, the real obstacles lie in the external dependent relations of these countries with advanced capitalist countries. In this sense, the role of capitalism and communism in the process of Third World development has been highlighted by dependency theorists.

The autarkic way of development was suggested by dependency theorists as the logical alternative for development in this situation. They claimed that the main obstacle to development of the Third World is capitalist "imperialism." The obstacle should be removed; that is, the imperialist expansion should be stopped and the revolutionary socialist way should be adopted. The socialist alternative was regarded mainly as self-reliant development by dependency theorists.

Dependency theory was criticized by the Marxist "mode of production" theorists in that it focused extensively on capitalist "imperialism" in which "socialism" was minimized (Brenner 1977). Unlike classical Marxists, those theorists of dependency/world system, such as Frank and Wallerstein, see capitalism as a world system of international trade, investment and division of labor, which dates from the sixteenth century. This is a system of exploitation of one area by another. In contrast, classical Marxists recognize the progressive role of capitalism in developing the forces of production. Capitalism, in their view, creates the material preconditions for a better (socialist) society, as well as the class forces that will bring it about. Since dependency theorists assert that the Third World is exploited by the "core" countries in the capitalist world system, the logical alternative for development in the Third World is not socialism, but autarky. Dependency theory tells us much more about what is wrong and why than about what is correct and how it is achieved.

Dependency theory is encumbered with further problems. First of all, the theory has not been able to offer adequate explanations of recent economic development in the Third World. In seeming contradiction of dependency theory's contention, Asian and Latin American Newly Industrializing Countries (NICs) have achieved successful development while opened to the capitalist world economy, though, at least until recently, political democratization does not appear to have come with development (Lim 1985, Evans 1979, O'Donnell 1973). Asian NICs also achieved moderate income equality. These countries, especially in the 1980s, have been reshaped into a "semi-periphery," which is used as an explanatory "limbo" in dependency theory. Moreover, its analysis focuses only on dependency as an American phenomenon, with scant attention paid to the Soviet Union. American imperialism is viewed as the source of all evil in the developmental process. And finally while dependency theorists suggest an ideological substitution of public enterprise for private enterprise as a mechanism for solving the problem, they pay little attention to problems of incentive, corruption, and innovation that are commonplace problems of Communist economies.

The classical Marxist theory, emphasizing the mode of production, has been criticized in that, unlike its prediction, the revolutionary process it assumes is associated with the early stages of capitalist industrial development rather than the later stages (Gidden, 1973:152-3). It grows out of the situation of underdevelopment. Kautsky (1968) discussed why the Communist development model tends to appeal to the Third World. He has explained that it is because the Soviet experience of backwardness in the post-revolutionary years seems sufficiently similar to the recent history of underdeveloped countries that it could appear a relevant development model to Third World countries. As in the Soviet Union, communism or socialism in the Third World did not spring from the rotting corpse of a fully developed capitalism— a capitalism that would eventually fall prey to its own internal contradictions, overthrown by a revolutionary movement led by a radicalized working class. It seems rather to have been, in part, a consequence of the expansionism and machinations of the Soviet Union and its allies.

Modernization theorists have generally shown little interest in Communist societies, thinking that the world is still dominated by a capitalist world economy in which the communist societies are somehow marginal and unimportant. Dependency/world system theorists have therefore focused only on the problems of the capitalist Third World, not on the socialist, supposing that the capitalist one will ultimately be transformed into the communist one and that Communist societies have, in any case, transcended the problematic capitalist stage. In some cases, it has been presumed that the Third World has adopted a "third way" of development, which is supposed to avoid the pitfalls of both Western capitalism and Soviet-type socialism. Although this notion contains certain truths, it still incorporates in great degree the essentials of the two competing ideologies. In reality, the Third World has been deeply involved in the arena of a First World and Second World struggle (Horowitz 1982, ix). The Third World today follows, officially or nonofficially, either a capitalist or Communist (or, socialist) development model.

The postwar decade was characterized by a radical realignment of the balance of economic and political power, with the ascendancy of the United States as the dominant power of the capitalist world and the concomitant consolidation of the power of the Soviet Union and the victory of the Chinese Communist Party. In that period the powerful resurgence of national liberation movements and the dismantling of the colonial system became central. Historical evolution was presented in terms of movement from colonialism to independence. The newly born nations were especially vulnerable to involvement in the ideological conflict of the superpowers (Shulman 1986) and national liberations took one of two directions. There were countries where liberation took the form of a radical break with the framework of world capitalism and with an effective social revolution of varying characteristics and internal dynamics. Independence movements in other countries did not try to break with the institutions and the international framework of the capitalist world or radically overturn their own class structure. The former followed various forms of socialism and the latter adopted capitalism.

The division of Korea into two ideologically opposing camps is a reflection of the divided world at large. The nature of the separate development of the two Koreas does not appear to fit any of the tenets of the three theories discussed so far. The autarkic way of North Korean development has not produced sustained developmental results. North Korea, which achieved rapid growth in the very early period, is now suffering from internal stagnation and international backwardness. It seems to have created another kind of dependency on the Soviet Union, owing much to Soviet finance and technology.

South Korea has made great progress in industrialization, depending heavily upon foreign capital, technology, and trade. Its industrialization has produced an accumulation of capital and a complex differentiation of productive structure. During the course of rapid industrialization, however, South Korea has suffered an authoritarian transformation that manipulated the electoral process and made abrupt constitutional changes. In order to sustain rapid industrialization, the authoritarian regime has also tended to exclude the popular sector from the fruits of growth. In a word, the development has more or less been accompanied by the impeding of democracy and equality in South Korea.

Many Communist states, including those recently dissolved, came into being in the capitalist-dominated world since the end of the Second World War. Before 1945, there were only three Communist countries in the world: the Soviet Union, Mongolia, and Albania. Today, although some Communist regimes in Eastern Europe were dissolved, capitalist and communist (or socialist) systems still seem to be the world's two predominant systems of political economy, even within the Third World alone. Communist countries account for about a third of the world's population, for up to 30 to 40 percent of its industrial production, and for a substantial proportion of its military might. In 1987, 38 out of 167 countries (22.8 percent) belonged to the socialist world and 84 countries (50 percent) to the capitalist (Gastil 1988, 74–75). A similar division is found in the Third World alone: about 21 percent of all the Third World is communist or socialist, while 46 percent is capitalist.

Since late 1989, the communist world has changed radically with the dissolution of the Communist regimes. It has happened all over Eastern Europe, where the accelerating pace of reforms gave birth to the observation that "Poland took ten years, Hungary ten months, East Germany ten weeks, Czechoslovakia ten days, . . . and Rumania ten hours (Nelan 1990, 34)." The Soviet Union has recently allowed individual property ownership and adopted a presidential system.

The nature of the capitalist world economy has changed as well. Since the late 1950s, with the growing awareness of revolutionary pressures and the emergence of the Soviet bloc as a provider of aid to the Third World countries, the aid policies of the advanced capitalist nations were placed on a new footing and coordinated through the World Bank and, later, the International Monetary Fund. Through these bodies, the advanced capitalist countries collectively confronted individual Third World societies, which involved detailed consideration and stringent conditions concerning Third World internal economic policies. In addition, the rise of multinational corporations has contributed to the mitigation of international economic rivalry. The coordination of policies imposed collectively by the advanced capitalist countries differs considerably from the unmitigated interimperialist rivalry that was at the center of Hobson's and Lenin's analysis of early imperialism.

Awareness of changing realities has brought about intermediary approaches between the modernization and dependency theorists. Those approaches have appeared in different contexts of recent developmental literature: developmentalism (Horowitz 1982, 1972), latecomer effect theory (Yang 1982), neo-Weberianism (Offe 1985; Giddens 1984; Moore 1966), associated development (Cardoso 1973), dependent development (Evans 1979), bureaucratic-authoritarianism (O'Donnell 1973), and so on. The explanatory strategy of these approaches is to focus on any one of several internal sectors, such as state, class, or culture. They consider external pressures and internal dynamics in the development process and leave open the possibility that priorities may shift within a nation. Policymaking, evaluation studies, and reshuffling social indicators may change the very nature of the development process. Cardoso, O'Donnell, Yang, and Evans have suggested that capitalist development in the Third World is possible and can be successful within the capitalist world economy. Jameson and Wilber (1981) have suggested varieties of socialist development in the Third World that diverge from the dominant Soviet and Chinese models of socialism. Wilczinsky, Wiles, Horowitz, and Giddens try to compare capitalist and socialist development, rather than discard either one. From these perspectives, both capitalist and Communist development can be compared for theoretical elaboration.

This book has several unique features. This is the first comprehensive analysis of the two Koreas' development during the post-liberation period. The collection of GNP data and the analysis of GSP and living standards are parts of its contribution as is the data analysis comparing income inequality in the two Koreas.

This book attempts to provide an empirical analysis of this special test case for evaluating the relative merits of capitalist and Communist claims. The sociological study of national development has sought safety in its own world of capitalism. It has neglected theories of Communist development and/or comparisons between capitalist and Communist development. Until now, little research has taken up these empirical cases for comparison. Modernization theory has show little interest in communist societies, assuming that since the world is dominated by capitalism, Communist societies are somehow marginal and unimportant. Dependency theory has limited its focus to the problems of the capitalist Third World, predicting that the capitalist world will ultimately be transformed into a Communist one and that Communist societies have, in any case, transcended the problematic capitalist stage. "Actually existing communism" needs to be brought into comparative perspective and the case of the two Koreas meets the criteria. the important task in the current sociology of development should be "the continuing elaboration of theory and examination of real situations for a deeper understanding of capitalism and socialism in the contemporary world" (Chilcote 1984, 132). Competing developmental systems with divergent strategies which produced a differentiated pace and pattern of development offer a unique opportunity for investigating all aspects of the relationship between the political economic system and developmental patterns and outcomes.

The book contains a theoretical dimension that seeks to test basic theorems in the sociology of development in the light of the Korean experience. The two Koreas case radically departs from extant sociological theories of modernization and dependency. The two Korean developments are not consistent with the tests of modernization theory not only because South Korean growth does not correspond to modernization as independent capitalist development, but also because the independent (socialist) development of North Korea does not follow a pattern of sustained development. Korean development also shows the inadequacy of dependency theory in explaining the two Korean developments in that dependency has not been associated with economic stagnation or underdevelopment in South Korea, nor have stagnation and underdevelopment been associated with dependency.

Another contribution of the book is that in terms of methodology it defines such problematic variables as the starting point of development, racial and ethnic difference in human capacity, historical background, and cultural tradition, which might be arguable in a study of comparative development. In a comparison of the United States and the Soviet Union, for example, the evaluation may be problematic because of the confounding variables. The natural conditions of the artificially divided Korea solve these problems. Before the division, the two Koreas had had a common historical, linguistic, and cultural tradition. Modern development started from the same historical point— the defeat of the Japanese Empire in 1945. Although there were some regional differences in the location of raw materials and industrial facilities, these were minimal in light of how much was commonly shared. What has been produced after the division can be regarded as the primary consequences of the two ideological states.

Finally, the analytic framework by which the two economic developments are compared is particularly valuable in a comparative context. The book attempts to contrast paths of development that systemically diverged and that are endemic to the systems of capitalism and communism. In this sense, the book attempts to advance the methodology of comparing the two systems by combining both theoretical approaches and empirical comparisons in a systematic fashion. In analyzing the systemic characteristics of the divided development being compared, these features were considered: the process of original capital accumulation and industrialization, the pattern of equalization through land reform and/or education, the role of the military and militarization, mobilization and incentive policies, the role of the new middle class and capitalists in development, and so on. A strong state, a Confucian culture, and a relatively equal distribution of income are further analyzed in both Koreas to see how these elements work in each system and how Confucianism has diverged in the two systems.

The comparison of development in South and North Korea may help to explain the degree and kind of development and underdevelopment that the Third World is faced with and to suggest the systemic implications of development. Comparative study will also contribute to the elaboration of the extant sociological theory of modernization and dependency. Despite such limitations as regional differences of raw material distribution between the two Koreas, many variables common to both sides before the division make the comparative study significant. Although comprehensive comparative study will require more data on North Korea than have thus far been available (in fact, there are no comprehensive data on GNP for the two Koreas), it is possible, even at present, to undertake a limited comparative study with available data and it should be encouraged.

Methodology of the Study

The term *development* is defined in this book as the maximization of the growth potential of a society. It combines social and economic development. Development means growth, but not in the simplistic sense that some index becomes larger. Development involves the ability to fulfill basic human needs. It may be understood as an increase in national income, as wealth creation, as poverty reduction, as basic needs fulfillment, as creation and maintenance of an infrastructure, and as international competitiveness. Development is evaluated not only by social and economic indicators, but also by time series. Economic development is normally taken to mean growth in national production and income. Social development may be considered in a broad sense as the pattern of evolution that a society follows, resulting from factors such as changes in the pattern of social stratification, demographic trends, the alteration of cultural values, and so on.

The socioeconomic development that the two Korean states have undergone from 1945 to 1988 (1989 and 1990 in some cases) is the dependent variable. Economic development is evaluated in terms of Gross National Product (GNP), GNP per capita, Gross Social Product (GSP), industrial structure, and trade that the two states have produced from 1945 to 1988. The period for which economic performances are evaluated is divided into five decades, so that historical shifts are taken into consideration in assessing economic development. Social development is evaluated in terms of education, health care, labor force and class structure, urbanization, income distribution, and standard of living.

Independent variables to explain socioeconomic development are factors related to the nature of the different political economies of South and North Korea. They are analytically categorized into political, economic, social, and military factors. They are further interrelated as they may affect socioeconomic development. Political factors refer to political ideology, leadership, socialization, and mobilization. Economic factors refer to strategies of development, international capital, service sector, and the size of the economy and industries. Social factors include labor force structure, education, income equalization, the new middle class, incentive policy, and religion. Military factors include defense burdens and the Korean War.

Different aggregate national accounts were used for both Koreas before and after the year 1967 when North Korea stopped publishing comprehensive data. The data for the early period until 1967 refer to National Income (NI) rather than GNP to which the data for the later period after 1967 until 1988 refer, because of data availability. The NI data for the early period was collected from primary governmental sources. Per capita NI was derived by dividing the national income by population figures of a corresponding period. In this case, however, it raises the problem of foreign exchange rates which entailed some difficulties. First of all, it was difficult to convert South Korean NI into dollar values. For this matter, the revised exchange rates were applied to the Korean *won*. In earlier years, the official exchange rates rapidly increased, but for certain years the official rates lagged far behind the reality. In 1961, however, a reasonable base point was found, and the official exchange rates were regarded as the applied rates. The applied rates in other years are calculated by extrapolating between 1945 and 1961. It is understandable that the military coup occurred in 1961 and that the military junta probably needed the true facts of the economic situation, so that they would have a sound basis to criticize the corrupt Rhee regime. The official rate of 130 *won* to one dollar was applied for the year 1961, and since 1964 the official data were applied without any revision. NI for the years before 1961 were derived simply by multiplying the applied exchange rates, which were calculated by extrapolation between 1945 and 1961.

North Korean exchange rates are simple to apply for the years until 1967. Official rates were about one *won* per dollar, and commercial rates for most foreign trade were about 2.5 *won* per dollar. This number was adjusted by scholars to reflect reality. P.S. Lee (1972, 170) estimated an approximate rate of 1.66 won per dollar applying purchasing power parity (PPP) exchange rates. The estimates of North Korean NI for the early years between 1945 and 1967 were applied by the 1.66 rate, and those for the years after 1967 by the 1.00 rate.

GNP data for the years after 1967 until 1988 were derived by multiplying the revealed per capita GNP by the total population. The per capita GNP data since 1967 were drawn from the U.S. Arms Control and Disarmament Agency (ACDA), the International Institute for Strategic Studies (IISS), the U.S. Central Intelligence Agency (CIA), the Far Eastern Economic Review (FEER), and the World Bank. Selected base years have been used for the reasonable construction of the data because each one of these sources appears to be more reliable for a certain period of time than others. The CIA source seems reliable for the early 1970s, the World Bank source for the late 1970s, ACDA for the early 1980s, and FEER for the late 1980s. The years 1970, 1975, 1980, 1985, and 1988 were selected in order for the per capita GNP to be derived from each reliable source.

For 1988, the North Korean GNP was derived by cutting the official North Korean figure in half because in common with the experiences of East European Communist countries, the official GSP of North Korea is twice the national income (P.S. Lee 1972,520). The South Korean GNP was derived by taking the medium point between the FEER source ($4,040) and the World Bank estimate ($3,650). The

FEER figure in that year simply followed the official South Korean figures which seem highly overestimated.

This book is designed to achieve a deeper and more meaningful analysis of Korea's development experience in the postwar period. The primary aim is to move from a simplistic economic or political discussion of Korean development to a historically and structurally guided sociopolitical analysis of Korean development that captures its systemic nature in detail. A case study proves to be useful in generating assumptions and refining existing observations, though it may suffer from limitations in establishing causal relations among mechanisms and outcomes. Smelser argues that qualitative historical methods must be used when the number of relevant cases is too small to permit use of multivariate statistical techniques (Smelser 1973,199). "This method is," he wrote, "often required in the comparative analysis of national units or cultures—where the sample is often small." In order to compensate for this shortcoming, this book discusses in brief other divided countries in chapter 2.

This book is based on the "method of difference" that Skocpol discussed as a comparative historical analytic framework (Skocpol 1984). The method of difference contrasts the two cases in which the phenomenon to be explained and the hypothesized causes are present or absent in either, even though the other is as similar as possible in other respects. The differential development between the two Koreas is due to the wide differences in the independent variables previously discussed.

This analysis basically assumes that a country's development experience emerges as a historical process through the interactions of domestic factors and international factors. In these interactions, a variety of linkages between domestic and international factors are established in ways that affect the entire process of national development: these linkages are deemed to be closely associated with both the country's particular relations with the international political and economic system and that its particular responses spring from unique sociohistorical conditions and unique political leadership. The development strategies of the two Korean states are molded by the interaction between the international politics and economy of the four superpowers (U.S., USSR, China, and Japan), on the one hand, and the special experience during the time of Korea's opening and the Korean War.

Statistical data sources used in the book are drawn from World Development Report (World Bank), Asia Yearbook (Far Eastern Economic Review), The Europa World Yearbook, Background Notes (U.S. Department of State), SIPRI Yearbook (SIPRI), World Military Expenditures and Arms Transfers (ACDA), The Military Balance (IISS), Statistical Yearbook (U.N.), and Country Profile (EIU). Korea Statistical Yearbook (EPB), Korean Economic Indicators (EPB), Social Indicators in Korea (EPB) are also used for the data on South Korean development. Limited data sources produced by North Korea, and travel reports and video tapes are used for comparison and to complement other data.

Limitations of the Study

Several difficulties and limitations remain in this book. A primary difficulty lies in the absence or reliability of the data on North Korean development. Lack of information on North Korean development constrains the comparative study. Most materials focus almost exclusively on issues of South Korean development. The literature on issues of North Korean development is distressingly small. The lack of information on the development of the North is mostly due to the North Korea's not releasing the information. North Korea has not published systematic data since 1965. What piecemeal figures are available in its publications are mostly for overseas consumption, calling in question their reliability. Since no precise calculations are possible, only rough comparisons between South and North Korea are feasible. The North Korean GNP figures are only rough estimates, involving complex adjustments of the possible statistics of the Net Material Product in inconvertible currency to the Western GNP in a convertable currency.

The lack of data also raises the problem of the reliability of information. Where different social systems are involved, the problem is magnified because the basis, method, and consistency of valuation differ fundamentally. Where value judgments have to be made, as in the case of national income, industrial output, and foreign trade, the problems become more serious. The different concepts and the lack of appropriate measurements for a comparison of national wealth and welfare in the two countries makes the comparison difficult.

In most Korean studies achievements made under the system of the writer are usually exaggerated, while those of the other system are belittled or ignored. This has produced a wide range of estimation on North Korean GNP. The South Korean National Unification Board estimates North Korean per capita GNP in 1983 as only $765, while North Korean claims are much higher than the South's estimates. It was claimed that per capita national income exceeded $1,000 in 1975, reached $1,920 in 1979, and $2,400 in 1986 (Pang 1988,152-3), whereas the World Bank suggest, medium estimates for 1979 of $1,130. The difficulty in determining the appropriate exchange rate is also among the limitations. A dual system of exchange rate operated in North Korea and the lack of an appropriate standard of the exchange rate operating in South Korea during the 1950s, in particular, hinders the reasonable comparison of the two Korean developments.

References

Amin, Samir et al. 1982. *Dynamics of Global Crisis*. New York: Monthly Review Press.

Brenner, Robert. 1977. "The origins of capitalist development: A critique of neo-Smithian Marxism." *New Left Review* 104:25–92.

Brun, Ellen and Jacques Hersh. 1976. *Socialist Korea: A Case Study in the Strategy of Economic Development*. New York: Monthly Review Press.

Bunge, Frederica M. (ed.). 1981. *North Korea: A Country Study*. Washington, D.C.: American University Press.

Cardoso, Fernando Henrique. 1973. "Associate-dependent development: Theoretical and practical implications." Pp. 142-76 in Alfred Stepan (ed.), *Authoritarian Brazil: Origins, Policies, and Future*. New Haven: Yale University Press.

Chilcote, Ronald H. 1984. *Theories of Development and Underdevelopment*. Boulder, CO: Westview Press.

Chirot, Daniel. 1977. *Social Change in the Twentieth Century*. New York: Harcourt Brace Jovanovich.

Chung, Joseph Sang-hoon. 1983. "Economic Policy in North Korea." In Scalapino and Kim (eds.), *North Korea Today: Strategic and Domestic Issues*. Berkeley: University of California Institute of East Asian Studies.

———. 1980. "The Economic System." Pp. 274-300 in H.K. Kim and H. K. Park, *Studies on Korea: A Scholar's Guide*. Honolulu: University Press of Hawaii.

———. 1974. *The North Korean Economy: Structure and Development*. Stanford: Hoover Institution Press.

Clough, Ralph N. 1987. *Embattled Korea: The Rivalry for International Support*. Boulder, CO: Westview Press.

Cole, David C. and Princeton N. Lyman. 1971. *Korean Development: The Interplay of Politics and Economics*. Cambridge, MA: Harvard University Press.

Cumings, Bruce. 1984. *The Two Koreas*. Foreign Policy Association, No. 269. New York: Hadline Series.

_____. 1981. *The Origins of the Korean War: Liberation and the Emergence of Separate Regimes 1945-1947*. Princeton, NJ: Princeton University Press.

Economic Planning Board (EPB). 1989. *Korea Statistical Yearbook 1988*. (No.35). Seoul: National Bureau of Statistics, EPB.

_____. 1989. *Korean Economic Indicators*. Seoul: EPB.

_____. 1989. *Social Indicators in Korea*. Seoul: EPB.

Economist Intelligence Unit (EIU). 1990. *Country Profile 1988-89*. London: The Economist Intelligence Unit.

Europa World Yearbook, The. 1990. *The Europa World Yearbook 1990*. 2 vols. London: Europa Publications.

Evans, Peter. 1979. *Dependent Development: The Alliance of Multinational, State, and Local Capital in Brazil*. Princeton, N.J.: Princeton University Press.

Far Eastern Economic Review (FEER). 1990. *Asia Yearbook 1990*. Hong Kong: FEER.

Foster-Carter, Aidan. 1985. "Korea and dependency theory," *Monthly Review* 37(5):27-34.

Frank, Andre G. 1981. *Crisis: In the Third World*. New York: Holmes & Meier Publishers.

Gastil, Raymond D. 1988. *Freedom in the World, 1987-88*. New York: Freedom House.

Giddens, Anthony. 1987. *Social Theory and Modern Sociology*. Cambridge: Polity Press.

_____. 1984. *The Constitution of Society*. Berkeley: University of California Press. .

_____. 1973. *The Class Structure of the Advanced Societies*. London: Hutchinson & Co.

Gregor, A. James. 1990. *Land of the Morning Calm: Korea and American Security*. Washington, D.C.: Ethics and Public Policy.

Halliday, Jon. 1987. "The economies of North and South Korea." Pp. 19–54 in Sullivan and Foss, *Two Koreas—One Future?* Lanham, MD: University Press of America.

_____. 1981. "The North Korean Enigma." Pp. 114–154 in White, Murray and While (eds.), *Revolutionary Socialist Development in the Third World*. Lexington: The University Press of Kentucky.

Horowitz, Irving Louis. 1982. *Beyond Empire and Revolution*. New York: Oxford University Press.

_____. 1972. *Three Worlds of Development*. New York: Oxford University Press.

International Institute for Strategic Studies (IISS). 1990. *Military Balance 1989-1990*. London: IISS.

Jameson, Kenneth P. and Charles K. Wilber. 1981. "Socialism and development: Editor's Introduction," *World Development* 9(9/10):803-11.

Jones, Leroy P. and Il Sakong. 1980. *Government, Business, and Entrepreneurship in Economic Development: The Korean Case*. Cambridge, Mass.: Harvard University Press.

Kautsky, John H. 1968. *Communism and the Politics of Development*. New York: John Wiley & Sons, Inc.

Kihl, Young Whan. 1984. *Politics and Policies in Divided Korea: Regimes in Contest*. Boulder, CO: Westview Press.

Kim, Hak-Joon. 1977. *The Unification Policy of South and North Korea, 1948-1976*. Seoul, Korea: Seoul National University Press.

Kim, Il-pyong J. 1975. *Communist Politics in North Korea*. New York: Praeger Publishers.

Kim, Joung-won Alexander. 1975. *Divided Korea: the Politics of Development, 1945-1972*. East Asian Research Center, Cambridge, Mass: Harvard University Press.

Kim, Young C. and Abraham M. Halpern (eds.). 1977. *The Future of the Korean Peninsula*. New York: Praeger Publishers.

Koo, Hagen. 1987. "The interplay of states, social class, and world system in East Asian development: the case of South Korea and Taiwan." In F. Deyo, *The Political Economy of the New Asian Industrialism*. New York: Cornell University Press.

Kuznets, Paul W. 1977. *Economic Growth and Structure in the Republic of Korea*. New Haven: Yale University Press.

Lane, David. 1976. *The Socialist Industrial State: Towards a Political Sociology of State Socialism*. Boulder, CO: Westview Press.

Lee, Byoung-Young. 1980. "Comparison of the economic power between South and North Korea," *Korea & World Affairs* 4:448-63.

Lee, Chong-sik. 1978. *The Korean Worker's Party: A Short History*. Stanford: Hoover Institution Press.

Lee, Chong-sik (trans. and ed.). 1977. *Materials on Korean Communism 1945-1947*. Center for Korean Studies, Hawaii: University of Hawaii Press.

Lee, Pong S. 1982. "The Korean People's Democratic Republic," in Peter Wiles (ed.), *The New Communist Third World*. New York: St. Martin's Press.

_____. 1972. "An estimate of North Korea's National Income," *Asian Survey* 12(6):518-526.

Lee, Seung-Sang. 1989. *Bukhan bukhan saramdul*. (North Korea and North Korean People.) A video tape.

Lim, Huyn-Chin. 1985. *Dependent Development in Korea, 1963-1979*. Seoul: Seoul National University Press.

Michell, Tony. 1988. *From a Developing to a Newly Industrialized Country: The Republic of Korea, 1961-82*. Geneva: International Labour Organization.

Moore, Barrington. 1966. *Social Origins of Dictatorship and Democracy*. Boston: Beacon Press.

Nelan, Bruce W. 1990. "Slaughter in the Street." *Time*, 1 January 1990: 34-37.

O'Donnell, Guillermo A. 1973. *Modernization and Bureaucratic-authoritarianism*. Berkeley: University of California Press.

Offe, Claus. 1985. *Disorganized Capitalism*. Cambridge, Mass.: MIT Press.

Pang, Hwan Ju. 1988. *Korean Review*. Pyongyang, Korea: Foreign Language Publishing House.

Park, Yho-Han. 1989. *88 nyun gyuool booknyukttang*. (The Northern Land in Winter 1988.) A video tape.

Petri, Peter A. 1988. "Korea's export niche: Origins and prospects," *World Development* 16(1):47-63.

Scalapino, Robert A. (ed.). 1960. *North Korea Today*. New York: Praeger Publisher.

Scalapino, Robert A. and Chong-sik Lee. 1972. *Communism in Korea*. 2 vols. Berkeley: University of California Press.

Shulman, Marshall D. (ed). 1986. *East-West Tensions in the Third World*. New York: W.W. Norton & Company.

Skocpol, Theada (ed.) 1984. *Vision and Method in Historical Sociology*. Cambridge: Cambridge University Press.

Smelser, Neil J. 1973. "Toward a Theory of Modernization." Pp. 268–84 in Etzioni and Etzioni-Halevy (eds.), *Social Change: Sources, Patterns, and Consequences*. New York: Basic Books.

Stockholm International Peace Research Institute (SIPRI). 1990. *SIPRI Yearbook 1990: World Armaments and Disarmament*. New York: Oxford University Press.

———. 1988. *SIPRI Yearbook 1988: World Araments and Disarmament*. New York: Oxford University Press.

Suh, Dae-Sook. 1970. *Documents of Korean Communism 1918-1948*. Princeton, NJ: Princeton University Press.

United Nations (UN). 1989. *Statistical Yearbook*. New York: U.N.

U.S. Arms Control and Disarmament Agency (ACDA). 1988. *World Military Expenditures and Arms Transfers 1987*. Washington, D.C.: US ACDA.

U.S. Central Intelligence Agency (CIA). 1978. *Korea: The Economic Race Between the North and the South* (ER 78-10008). Washington, D.C.: National Foreign Assessment Center, U.S. CIA.

U.S. Department of State. 1987. *Background Notes: South Korea*. Washington, DC: US Department of State, April 1987.

———. 1986. *Background Notes: North Korea*. Washington, DC: US Department of State, May 1986.

Wallerstein, Immanuel. 1989. *The Modern World-System III: The Second Era of Great Expansion of the Capitalist World-Economy, 1730-1840s*. New York: Academic Press.

———. 1984. *The Politics of World-Economy*. New York: Cambridge University Press.

World Bank. 1989. *World Development Report 1989*. New York: Oxford University Press.

Yang, Jonghoe. 1982. "Sectoral shift of the labor force in economic growth—A cross-national study" (Ph.D. diss. Department of Sociology, SUNY at Buffalo).

2

Capitalism, Communism, and Third World Development

The evolution of the two Koreas can be elucidated broadly by three groups of theoretical approaches, each grasping a significant part of the nature of capitalism and communism in national development. First, developmental patterns and unique characteristics of divided nations help us understand the divided development of Korea. Second, the analysis of dominant features of market and planned economic systems helps us understand the ideologically opposing institutions built in the two states. And last, sociological theories of Third World development help elucidate the patterns and problems that the two Koreas as Third World countries experience in the process of their development.

Divided Nations and Developmental Patterns

This section takes three nations, China, Germany, and Vietnam, and examines how the economic, political and cultural formations of each of these three divided nations help to explain the Korean case. Admittedly, there are serious difficulties in such an approach: Germany has already achieved formal unification, moving fast toward full integration since the Berlin Wall collapsed in late 1989; China is divided from Taiwan by a body of water, which contributes to the significantly unbalanced nature of the division including a size imbalance; Vietnam is a case in which the separation of North and South has already been resolved by the termination and conclusion of its civil war. Nonetheless, geographical and even military differences notwithstanding, this type of analysis is helpful. For the ability to establish as a constant a series of divided nations provides us with a subset of developmental themes involving economic (free market vs. planning system); political (multiparty parliamentary systems vs. single party, and essentially dictatorial regimes) and sociocultural (modernization vs. traditional modes of behavior) models.

The purpose, then, of this section is to explore a subset of developmental patterns, one that allows us to better understand and place in a global context the divided nations syndrome. This type of analysis does not disappoint: we find some powerful sets of commonalities that need to be explored in more general social and economic analysis. These, in turn, give rise to fundamental reasons for the ferment and discontent found in welfare states and in Communist states economically, and no less, in the cultural formations of Western democratic societies. If this sort of analysis elucidates the larger issues, it would be fine. But for our purpose, the analysis itself rather than the model which ensues will suffice. Whatever one's attitude may be toward specific developmental, or modernization, or dependency approaches, the fact of the bifurcation or division of a nation is so unique and so central, that such an analysis as is herein proposed needs no elaborate rationalization beyond the fact of division itself.

Two Germanys

The competition between the two Germanys seems to have ended with a capitalist victory. The opposite is the case for Vietnam at least thus far. The two Germanys have represented capitalist and communist development in the context of highly industrialized countries. Each has been the most important member (outside the superpowers) of its respective alliance system both in terms of economic and military power. As of 1988, per capita GNP of West Germany ($14,260) was a little ahead that of East Germany ($12,480) (Rubenstein 1989, 22). The gap was greater in the early 1980s (table 2.1): In 1981, per capita GNP of West Germany ($13,450) was far higher than that of East Germany ($7,180).

Geographically, East Germany is less than half the size of West Germany. West Germany comprises a territory of 248,690 square kilometers—about the size of Oregon, and East Germany 108,177

TABLE 2.1
Major Indicators between East and West Germany

		East Germany	West Germany
Pop. (mil.)	1988	16.6	61.0
Pop. Inc. Rate	60–87	−0.5	+5.6
Per Capita GNP,	1981	7,180	13,450
($)	1988	12,480	14,260
Life Expectancy	1988	73	76
Trade (bil.)	1988	61.7	574.0

Sources: The Europa World Yearbook 1990.
Moreton, *Germany between East and West* (1987) pp.123–4.
Rubenstein (1989), "The economic wall," *National Review,* 22 December 1989, p. 22.

square kilometers, comparable to that of Ohio. The population of East Germany is about one-fourth of West Germany's: population in 1988 was 61.0 million in West Germany and 16.6 million in East Germany.

After the defeat of the Third Reich in 1945, Germany was divided into American, Soviet, British, and French occupation zones. After the failure of negotiation to establish a unified Germany, the three Western-occupied zones were integrated economically in 1948, and the Federal Republic of Germany (FRG) was established on 21 September 1949. In response to the initiative, the Soviet-occupied zone declared itself the German Democratic Republic (GDR) on 7 October 1949. At the beginning of its development, East Germany was at a tremendous disadvantage in terms of natural resources, and industrial, transportation, and communications capacity. Although East Germany is abundant in lignite, raw material deposits are generally more scarce in the communist East than in the capitalist West. This was very much the opposite situation from Korea and Vietnam at their starting points, where natural resources and industrial facilities were more scarce in the capitalist South than in the communist North. Moreover, between May 1945 and 1953 the Soviets carted off some 45 percent of East Germany's total prewar industrial equipment, in addition to the approximately 20 percent that had been destroyed during the war (Dornberg 1974, 135). During the first postwar decade, East Germany had to pay the Soviet Union $10 billion in direct reparations. West Germany, like the East, had to pay out billions in restitution to Israel and to individual Jewish victims of Nazism. However, West Germany

TABLE 2.2
Labor Force and Production by Industry in Two Germanys

| | 1960 | | 1980 | | 1985 | |
	E.G.	W.G.	E.G.	W.G.	E.G.	W.G.
Labor Force						
Agri. etc.	18%	14%	10%	6%	10%	5%
Industry	48%	48%	50%	44%	41%	39%
Service	34%	38%	40%	50%	49%	56%
Production as % of GNP						
Agri. etc.	—	5.8%			8.1%	1.7%
Industry	—	53.2%			70.0%	42.8%
Service	—	41.0%			21.9%	55.5%

Sources: World Bank, World Development Report 1983 and 1987.
The Europa World Yearbook 1988, pp. 1153–67, 1131–40.

received $3.8 billion in aid from the United States which offset resti-
tution. Between 1945 and 1961, some 3.5 million East Germans fled
to the West, which caused a serious shortage of labor in East Germany.

As shown in table 2.2, the population engaged in agriculture and
industry is lower in the West (5 and 39 percent, respectively) than in
the East (10 and 41 percent, respectively), while that in service is
higher in the West (56 percent) than in the East (49 percent). In
general, labor force structures tend to converge in the 1980s: the population occupied in agriculture and industry has declined, while that of
service increased on both sides. It is a sharp contrast, however, that
industrial production takes a much higher composition of GNP in East
Germany (70 percent) than in West Germany (43 percent).

West Germany achieved considerable economic development since
the division. The new currency reform was introduced into the western
zones by the allied military government in 1948. Under the chancellorship of Konrad Adenauer (1949–63) and the direction of Economics
Minister Ludwig Erhard, who succeeded Adenauer until 1966, West
Germany rebuilt itself rapidly to become one of the most affluent and
economically dynamic states of Europe (Gottlieb 1960). Their parties,
the Christian Democratic Union (CDU) and the Christian Socialist
Union (CSU), encompassed a broad range of the population. Erhard
implemented an economic policy according to the principles of "social

market economy," which is a regulated and/or socially conscious free market economy. The role of government became one of implementing social programs, though not intervening too far in the direction of planning or economic control.

The expanding role of the state brought about uneven development. During economic recession of 1966–67, urban unrest, centered in the universities in the 1960s, persisted into the 1970s. In coalition with the Free Democratic Party (FDP), Willy Brandt (1969–74) and Helmut Schmidt (1974–82) of the Social Democratic Party (SPD) could undertake an ambitious reform program in part because the lasting effect of the student protest had been to create a new awareness of the need to democratize a society that became somewhat fossilized in the Adenauer era. As the FDP moved to the right in 1982, the CDU/CSU-FDP coalition formed under the chancellorship of Helmut Kohl. Unemployment is a chronic problem in West Germany. It increased by 1.1 million by 1975 and reached 2.2. million in 1985.

Until the introduction of the New Economic System (NES) in 1963, East Germany practiced Stalinist Soviet-style central planning and management. In 1945, the Soviet military government ordered the confiscation of all properties belonging to former Nazis. In 1946 the land reform began and all large-scale industrial concerns became state owned. Walter Ulbricht (1950–73) of Socialist Unity Party of Germany (SED) continued this policy. Ulbricht's plans for the "building of socialism" announced in 1952 laid emphasis on rapid industrialization and on the collectivization of agriculture. They were accompanied by punitive measures against farmers, the middle classes, and the churches. The policy concentrated on the expansion of heavy industry at the expense of consumer goods. In 1958, collectivization was extended to the remaining small businesses and shops which resulted in immediate stagnation: the 8 percent growth of the 1950s fell to 2.3 percent between 1960 and 1962.

In 1957, however, the Soviets started to help East Germany, delivering vast amounts of raw material and semi-finished goods, and adding a $350 million loan. Forced collectivization of agriculture was put into action in 1960. The New Economic System introduced in 1963 served as an experimental laboratory for the Soviet Union. The NES emphasized quality instead of quantity, decentralization of the decision-making process, incentives and bonuses, and profitability. Although the reform produced fast growth, it created serious "distortions" and "unplanned" growth.

Erich Honecker who replaced Ulbricht in 1971 intensified socialist production. In order to respond to Brandt's *Ostpolitik*, a new strategy needed to be brought to the centralized, administrative direction of the economy. What remained of the NES was its valued emphasis on the "scientific technological revolution (STR)." In East Germany, industry is run by several thousand "people's owned enterprises." These are organized in eighty "associations of people's owned enterprises." Each association is like a huge, powerful trust, comparable in many ways to a large conglomerate or monopoly. In early 1980, East Germany created giant amalgamations of industrial enterprises—the *Kombinate*—and restored the private profit.

West Germany was, of course, far more democratic than East Germany. West Germany's constitution, or Basic Law, was drafted in the ivory tower atmosphere of Bonn and instituted a practicing multiparty parliamentary system. East Germany was a totalitarian state with power vested in the ruling Socialist Unity Party (SED). It had no free elections, no choice of political parties or candidates. There have been a centrally controlled press with censorship and a vast secret police organization that kept a sharp eye on all citizens.

Although per capita GNP figures show only a 14.3 percent advantage for West Germany, the actual gap in living standards is many times larger, since East German central planners channel the bulk of GNP into heavy industry, chemicals, and other exports, while giving short shrift to consumer products. The real problem here is that, although per capita GNP in East Germany increased steadily, the gap between the state's "material" production and people's consumption was wider during the 1980s. The East German development was in far worse shape than portrayed in GNP terms.

Two Chinas

The Chinese case is one of sharp contrasts in all its aspects. China occupies 9,561,000 square kilometers, about the same size of the Untied States, and Taiwan occupies only an island of 36,000 square kilometers. In terms of size, China is 266 times larger than Taiwan.

And, the population of China in 1988 (1.1 billion) is fifty-five times larger than that of Taiwan (20 million).

The population of China is still predominantly engaged in agriculture. As shown in table 2.3 about 63 percent of the total labor force was in agriculture in 1987, but only 17 percent in Taiwan. The industrial population constitutes a much smaller portion in China (21 percent) than in Taiwan (41 percent). In spite of the smaller portion of the population in the industry sector in China, the portion of industry in GNP was somewhat higher in China (59 percent) than in Taiwan (51 percent).

Taiwan was ceded to Japan after the Sino-Japanese War in 1894. In 1911 the Ch'ing Dynasty, the last dynasty of China, was overthrown by the forces of Sun Yat-Sen. Chiang Kai-Shek had led the Kuomintang (KMT) since 1926. After the defeat of Japan in 1945 the Communists, led by Mao Zedong, who had established themselves in the north, brought the entire country under their control. The People's Republic of China was proclaimed on 1 October 1949. The Republic of China moved to Taiwan in December 1949. Mao died in 1976, and Hua Guofeng assumed the party chairmanship. Hua resigned to be replaced by Zhao Ziyang in 1980. In 1981 Hua resigned from the party chairmanship, replaced by Hu Yaobang whose death touched off the prodemocratic movement in Tiananmen Square in June 1989. Deng Xiaoping became head of the Party Advisory Commission at the 12th Party Congress in 1982. He was succeeded by Party General Secretary Zhao Ziyang at the 13th Party Congress in 1987. Zhao Ziyang was removed after the Tiananmen Square incident in 1989. After the installation of Jiang Zemin as party leader, Deng finally stepped down from his party post in November 1989, while remaining the recognized paramount leader. Taiwan was expelled from the U.N. in 1971. Chiang Ching-Kuo, the son of Chiang Kai-Shek, became president in 1978. The father-son succession forms an interesting parallel to that of North Korea. Chiang died in 1988 and Vice-President Lee Teng-hui, a Taiwanese technocrat, succeeded to the presidency, becoming head of state and head of the ruling KMT.

The two Chinas have achieved rapid economic growth. The Communist Chinese economy achieved annual average growth rates of 4.8 percent during the 1965–85 period and produced the annual 6.0 and 7.9 percent in real national income and real GNP, respectively, be-

TABLE 2.3
Major Indicators of Economy in China and Taiwan

	China	Taiwan
GNP per capita 1963	—	178
($) 1973	—	695
1985	310	3,468
1988	283	5,520
Labor Force, 1987		
Agriculture, etc.	62.5%	17.0%
Industry	20.9%	40.6%
Service	16.6%	42.4%
Production as % of GNP, 1987		
Agriculture, etc.	20%	5.6%
Industry	59%	51.4%
Service	21%	43.0%
Trade as % of GNP		
1981	14.0%	98.0%
1987	28.0%	92.6%
1988	29.0%	98.5%

Sources: World Bank, World Development Report 1984 and 1987.
FEER, Asia Yearbook 1990, pp.6–9.

tween 1952 and 1982. The growth rate of Taiwan was 7.2, 10.4, and 10.0 percent for the 1950s, 1960s, and 1970s, respectively, though the growth in the 1980s fluctuates from 3.8 percent in 1982 to 10.8 percent in 1986 to 11.6 percent in 1987. Ka and Selden (1986) pointed out that as far as original accumulation is concerned, the states of both China and Taiwan played a crucial role in transferring resources from agriculture to industry and from the private sector to the state and institutions it controls.

Chinese development since 1953 has been within the framework of five-year plans. Until 1975, in general, a heavy industry-oriented strategy had been pursued by the Mao government. After the first five-year plan (1953–7) was applied according to the Soviet model, creating the Great Leap Forward Movement, Mao changed the policy from the Soviet-type heavy-industry-first to that of emphasizing agriculture and light industry where capital-output ratios are lower and economic returns quicker. The principle of local initiative in industrialization reflected a wider emphasis on decentralization to local units. The "reformist" Maoism had gradually developed into a new paradigm of "radical" Maoism, the Cultural Revolution, which targeted the entire society. Since 1978, the Chinese development strategy has been more balanced. The heavy-industry-first policy was adjusted slightly to a consumption-oriented policy. Trade also increased continuously from about 5 percent of GNP in 1965 to level of 29 percent in 1988. These trends reflect the rapid liberalization of China's international trade since 1975.

The rapid growth in Taiwan was caused in large part by a substantial structural transformation of the economy from an agricultural to an industrial one. Agriculture's proportion of GDP (Gross Domestic Product) fell from 38 to 5.6 percent between 1953 and 1987, while that of industry sharply increased from 11 to 51.4 percent over the same period. Industrial growth in Taiwan was not concentrated in a few urban areas. Rather, a wide dispersal of manufacturing enterprises occurred because of an excellent transportation infrastructure, the rural electrification program, and a fairly well-educated population. For example, the percentage of people employed in manufacturing establishments in rural areas actually rose from 47 to 52 percent during the 1956–66 period. Small- and medium-sized companies are well developed.

Rapid growth in Taiwan was generally associated with low levels of unemployment and inflation. Unemployment fell steadily from about 6 percent in 1953 to 2 to 3 percent since 1967 except in the "oil shock" years of 1974 and 1980 (Clark 1987, 4–5). This pattern of industrialization was also accompanied by a major deviation from the normal pattern of "dependent development" in which the state enterprises take a very active role.

Two Vietnams

The two Vietnams ended in 1975 and the competition between the two appeared to end with the "socialist victory." Since the fall of Saigon in 1975, the unified Socialist Republic of Vietnam has made an effort to develop the country, launching consecutive Five-Year Plans. Nevertheless, Vietnam has remained one of the poorest countries in the world, suffering from food shortages and inflation. Per capita income was $195 in 1983 and was estimated at between $100 and $150 in 1988; 73 percent of the labor force was engaged in agriculture in

TABLE 2.4
Major Indicators of Two Vietnams

	South Vietnam	North Vietnam
GNP per capita, 1968	$276	$100–$150 (1988)
Production as % of GNP, 1968		
Agriculture, etc.	30.0%	73% (1988)
Industry	9.2%	
Service	60.8%	
Selective Products, 1961		
Rice (thou.tons)	4,200	4,000
Rubber (thou.tons)	83	negligible
Coal (thou.tons)	25	2,800
Cement (thou.tons)	200	455
Cattle (thou.tons)	1,940	1,800
Electr. (mil.kwh)	293	254
Textile (mil.meter)	144	68

Sources: *Asia Yearbook 1970, 1990* pp. 6–9
Fall, *The Two Vietnams* (1963), p. 302 for the years 1955 and 1961.
The Europa Yearbook 1988, pp. 3035–7.

1988 (See table 2.4). In 1987, Vietnam introduced a series of economic reforms to remedy the chronic underdevelopment, allowing material incentives, private businesses, and foreign investment.

Vietnam had been under Chinese influence until Cochinchina (the southern part of Vietnam) and Annam and Tonkin (central and northern Vietnam) became a French colony in 1863 and 1883, respectively. Later all three were merged with Cambodia and Laos to form French Indochina. During the colonial period, nationalists and revolutionary groups developed. The nationalists formed the Revolutionary League for the Independence of Vietnam, known as the Vietminh when Japanese forces began to occupy Vietnam in 1941 taking control from the French in March 1945. Following Japan's defeat in August, the Democratic Republic of Vietnam (DRV) was proclaimed in Hanoi on 2 September 1945. Fighting with the French power, which returned after World War II, broke out at the end of 1946 and continued until the Geneva Agreement of July 1954, when DRV, under Ho Chi Minh, received the territory north of the 17th parallel on what was supposed to be a temporary basis. Ngo Dinh Diem, backed by the U.S., became president of South Vietnam.

North Vietnam initiated and supported a liberation movement that gained popularity because of traditional nationalistic feeling and the ineptness of Diem's leadership. Rebellion broke out in 1959 and 1963 in South Vietnam. Diem was murdered during a military coup allegedly backed by the U.S. A series of short-lived military regimes held power until 1965, when some stability was restored by Lieutenant General Nguyen Van Thieu. Civil war broke out and intensified and resulted in direct involvement by the U.S. forces. In January 1973, the Paris Peace Agreement put an end to it and prescribed a ceasefire in South Vietnam, but the agreement was not fulfilled before the fall of Saigon in 1975.

Both North and South Vietnam comprised about the same amount of territory: North Vietnam occupied 63,360 square miles and the South 66,263 square miles. The population of North Vietnam exceeded that of South Vietnam: 19.5 million to 14 million. By 1975, it had increased to 24 million in the North to 21 million in the South. The North possessed all the mineral wealth necessary for industry; the South had an output of highly diversified agricultural products and rubber. Both populations were generally homogeneous in spite of several ethnic minorities (Fall 1963, 151), and the South had the burden of 860,000 refugees. The exodus did not seriously hurt the labor force of the North. It rather helped North Vietnam politically because most of the people who fled the North were Catholics, potentially the most powerful opposition force to the Northern regime. Moreover, the exodus created political tensions in the South which is largely Taoist, spiritualist, and Buddhist. President Ngo Dinh Diem immediately used the Northern Catholics as a major base of political power since he and his closest associates were Catholics. As in the Vietnamese case, the outflow of labor from the Communist to capitalist side occurred in Korea and Germany. Unlike the case of Vietnam, however, North Korea and East Germany seriously suffered from the loss of labor.

By 1954 North Vietnam had been heavily ravaged by wars. Its land had been plundered by the Japanese and Chinese and its communications bombed by the U.S. Air Force in 1944–45. The North had also sustained much damage from the war with France. Both Vietnams received a large amount of foreign aid. In 1954 the French Army had spent more than $500 million in support of the South apart from U.S.

aid and 120,000 Vietnamese served in the French armed forces. In 1974, North Vietnam received about $800 million worth of economic aid from the socialist bloc, and the U.S. administration had proposed for South Vietnam a similar amount of economic aid (FEER 1985, 245).

South Vietnam never reached prewar levels, despite French efforts to reconstruct the economy through the Monnet Plan in 1947. The North Vietnamese regime launched one-year economic plans for both 1956 and 1957, aiming mainly at preparing the economic-administrative base for later longer-range plans: an intermediate three-year plan covering the years 1958 through 1960, and then the first five-year plan covering the years 1961–65. Land reform was carried out during the period of 1955–58. The North Vietnam issued the "Population Classification Decree" on 2 March 1953, which classified people into five categories, ranging from "landlord" to "agricultural worker" (Fall 1963, 155). The same classification was applied to intellectuals, artisans, professionals, and so on. There was an uprising in opposition to land reform in 1956. Probably close to 50,000 North Vietnamese were executed in connection with the land reform and at least twice as many were arrested and sent to forced labor camps where some 6,000 farmers died (Fall 1963, 156).

The 1974–75 Two-Year Economic Plan and the 1974 State Plan were announced to reorganize retail trade and squeeze private entrepreneurs, reemphasizing heavy industry for what they called the base of the development of agriculture and light industry. This was a significant departure from the policy followed in 1973, which tolerated the market as an incentive to greater productivity (FEER 1975, 244–5).

It is overwhelmingly clear that the economic performance of capitalist or free-market societies far outstrips their Communist rivals, although it should be added that the social welfare component is much greater in the West German, Taiwanese, and former South Vietnamese regimes rather than, say, in the United States. In this sense, the power of the state in other divided nations, as well as in South Korea shows a mixed model pattern: that is, high development of market mechanisms, though aided and abetted by the state. One also sees a rapid internationalization of culture, a modernizing phenomenon that goes against the grain of traditionalism.

In the Communist portions of these divided nations, the contrary obtains: poor economic performance, tight political controls, and strongly retentive, traditional patterns of culture. There is more labor force input in the agricultural sector, and industrial production makes up a much higher proportion of GNP. Thus, what emerges in divided nations is less a unique "model" and more a special combination and permutation of available models of development elsewhere. One might argue that these unique features are aberrations, but, as in the case of Korea, when a divided nation is defined by more than forty years' duration (and Germany too can be added to this), it is important to appreciate the extent to which basic models are fundamentally altered by such special geographic and military circumstances.

In the process of development in divided countries, such unique phenomena as "division effect" and "comparison effect" are observed. The "division effect" shows that a significant number of people in the communist countries fled to the capitalist counterparts. This shift of population caused a serious problem of labor force shortage in the communist camp. As many as 860,000 North Vietnamese fled to the South fearing a Communist crackdown on the bourgeoisie and religious people. About one million people fled to Taiwan to establish a new government. The German case shows a much more serious effect. Between 1945 and 1961 some 3.5 million East Germans fled to the West. This certainly caused a chronic shortage of labor throughout the entire process of East German development.

The "comparison effect" is an important factor that each side of a divided country is mutually influenced by. Direct military threats and economic boom from one side significantly affect the other. In the case of Vietnam, the North instigated a revolution in the South that brought about rebellion in 1959 and in 1963 in the South. The direct military threat from the Communist North Vietnam required South Vietnam to adopt a more authoritarian measures to cope with a critical situation. Likewise, the father-son succession in Taiwan was allowed in the face of potential danger from the Communist China.

The "comparison effect" in the economic sense is equally significant. A change in economic policy on one side directly affects the other. Erich Honecker in East Germany introduced a new economic strategy in response to Willy Brandt's open politics in the early 1970s. East Germany, which had pursued the expansion of heavy industry at the expense of consumer goods, began to emphasize scientific and technological development in order to catch up with West German performance. In general, divided countries are so sensitive to each other that virtually all aspects of the system and any change on one side affect the system of the other.

Market vs. Planned Economy

The Koreas have pursued capitalism and communism originally transplanted by the U.S. and the USSR, respectively. The ideal types of capitalism and communism, based on the experiences of advanced countries, particularly the U.S. and the USSR, help us to grasp some general characteristics of the two Korean systems and developments. Whereas Adam Smith and the United States defined a pattern for capitalist development, Marx and the Soviet Union played the same role for socialism and socialist development. They provided a theoretical framework for observing and understanding reality and an actual experience of operationalizing the theory. The steps taken to change an economy toward capitalism or socialism, the institutions developed, the control mechanisms established, the successes and the failures, all of these would appear to be of aid to countries seeking to follow a capitalist or socialist development strategy.

There is much controversy over the basic nature of market and planned economies, but a general consensus is reached on their inner logic. Capitalism in the sense of an ideal type entails a multiparty system of government, the predominantly private ownership of the means of production, the operation of the market machanism, and freedom of enterprise spurred basically by the private profit motive. In contrast, socialism is characterized by the single party system of government, the social ownership of the means of production (land and capital), and economic planning guided by social interest as interpreted by the ruling party.

The market system is an arena of action of mostly privately owned corporations, industries, and business enterprises, acting on their own behalf and at their own risk. The production of goods is designed for profit, and it is directed toward the market. The market situation and supply and demand are essentially the major mechanisms that regulate what is produced for sale. Of course, other factors also affect the market situation—state controls, subsidies, duties, the situation in the labor market, and so on. In short, the economy is an arena of competitive interactions between the many parties that are seeking profits and sources of income on the one hand, and the commodities needed for consumption on the other.

In a planned economic system, production is ordered by the state, and it is controlled by the party. All enterprises are as a rule owned by the state. The state decides what is to be produced, with what quantity, and at what price. The state is the sole monopolistic employer. The more important jobs in all fields are under the management of their respective party committees. The state owns nearly all business enterprises, wholesale and retail stores, restaurants, and so on. It provides the citizens with recreation. Bargaining over prices, wages, or salaries is practically nonexistent. Strikes are banned. The function of the trade union is to mobilize the workers to increase their productivity and to provide some social services.

Horowitz (1982) gives further analyses of market and planned economies based on the experiences of the advanced economies. A market economy is typically based on individual entrepreneurial initiative, with little centralized planning (and that generally in social welfare sectors). Services and consumer goods production are emphasized. The domestic market is open; a high degree of international integration is created by financial and commodity markets with slight regulation. Savings policies are individiual-voluntary and based on a democratic tax system. Investment is private, unrestricted, and uncoordinated. Sources of investment funds are varied, based on decisions taken by households, businesses, financial institutions such as banks, and the international capital markets. Currencies are stable. Establishing terms of trade that are mutually favorable is difficult, given protectionist ideologies. Growth rates tend to be low, but seem adequately balanced for the needs of an industrial society.

A planned economy is typically geared toward "proletarian" values. Heavy industrial production is emphasized. Internal and external markets are highly regulated on the basis of economic considerations. Trade agreements are largely confined to formal allies and are not subject to severe fluctuations. Savings are nonvoluntary, state-determined, and government-controlled. Investment is confined to the public sector and is highly restricted and coordinated. Sources of funds are stable, based on public budgeting. Currencies are generally stable. Direct and manifold controls on production and distribution of consumer goods are maintained to discourage consumption as a deterrent to industrial development.

Wiles (1977) has analyzed the common and different characteristics of the STE (Soviet-Type Economies) and ACE (Advanced Capitalist Economies). He found that the "laws of production" are the same in both systems. Returns increase with scale under all systems: cost of production falls as producing units grow until they become too big to run in the old centralistic way. Both systems lay much weight on the technological fact that skill and development are improved by specialization. Alienation increases with specialization and the scale of the enterprises regardless of the system.

There are some differences across the systems. Some of the functions of money are cut away by the STE, where interenterprise money is "passive," that is, does not normally affect anyone's decisions. Aspiration levels decline in communes (kibbutzim, for example) and under communism as in the Cuban economy, while it increases under capitalism. Income distribution between individuals depends greatly on systems.

Wiles concludes that systems do not alter human nature, but they can suppress some of its symptoms. Systems do not change technology or other knowledge, but they do change our ability to discover it and adapt ourselves. The nationalization of the means of production, the substitution of command and plan for markets, the evolution of the STE into full Communism—none of this makes any difference at all in bringing out greater equality and rapid growth. What is important for the results is the procedures within each system. The very procedures adopted by computers and planners consciously simulate a perfectly competitive market. If they do not, total failure is the outcome.

Wilczynski (1983) has commented on the role of the state in industrial relations between market and planned economies. In market economies, the relations are characterized institutionally by a tripartite setup—labor (represented by independent trade unions), owners (or managers), and the state. The state is an institution that endeavors to mitigate industrial disputes between the other two parties and create better conditions for the avoidance or settlement of conflicts. Admittedly, it may be biased, sometimes toward capital, other times toward labor, depending largely on the domestically elected political party in power. The state as the holder of public authority is a separate entity from the state as employer. Higher wages and other improved conditions of work must be won from the state through bargaining and industrial actions as with private firms.

In contrast, in planned economies, the state is the owner and manager—the enterprise "director" is appointed by the state and he or she answers to it under the one-person managerial responsibility prevailing in all socialist countries. Although the enterprises generally have a legal status, the general rule for management, wage scales, bonuses and prices, and the provision of amenities arc fixcd by the state which is a party to industrial disputes. Moreover, the same state is also the central planner, the mouthpiece of the party in power, the legislator, and the law enforcer abetted by an overdeveloped police force.

Both Korean developments seem somewhat aberrant, deviating from the general categorization of both market and planned economies drawn from advanced experiences. Kihl (1984) summarized the typology of South and North Korean models of political economy as respectively authoritarian vs. totalitarian, state capitalist vs. state socialist, government-managed vs. centrally planned, dependent development vs. independent development. The means of achieving development objectives varied, with South Korea building light industry first and heavy industry later, and North Korea building hcavy industry first and light manufacturing later. In terms of market processes, South Korea moved from concentrating on the domestic market to exporting its manufactured goods to earn foreign currency for further investment in the economy; North Korea continued to concentrate on the domestic market. While South Korea has moved toward an export-led strategy of industrialization, North Korea has relied on an 'export-substitution' strategy. North Korea has consistently given priority support to both the agricultural and industrial sectors, whereas South Korea initially supported only the urban and industrial sectors but soon expanded its support to include the rural and agricultural sectors.

Sociological Theories of Third World Development

Both Koreas as Third World nations have been faced with problems and difficulties similar to those of most other Third World nations. The two-Korea development can be analyzed by sociological theories that explain the processes of the Third World in the context of the two world systems. These theories give helpful insight into how each Korea has attained its successful achievement or failure in the dynamic relations of domestic and international forces.

The question of capitalist and Communist development has been widely touched on by sociological theories of national development. The contributions of sociology to the field of Third World national development has been substantial, but they have focused extensively on the capitalist road. There are three theories that find the explanations for the uneven development in the social configurations of societies. These theories are modernization theory, developmental theory, and dependency theory.

Modernization Theory

Modernization theory presumes a dualism that there are two sectors of society in every developing country, the modern sector and the traditional sector. The traditional sector, usually associated with rural areas, is precapitalist. This sector exists in economic isolation from other outside sectors of the economy; it is untouched by market forces. The theory asserts that development takes place as a country moves from the traditional end to the modern end of the continuum. The main cause of underdevelopment is inherent in the traditionalism of Third World countries themselves. The major triggers of development lie in the introduction of capital, technology, values, and institutions from advanced capitalist countries to remove the international obstacles to development. Although such international interactions are emphasized, it is in a national society that various aspects of development processes are aggregated.

The theory also presupposes stages of development; every country must pass through a series of predetermined stages during the course of development. In this restricted sense the theory agrees with Marxist doctrine that the industrially advanced country presents the less advanced country with the image of its future. In Rostow's version (1960) of the theory there are five stages of development with the third stage being "takeoff." In this stage, the country has accumulated enough capital to begin self-sustained growth. High growth rates come only after large amounts of capital have been amassed.

A number of social-psychological extensions of modernization theory have been worked out. Inkeles (1974) argues that individual attitudes and values undergo systematic changes as societies progress through the five stages of development. McClelland (1961) makes a similar argument, which spawned a series of efforts to create entrepreneurs in developing countries. McClelland argued that on the basis of content analyses of stories produced by people in developed and developing societies, people in developed societies score high on indices of need-achievement while people in developing countries score high on need-affiliation indices.

The modernization perspective has produced plenty of literature on South Korean development, but little on North Korean development or underdevelopment. Sociological modernization theory has placed greater emphasis on the analogy between South Korean and Western societies. The process of social change in South Korea is understood merely as a phenomenon typical of historical latecomers to development, treading the same path already followed by Western countries. Much attention is given to structural differentiation and value changes, mainly in the area of urbanization, institution building, communal and occupational structure, kinship organization, education, and so on (M.G. Lee 1973, K.D. Kim 1979). Such an explanation has contributed to the understanding of the sociocultural and structural characteristics of South Korean society in transition, but it has failed to take into adequate account the impact of external economic and political dependence on the formation of internal social structure and values in South Korea.

Neomercantilist economists have focused on economic growth and structural change in South Korea (Kuznetz, 1977, K.S. Kim and Roemer 1979). This theory has encouraged Korea to adopt an "outward-looking" development policy as a viable means of spurring industrialization. However, it overlooks the possible adverse effects of such participation on the internal processes of economic development. While such participation has contributed to rapid economic growth and structural change, it has brought about balance of payment difficulties, and foreign indebtedness. Political development theory has paid much attention to nation-building in South Korea. Political stability can be achieved in the process of greater institutionalization of political organization, such as parties and bureaucracy. This theory places a particular stress on political stability as a necessary condition for the strengthening of the state's role in mobilizing manpower and resources for industrialization (Cole and Lyman 1971, Jones and Sakong 1980). But the validity of this explanation is quite questionable when it analyzes the emergence of authoritarian regimes in South Korea only in terms of the lack of satisfactory political institutionalization.

While the idea itself of modernizing a nation has been widely accepted by South and North Korea, most of the theory became invalidated by suggesting an unconvincing explanation of development of Korea. What is central to the modernization theorists was the concept that development can be achieved with the creation of a social structure and values similar to those of Western countries, with the pursuit of outward-looking development policy, or with the formation of a strong state that can effectively mobilize manpower and resources for industrialization. Yet the doctrine was radically rejected by North Korea. And, by focusing on the factors that are endogenous to South Korea, these explanations have not succeeded in relevantly addressing the influence of the international economic and political system with which those factors interact in South Korea's development process.

Dependency Theory

The theoretical tradition of dependency theory developed in reaction to modernization theory. Modernization theory emphasized the importance of forces internal to a country in national development; dependency theory has emphasized the importance of international forces in national development. Dependency theory focuses on factors exogenous to Third World countries, such as foreign aid, trade, resources, technology, multinational investment, and so on. By envisaging capitalism as an imperialist system, dependency theory, first of all, asserts that for various reasons little or no further development is possible for Third World countries within the constraints of the world capitalist system (Wallerstein 1989, 1984; Amin et al. 1982, Frank 1981, Chirot

1977). Hypothetically, the greater the degree of reliance on foreign investment/assistance and trade in a country, the slower the rate of economic growth. Therefore, capitalism has a negative impact on development in the Third World.

The reasons for underdevelopment are many: dependent countries suffer from direct exploitation; foreign firms repatriate profits overseas rather than reinvesting them in the local economy; core countries tend to transfer outmoded equipment and technology so dependent countries cannot compete effectively in international markets or grow very fast; because of foreign economic interest, the state of dependent countries becomes weak and cannot play effectively its necessary role in protecting domestic industry and fostering economic growth; finally, the domestic market becomes flooded with imported consumer goods while exports to pay for them are harmed by the instability of world demand and prices, which leads to trade deficits, growing indebtedness, and less capital to invest.

Foreign trade is a specific focus of dependency theory. It generally analyzes the negative features of foreign trade and investment. A specific version of the assertion is characteristic. It says that trade under certain conditions hinders growth: (1) countries with a "vertical" type of trade pattern only export raw materials and always import manufactured goods; (2) the export goods all experience large fluctuations in price; and (3) the stock of direct foreign investment is large; enclaves of foreign investment and workers characterize the economy; usually the industries are highly technical such as petroleum or mining.

The theory asserts that the economic underdevelopment of the Third World leads to internally uneven development in class structure, the system of economic production, and its political processes. Foreign investment, external aid, and trade lead to large-scale distortion in the structure of peripheral economies, which in turn results in inequality of income, intense social conflict, and ultimately in harsh state repression in dependent societies. In hypothetical form, this tenet of dependency theory states that the greater the degree of reliance on foreign investment and foreign aid in a country, the greater the inequality of incomes and power in that country.

Foreign investment in Third World agriculture and industry generates a bias toward the use of capital-intensive techniques in productive processes. These tendencies reduce the number of jobs in agriculture and create incentives for rural-urban migration at the same time that they limit the number of industrial jobs being created in urban areas. The only opportunities for employment in urban areas are therefore in the service sector. Roberts (1979) has examined the relationship between the service sector and the increased income inequality induced by foreign investment. Foreign investment leads to higher rates of income inequality, which in turn spurs urbanization and rapid growth in the service sectors of these economies.

Dependency theory further suggests, implicitly or explicitly, that the road to development (the alternative for nondependency) is to "close off" from external control and to be liberated from the internal structure of inequality that this is said to promote. Based on their first assertion discussed above, the dependency theorists advocate less and less foreign investment, assistance, and trade in order to facilitate development. In order to reduce inequality, according to the theory, theorists have suggested reducing the service sector and the gap between urban and rural.

General historical experiences of Latin America seemed to fit the assumptions of dependency theory. However, it was increasingly recognized by the mid-1970s that some Third World countries, such as Brazil, Mexico, Taiwan, South Korea, Hong Kong, and Singapore, enjoyed the benefits of international interactions by pursuing an outward-looking development policy. These countries did not manifest many negative features of underdevelopment, and even showed some possibilities of independent capitalist development. The concept of dependency is used as an ideological rather than as a scientific construct.

Dependency theory has given primary attention to South Korea's heavy dependence on foreign capital, which has resulted in economic exploitation, foreign indebtedness, and political repression (Long 1977, H.H. Sunoo 1978). South Korea has been looked upon as a foreign-controlled economy exploited for the exclusive interest of multinational corporations (MNCs). The central argument of this explanation is that South Korea's outward-looking development policy merely serves the economic interests of MNCs. The impact of such a policy is quite negative, resulting in greater foreign debt burden, mass poverty, and political repression.

According to the logic of dependency theory, it is North rather than South Korea that offers the more soundly based and durable economic model for Third World development. But, Korea has a way of being more complicated than most dependency theorists assert. The theory has reduced the process of South Korean development to the mechanistic logic of global exploitation by international capital, mainly the multinationals. It has failed to take into consideration the importance of both the internal sociocultural tradition, natural endowment, and the state role, as well as international and inter-Korean political and military competition operating in the process of Korean development.

Development Theory

Intermediate theories tie the national and international forces together in historically contingent ways. Changes in international capitalism modify the patterns of dependency that conditions development policy of the Third World. Capitalist centers have been diversified among the U.S., West Germany, Japan, and other powers in the Third World. This helps to strengthen the bargaining power of the state in the Third World vis-à-vis multinationals and to give greater opportunities to domestic capitalists within the Third World nation.

Evans (1979) has generated a sophisticated theoretical framework, based on his case study of Brazil, for analyzing the mechanisms and outcomes of dependent development in the Third World. Following Cardoso and Faletto (1979), he stresses that the concept of dependency should be replaced in a wide range of disparate situation. It does not refer to any fixed relations by which a country is economically dependent upon the world capitalist system. The concept of dependency means rather that the historical process of capitalist development occurs in a dependent country in accordance with the interaction of its internal political and economic alliances with international capitalism. This process is bound to be divergent across time and space. "Dependent" development is a special instance of dependency in which development occurs with capital accumulation and differentiation of productive structure. It alludes to the generation of capital accumulation, the differentiation of productive structure, the emergence of a sophisticated state apparatus, and the structuring of class relations. Nonetheless, it does not necessarily imply the achievement of a more democratic and egalitarian society.

The mechanisms of dependent development are governed by the triple alliance of the state, multinationals, and local capitalists. The relationships among these actors are characterized by both cooperation and conflict, as each holds different interests, objectives, and leverages (Evans 1979,34–54). The state acts as a central agent of capital accumulation. Usually growing out of a military coup, the state exercises control over the economic and political actors in the development process. The strong state tries to legitimize its authority by achieving rapid industrialization. It induces the participation of both multinationals and the local bourgeoisie in capital accumulation. Multinationals bring capital-intensive technology that is not appropriate for a dependent country's productive structure, and invest mainly in consumer goods suitable to the core nations but affordable only by the middle and upper classes in the dependent country. Most local capitalists have a comparative advantage in the manufacturing sector that does not need intensive capital and high technology input. Their source of leverage over the state comes from their function of legitimizing the state's policy of capital accumulation.

The outcomes of dependent development are, however, contradictory. They combine a considerable degree of economic growth and structural change with disarticulation, exclusion, and repression in the social, economic, and political realms. In order to mitigate widespread opposition from the masses of the population, the state must legitimize its development policy. This necessarily leads the state to manipulate the electoral process by making abrupt constitutional changes (Cardoso and Faletto 1979,164–71). The advent of an authoritarian military or authoritarian regime is an essential part of dependent development.

This phenomenon can be located in the context of the emergence of the Bureaucratic-Authoritarian (BA) regime. O'Donnell (1973) has argued that such economic contradictions as trade imbalance and the worsening of balance of payments involved in the transition from the horizontal industrialization on intermediate and capital goods leads the state to resolve these contradictions by creating a repressive bureaucratic-authoritarian regime, as illustrated by the cases of Brazil in 1964, Argentina in 1966, Chile and Uruguay in 1973, and South Korea in 1972.

Developmentalists perceived a breakdown in the identity between modernity and freedom. For development theories, the relative position of any state or society in an international framework, or different sectors, classes, and subclasses within a state and society, affects events more than values, attitudes, or dependency. Policy became an even more important aspect of development, since questions of capitalism and socialism, democracy or authoritarianism, were matters of choice for new nations rather than historical inevitabilities (Horowitz 1982,77). At the same time, decisions concerning reform and/or revolution were determined by strategies and tactics, and not simply models of social change imported from an earlier European framework. One-party military rule can also serve as a political system. In this perspective the extensive military leverage of the social order emerges with a specific set of planning and developmental tasks.

Much more substantive attention has been devoted to South than to North Korea. This is because, except for the absence of North Korean data, South Korea raises the more complex and interesting questions regarding development. South Korea has been well analyzed within a modified dependent development framework by Lim (1985). Foster-Carter (1987) has advised that two Koreas' development be analyzed through a bipartisan approach from which the developmental outcomes of each can be celebrated as well as criticized avoiding ideological prejudices. He particularly pointed out that in spite of its claims, North Korea has depended considerably on the Soviet Union, whereas South Korea has taken a more independent pattern than its outlook would suppose.

The two Koreas are considered unique cases in a general discussion of the previous theoretical frameworks. It is not sufficient to view the countries' development simply in terms of any one model. All the existing modes of explanation of Korea's development emphasize only a particular aspect of the total processes. They may be valid to some degree, but they do not present an entire picture of the complex nature of Korean development. The division itself is in sharp contrast with the other cases. In Germany, there was the avowed intention and prearrangement among the Allied powers to make Germany impotent by means of partition. The German case was the prototype for division by international agreement. The division of Korea was not, however, intentional in the sense that there was no agreement or prearrangement of the nature of the Allied entry into and occupation of Korea. The case of Vietnam was also different from that of Korea. Like China, the division of Vietnam was due basically to civil war between Hanoi and Saigon. The Korean civil war was not the cause of the division but the result of the division imposed by external foreign powers.

Korea is a small country with meager raw materials, scarce capital, and a large population. Agricultural production is constrained by limited arable land that constitutes only 23 percent of the total. There are no significant raw materials and energy sources other than some deposits of medium-grade coal. The basic resource deficiency makes the Korean case different from others. Korea does not provide much incentive for multinational investment or the Soviet Union because of its meager raw materials. Their chief interest in Korea lies solely in cheap and disciplined labor, or in political-military reasons.

Korea has a long history, marked by a considerable degree of national identity, ethnic homogeneity, and cultural achievement. This national, ethnic, and cultural cohesiveness facilitates a great degree of elite solidarity and mass participation in the development process. There are substantial remnants of traditional Korean culture at work in modern Korea. Even more than in China, Confucianism overwhelmingly molded the social structure, values, economic activities, and political pattern of premodern Korea. One of the positive legacies of Confucian tradition is thought to be its impact on the formation of a well-educated and hard-working labor force. By 1988, Korea's literacy rate was about 99 percent on both sides, far higher than China's 73 percent, and slightly higher than Taiwan's 92 percent.

Korea has frequently been the object of foreign aggression. Located at the heart of Northeast Asia, it constitutes a protecting shield for China, Russia's outlet to the Pacific Ocean, and Japan's bridge to the Asian mainland. As the Cold War intensified, the Korean peninsula became the focus of East-West political and military rivalry that culminated in the Korean War in 1950. Korea had experienced the brutality of a civil war from which both sides suffered heavy destruction.

In addition, Korea received massive economic and military aid from the superpowers, through which the latter intervened in Korea's domestic political affairs.

The strong state characterizes Korea's historical development. The autocratic tradition embedded in the centralized Korea of the Yi dynasty, reinforced by the Japanese colonial legacy of authoritarian and coercive rule, has given clear continuity to the evolution of authoritarian regimes in modern Korea. Moreover, the impact of the two Koreas' competition with each other on its development process cannot be overlooked. Consciousness of continuing threats from the other side has imposed a heavy defense burden on both Koreas. These threats have also been used as an excuse for the suspension of democracy in the name of security, stability, and growth on each side. This awareness of the competition with the other side has motivated itself to surpass its archrival economically.

The above examination of the three approaches to capitalist and Communist development provides, for their own parts, helpful insights to grasp a significant part of the nature of the development of capitalist South Korea and Communist North Korea. Also, the specific parameters involved in the Korean case suggest to us that the existing modes of explanation of national development be revised and complemented based on the two Koreas' experiences.

References

Amin, Samir et al. 1982. *Dynamics of Global Crisis*. New York: Monthly Review Press.

Buttinger, Joseph. 1977. *Vietnam: The Unforgettable Tragedy*. London: Andre Deutsch.

Cardoso, Fernando H. and Enso Faletto. 1979. *Dependency and Development in Latin America*. Berkeley: University of California Press.

Carr, William. 1987. *A History of Germany, 1815–1985*. London: Edward Arnold.

Chau, Phan Thien. 1972. "Leadership in the Viet Nam workers party: The process of transition." *Asian Survey* 12(9):772–82.

Childs, David. 1983. *The GDR: Moscow's German Ally*. Boston: G. Allen & Unwin.

Childs, David and Jeffrey Johnson. 1981. *West Germany: Politics and Society*. London: Croom Helm.

Chirot, Daniel. 1977. *Social Change in the Twentieth Century*. New York: Harcourt Brace Jovanovich.

Clark, Cal. 1987. "Economic development in Taiwan: A model of a political economy." *Journal of Asian and African Studies* 22:1–16.

Cole, David C. and Princeton N. Lyman. 1971. *Korean Development: The Interplay of Politics and Economics*. Cambridge, Mass.: Harvard University Press.

Dornberg, John. 1974. *The Two Germanys*. New York: The Dial Press.

Europa World Yearbook, The. 1990. *The Europa World Yearbook, 1990*. (2 vols.) London: Europa Publications.

Evans, Peter. 1979. *Dependent Development: The Alliance of Multinational, State, and Local Capital in Brazil*. Princeton, NJ: Princeton University Press.

Fall, Bernard B. 1963. *The Two Viet-Nams: A Political and Military Analysis*. New York: Praeger Publishers.

Far Eastern Economic Review (FEER). 1990. *Asia Yearbook 1990*. Hong Kong: FEER.

_____. 1985. *Asia Yearbook 1985*. Hong Kong: FEER.

_____. 1975. *Asia Yearbook 1975*. Hong Kong: FEER.

_____. 1970. *Asia Yearbook 1970*. Hong Kong: FEER.

Foster-Carter, Aidan G. 1987. "Standing up: The two Korean states and the dependency debate—a bipartisan approach." Pp. 229–69 in Kyong-Dong Kim (ed.), *Dependency Issues in Korean Development: Comparative Perspectives*. Seoul: Seoul National University Press.

Frank, Andre G. 1981. *Crisis: In the Third World*. New York: Holms & Meier Publishers.

Gottlieb, Manuel. 1960. *The German Peace Settlement and the Berlin Crisis*. New Brunswick, NJ: Transaction Publishers.

Grosser, Alfred. 1971. *Germany in Our Time: A Political History of the Postwar Years*. New York: Praeger.

Horowitz, Irving Louis. 1982. *Beyond Empire and Revolution*. New York: Oxford University Press.

Inkeles, Alex. 1974. *Becoming Modern: Individual Change in Six Developing Countries*. Cambridge, Mass.: Harvard University Press. Originally published in 1950.

Jones, Leroy P. and Il Sakong. 1980. *Government, Business, and Entrepreneurship in Economic Development: The Korean Case*. Cambridge, Mass.: Harvard University Press.

Ka, Chin-Ming and Mark Selden. 1986. "Original accumulation, equity and late industrialization: The cases of socialist China and capitalist Taiwan." *World Development* 14:1293–1310.

Kihl, Young Whan. 1984. *Politics and Policies in Divided Korea: Regimes in Contest*. Boulder, CO: Westview Press.

Kim, Kwang Suk and Michael Roemer. 1979. *Growth and Structural Transformation*. Cambridge, Mass.: Harvard University Press.

Kim, Kyong-Dong. 1979. *Man and Society in Korea's Economic Growth: Sociological Studies*. Seoul: Seoul National University Press.

Kuznets, Paul W. 1977. *Economic Growth and Structure in the Republic of Korea*. New Haven: Yale University Press.

Lee, Man-Gap. 1973. *Hankuk nongchon sahoe eui kujo wa byunhwa* (The social structure of the Korean village and its change). Seoul: Seoul National University Press.

Lim, Hyun-Chin. 1985. *Dependent Development in Korea, 1963–1979*. Seoul: Seoul National University Press.

Long, Don. 1979. "Repression and Development in the Periphery: South Korea." *Bulletin of Concerned Asian Scholars* 9(20):26–41.

McCauley, Martin. 1983. *The German Democratic Republic since 1945*. New York: St. Martin's Press.

McClelland, David C. 1961. *The Achieving Society*. Princeton, NJ: Van Nostrand. Originally published in 1955.

Moreton, Edwin (ed.). 1987. *Germany between East and West*. New York: Cambridge University Press.

O'Donnell, Guillermo A. 1973. *Modernization and Bureaucratic-Authoritarianism*. Berkeley: University of California Press.

Roberts, Bryan R. 1979. *Cities of Peasants: The Political Economy of Urbanization in the Third World*. Beverly Hills, CA: Sage Publications.

Rostow, Walt W. 1960. *The Stages of Economic Growth: A Non-Communist Manifesto*. Cambridge: Cambridge University Press.

Rubenstein, Ed. 1989. "The Economic Wall." *National Review*, 22 December 1989. p.22.

Sunoo, Harold H. 1978. "Economic Development and Foreign Control in South Korea." *Journal of Contemporary Asia* 8:322–40.

Sweezy, Paul M., Harry Magdoff, and John G. Gurley. 1975. *China's Economic Strategy: Its Development and Some Resulting Contrasts with Capitalism and the U.S.S.R.* New York: Monthly Review Press. (Also *Monthly Review* 27(3).)

Urata, Shujiro. 1987. "Sources of economic growth and structural change in China: 1956–1981." *Journal of Comparative Economics* 11:96–115.

Wallerstein, Immanual. 1989. *The Modern World-System III: The Second Era of Great Expansion of the Capitalist World-Economy, 1730–1840s*. New York: Academic Press.

———. 1984. *The Politics of World-Economy*. New York: Cambridge University Press.

Wilczynski, Jozef. 1983. *Industrial Relations in Planned Economies, Market Economies, and the Third World*. New York: St. Martin's Press.

Wiles, P.J.D. 1977. *Economic Institutions Compared*. Oxford: Basil Blackwell.

World Bank. 1988. *World Development Report 1987*. New York: Oxford University Press.

———. 1983. *China: Socialist Economic Development*, vol. 1. Washington, D.C.: World Bank.

3

The Bases for Development

The two Korean developments in postwar period cannot be fully understood without a careful examination of the socioeconomic and cultural heritages of the Yi society and the Japanese colonial rule before 1945. Until the opening of its doors to the modern world by signing the Kanghwa Treaty with Japan in 1876, Korea had rigorously pursued a seclusion policy under the Chinese political and cultural umbrella. The opening of the nation led Korea to become the object of rivalry among several imperial powers for the quarter century after the treaty. Korea's fate was ready to be decided by the expanding powers of both the East and West. Japan ended this rivalry by defeating Russia in 1905, proceeding to make Korea its colony in 1910. The "hermit kingdom" was incorporated into the Japanese empire between 1910 and 1945. At the end of World War II, the colony became subject to the East-West conflict. The South was integrated into the capitalist world and the North into the communist.

Traditional Development and Exposure to the Modern World

The early nineteenth century represents the expansion of Western imperial powers who were turning their attention from Africa to East Asia. Using the Opium War (1840–42) as a pretext, Western nations forced China to open her ports in 1842. In 1854, America broke down the seclusion of Japan. Great Britain secured Hong Kong, Portugal had Macao, France occupied Cochin-China, Annam, and Tonkin, and Russia seized the northern territory of the Amur River region.

Entering the 1860s Korea had also become the object of the imperial powers, such as France, America, England, Russia, and Germany as well as China and Japan. While the Western powers provided the original impetus for opening Korea, it was Japan and China that played a decisive role in ending its isolation from the outside world. Japan, which sought to increase its national power after the Meiji Restoration in 1868, seized this opportunity to open up Korea by force in 1876 when its proposals for trade were turned down. Korea also signed a treaty with the United States in 1882, negotiated through China's good offices, giving the United States trade privileges. Similar treaties were concluded with Great Britain and Germany in 1883, Italy and Russia in 1884, and France in 1886.

The treaty made forcibly by Japan presented an immediate challenge to the position of supremacy that China had held over the East Asian world from early times because it declared that Korea was an independent state, which meant that Korea ceased to be a dependent state of China. Korea became a field for the practice of diplomatic intrigues, the "Balkans of the East" (Chien 1967,3). Situated at a crucial crossroad in Northeast Asia and occupying the heart of the strategic triangle of China, Russia, and Japan, Korea had been a focus of international contentions. China's influence over Korea came to an end with the Japanese victory in the Sino-Japanese War of 1894–5. The Japanese victory in the Russo-Japanese War of 1904–5 finally ended the struggle over the Korean peninsula and secured Japanese influence over Korea's future development path.

Faced with serious challenges from the changing external political environment, the Yi state could not manage the crisis. The Yi Dynasty (1392–1910) was a highly stratified aristocratic society with a weak monarchy (K.H. Kim 1980, Palais, 1975). Although the Yi state bureaucracy itself was a well-organized and influential agency in theory, the state was weak in practice because it was dominated by a landed aristocracy. There were four categories of status in Yi society: *yangban* (aristocrats), *sangmin* (common people), *chungin* (lowly artisans), and *chonmin* (the despised). Composed of powerful lineages with hereditary aristocratic status and concomitant political and social privileges, the *yangban* (literally, "the two divisions," referring to the civil and military branches of the officialdom) monopolized access to the civil and military bureaucracy (Palais 1975,17). The aristocracy was able to manipulate state power to preserve privilege. Their political power was reinforced by the Confucian precept that enjoined the ruler to honor virtuous officials. Confucian orthodoxy as the state ideology restricted social mobility in this hereditary and hierarchical status system.

The Yi state did not encourage commercial activities, since revenues came from agriculture, not from commerce, and Confucian ideology, particularly in Korea, disdained commercial activities and physical labor (Lim 1985, 33). Rejecting Western consumer goods and technologies, the *yangban* insisted upon a closed agrarian subsistence economy as a basic principle of socioeconomic organization. The policy of the Yi state basically discouraged the production of wealth. This resulted in economic stagnation throughout the Yi Dynasty. The general judgment until the 1960s at least was that "commerce and industry were not the sorts of activities one should engage in or be rewarded for" (Cummings 1981, 23).

Discouraging commercial activities, the Confucian ideology emphasized learning and meritocratic bureaucracy. The elites were recruited through state examination. Emphasis on learning has contributed to the formation of a well-educated, skilled, and disciplined labor force. Its civil servant concept has also been conducive to the emergence of an effective bureaucracy with well-trained administrators.

However, the limited number of posts available in the bureaucracy by "upward draft" led to factional struggles within the bureaucracy. Political factionalism has had a great influence on political behavior in both Koreas.

The Yi Dynasty's primary foreign relationship had been with China, in which the cardinal relationship was the *sadaechuii* (flunkeyism) (Kim and Kim 1967,12–13). The idea was derived from Confucian elder-younger relationship involving the obligation of protection in exchange for ritual allegiance. The *sadaechuii* helped to discourage the drive for national self-reliance in the Yi Dynasty (Kim and Kim 1967). This flunkeyism should not, however, blind anyone to a most important characteristic of Korea's traditional diplomacy: isolationism, or exclusionism (K.H. Kim 1980). For 300 years after the Japanese invasions of the 1590s Korea isolated itself from Japan, dealt harshly with errant Westerners washing up on its shore, and kept the Chinese at arm's length (C.S. Lee 1963,13). Thus, Westerners called Korea the Hermit Kingdom, describing the pronounced streak of obstinate hostility toward foreign power and the deep desire for independence that marked traditional Korea. North Korea has exercised a "hermit king-dom" option by remaining one of the most isolated states in the world. By Korean standards, it is South Korea that, since the 1960s, has been "revolutionary" by pursuing an open-door policy toward markets and seeking a multilateral, varied diplomacy.

There came about some reformist ideas during the crisis of the nation's opening in the late nineteenth century. *Sirhak*, a reform-oriented Confucianism and ideas of Western learning appealed to some of the ruling elites and some urban intellectuals of the *chungin* class (Choe 1986,226). Supported by King Kojong, the reformists launched a series of reform policies in the early 1880s. There was also an attempt to restore royal authority which had steadily eroded under the consort clans' domination of the state. These reform policies were possible because of their widening influence in the state bureaucracy.

The reformists gradually, however, lost their power because of checks by conservative *yangban*. The pragmatic reforms caused increasing resentment and opposition from the more orthodox Confucian literati (K.H. Kim 1980,337). The *Kabo* Reform in 1894 was also greatly constrained by the vested interests of powerful *yangban* landed aris-tocracy. The anti-Western and anti-Japanese foreign policy of the con-servative orthodox Confucians was able to get wider support among the population than the reformists (Choe 1986,231).

The peasants were so discontented with the existing structure of domination that they ceaselessly provoked uprisings. The discontent with state exploitation and imperialistic penetration culminated in the peasant war of 1894–5 that has been called the Tonghak (literally, "Eastern Learning") revolution in South Korea or *Kabo* (1894) peas-ant war in North Korea. The Tonghak revolution of 1894 was the beginning of the Korean nationalist movements and it carried in part a xenophobic nature of the Korean nationalist movements (C.S. Lee 1963,19–33).

Development Under Colonial Dependence

Prior to liberation, Korea had operated as a colonial economy. Pri-vate ownership was allowed, but tightly controlled by the Japanese Military Government (JMG). At the time of the annexation, Korea's

TABLE 3.1
Occupational Distribution of the Population
(May 1910)

Govt. Employed	15,758	
Unemployed	54,217	
Confucian Scholars	19,075	3.1%
Agriculture	2,433,450	85.2%
Fishery	33,646	
Industry	22,943	
Mining	1,429	.8%
Commerce	178,780	6.2%
Unemployed and others	135,479	4.7%
Total	2,894,777	100.0%

Sources: Kim and Kim (1967), *Korea and the Politics of Imperialism 1876–1910*, pp. 225–227.

occupational distribution reflected its agrarian structure, with 85 percent of all households engaged in agriculture and fishing and a tiny 0.8 percent engaged in mining and industry (Table 3.1).

Japanese authoritarian and coercive colonial rule has left a legacy of centralized state control in the development process in the postindependence period. Although the Yi state was strong at the center, it had weak links to the broad strata of the society. Japanese rule broadened by force the power of the state exercising it to the bottom of the strata. The Yi state soon possessed a comprehensive, autonomous, and penetrating quality that no previous Korean state could possibly have mustered. Compared with French colonial Vietnam in 1937, Korean bureaucracy in the same year was more centralized and was dominated by people from the motherland (Cumings 1981,11–12). The colonial state achieved the mobilization of the Korean upper class, finding important collaborators within the old bureaucracy and mobilizing others into pro-Japanese organizations.

During the Japanese colonial period, the economic growth of Korea was considerably promoted, although this growth was heavily lopsided and geared toward the advantage of Japan. Japanese colonialism left a moderately well-developed social infrastructure in Korea. To sustain both industrialization and the transport of agricultural produce, Japan

TABLE 3.2
Distribution of Korean Labor Force, 1944

Industry	Number in millions	% Japanese	% of all employed
Agr. & Fish.	7.5	6	72.8
Manufac. & Mining	.9	20	8.7
Commerce	.4	22	3.9
Public Services etc.	.3	38	2.9
Other	1.2	14	11.7
Total	10.3	(8.4%)	100.0%

Sources: Rosenberg (1975), "Economic Comparison of North and South Korea," p. 178.

set up an extensive communications network, particularly through railroads. This was, of course, geared not to the domestic needs of Korea, but "externally" to those of the Japanese empire, with the linkages going from mines to the coast.

The Japanese regime mobilized Korean peasants into industry by increasing the concentration of land holdings and the National General Mobilization Law. By 1936 heavy industry accounted for 28 percent of total industrial production (Cumings 1981,26). Industry expanded in Korea far faster than in China and its Taiwan colony. Through forced industrialization between 1910 and 1944, the agricultural and fishing population had decreased from 85 to 73 percent, while the population engaged in industry and mining had increased from .8 to 8.7 percent (Table 3.2). On the other hand, commercial activities had declined from 6.2 to 3.9 percent during the same period. Industrialization was also fostered by three big institutions: the Government-General, including national public companies, such as the Oriental Development Company and the South Manchurian Railway Company (SMRC); the central bank, such as the Bank of Chosun and the Industrial Bank; and the great zaaibatsu houses of Japan, such as Mitsubish, Mitsui, and Sumitomo (Cumings 1981,3–67).

The Japanese introduced a modern education system, which was designed to assimilate Koreans into Japanese society by obliterating Korean national consciousness. This included the degradation of Korean history and the elimination of Korean language. This had an adverse impact on Korea's future development.

TABLE 3.3
Distribution of Resources between South and North
Korea at Partition, 1945

Sector	South Korea	North Korea
Agriculture	63%	37%
Light Industry	69%	31%
Heavy Industry	35%	65%
Commerce	82%	18%

Source: U.S. Central Intelligence Agency (1978), National Foreign Assessment Center, *Korea:*
The Economic Race Between the North and the South, p. 1.

War-related industrialization after the 1930s created a dual economy. Heavy industry and mines were developed in the north; agriculture, the light industry and most of the service sector were developed mainly in the south. Table 3.3 shows the unbalanced distribution between the south and the north at the partition in 1945.

The major political, economic, and sociocultural legacies of the Yi Dynasty and Japanese colonialism were shared by both Koreas. The strong state and nationalism were formed, which had an influence on implementing policies and guiding procedures in the development process of both Koreas. Authoritarian human relationships and political factionalism were continued on both sides. The heritage of emphasizing education was pursued with great zeal.

Nevertheless, the same tradition has had a different impact on each system. The Japanese *oyabun-kobun* human relationship, mixed with the traditional Confucian elder-younger relation and flunkyism, imprinted itself on the Korean mentality. It has been transferred to modern Korean political behavior, fostering paternalism in politics. In the North, the paternalistic human relation of the entire society were intensified as the result of the Korean War that left a great many orphans. In the South, it formed a strong intraparty group whose members pledged loyalty to their boss, fostering political factionalism.

Some traditions were absorbed into, or radically rejected by the communists in the North, while naturally developing without any abrupt change in the South. The Confucian trait of disdaining commercial activity is echoed by the communist ideology of North Korea which regards them as "nonproductive." Strict nationalism and exclusionism were intensified in Communist North Korea. The old exclusionist trait of Korean nationalism was well fortified by the extremist anticolonialism of the Communist ideology, which affects the North Korean idea of *juche* or self-reliance.

The Japanese colonial rule brought forth an entirely new set of Korean political leaders, spawned by the resistance to Japanese colonialism. The emergence of nationalist and Communist groups dates back to the 1920s; it is really in this period that the left-right split of postwar Korea began (Cumings 1984,21). The nationalist anti-Japanese movement developed and touched off the March First Independence Movement in 1919 in which Christian nationalists played an important role. Anti-Japanese communist military groups also were formed in Siberia, China, and Manchuria. Following the March First Movement in Korea, the leading nationalists in coalition with the communists established the Korean Provisional Government (KPG) in Shanghai. The coalition, however, lasted less than two years. The Soviet Union rendered material aid in the form of money, weapons, and technical assistance (Scalapino and Lee 1972,63).

The distinctive character of Korean nationalism was created during this period by a group of Korean nationalists such as Shin Chae-ho, An Changho, and others. They were the originators of both *juche* and *chaju*, Park Chung-hee's concept of mastery in one's own house. Since the time of Korea's opening, Korea had waged persistent struggles to retain its national independence and identity against powerful, often expansionist neighbors. From the centuries-old struggles against foreign domination, a tradition of strong nationalism had developed among the Korean people.

Korean nationalism was to a great degree inspired by the Christian churches. A significant number of old-generation leaders were transformed in their thought patterns and behavior through close contact with the missionaries. Along with Christian ideas, the missionaries brought liberal Western thoughts upon which much of Korean nationalism was nurtured (C.S. Lee 1963,277). The churches provided not only spiritual leaders, but also reformers and educators. The careers of most South Korean political activists after the liberation reveal some kind of Christian connection as well as Japanese higher education and work in journalism (Scalapino and Lee 1972,235).

Communism also developed in Korea as part of the fight against Japanese imperialism. Communist activities were assisted by the Soviets and Chinese military forces and monetary resources. The first official Korean Communist Party (KCP) was formed in 1925. As the Japanese military government cracked down on communists and their activities, some influential communists performed their activities outside the country. The communist activists became the political leaders in North Korea after the liberation. In this way, Japanese colonialism provided political bases for South and North Korea.

The Setting of Divided Development

The idea of dividing the Korean peninsula originated at the time of the Japanese invasion in 1593 (H.J. Kim 1977,18). It was discussed between China and Japan when Toyotomi Hideyoshi proposed that of the eight provinces of Korea four in the north should be ruled by the King of Korea, and the remaining four in the south ceded to Japan. The negotiation failed, and the war continued until the death of Toyotomi Hideyoshi in 1598. At the time of the opening of Korea, the division of Korea was discussed again. When Russia was faced with a Japanese threat backed by English force, Russia "tried in Korea to establish the thirty-ninth parallel as the dividing line between the spheres of influence of the two nations" (Hatada 1969,106). Japan refused the offer and defeated Russia.

At the Cairo Conference of December 1943 the Allies had decided to strip Japan of all the territories it had acquired since 1894 as a result its expansionist drive abroad, among which Korea had been one of the first (Bunge 1981,17). The Soviet Union agreed on the same principle in its declaration of war against Japan. Although the Yalta agreement on February 8, 1945 between the U.S. and the U.S.S.R. confirmed an international trusteeship for Korea, no decision had been made on the exact formula for governing that nation in the aftermath of an Allied victory. The landing of Soviet forces compelled the U.S. to improvise a formula for Korea. On 15 August 1945, President Harry Truman proposed to Stalin the division of Korea at the 38th parallel. The Moscow Meeting of the Allied powers on 7 December 1945 imposed trusteeship over Korea for a five-year period during which a Korean provisional government would prepare for full independence. This was the third time a Korean division was discussed and carried out.

The division of the Korean peninsula created two distorted and unbalanced entities. Geographically, the Korean territory, shaped like New Jersey but 70 percent of which consisting of mountain, has been divided roughly into two halves since 1945. The North occupies about 55 percent of the total land area of Korean peninsula, or 122,370 square kilometers; about the size of state of New York, Louisiana, or Mississippi. The South occupies about 45 percent of the peninsula, or 99,200 square kilometers; about the size of the state of Indiana. The northern half is more mountainous, with only 17 percent of the land suitable for agricultural use; 24 percent of the land in the south is arable. The soil in the south is considered to be better. The northern climate is considerably colder and less favorable for agriculture, particularly rice growing, than the southern that allows two crops a year in the southernmost provinces. Before 1945, rice and barley were mainly grown in the south, which had 75 percent of all paddy land, while the north led in such crops as wheat and corn (Park 1971,476–513). In terms of the conditions of geographical size and natural resources, each Korea is comparable to the two Vietnamese cases.

One of the more important factors for the divided setting of South and North Korea is the distribution of resources. In general, the Korean peninsula is not rich in natural resources. There are iron ore and coal deposits throughout the territory, though of small quantity and low quality. More relevant are nonferrous minerals that are found largely in the north and tungsten, which is abundant in the south. Graphite, magnesium, limestone, mica, and fluorite are concentrated more considerably in the north than in the south (Park 1971,478): "The North is more favored in terms of mineral deposits" (NUB 1986,52).

The distribution of industrial establishments was somewhat uneven in 1945. Under Japanese colonial rule, Korea was to supply foodstuffs and raw materials for the Japanese economy. Therefore, the Japanese invested in irrigation facilities, mainly in the south, and in mining, mainly in the north. An extended railroad system, ports, and a communication network were also built by Japan. These facilities, however, were geared toward Japanese trade and military purposes. Because of the location of the major coal and ore deposits, the proximity to Japan, and the bridge position to Manchuria, the main industrial establishments for a limited production of iron, steel, cement, chemical fertilizer, and oil were situated in the northeast of Korea, with only some light industry established in the south. Thus, North Korea inherited the lion's share of the existing industries in 1945. But this legacy was seriously depleted when the North Koreans received it: The Japanese had monopolized all technical and managerial positions. When they left in 1945 they took all the plans and other know-how with them, and there was hardly anybody to run the factories.

It is certain in 1945 that the North had advantages over the South regarding the base for development. However, a consideration of the setting of the divided development cannot be confined to conditions in the base year 1945, when separate development began. Later outside influences on their respective evolutions, most importantly the impact of the Korean War and the input of foreign aid on both sides, must also be examined.

In conclusion, South and North Korea shared a common ethnic, cultural, and historical experience until 1945. They are geographically about the same size, the northern half containing more mineral resources while the southern half is more favorably endowed for agriculture. Since most of the Japanese industrialization in Korea was located in the North, North Korea had an advantage when the separate development began in 1945. However, this advantage was lost during the Korean War which brought more devastation for the North, and it was reversed by postwar aid and economic assistance which was at least seven times higher for South Korea than for the North. In this respect, differences in success had little effect in the long run on the rates of economic growth achieved by the two Koreas. The crucial differences were in the system and the policies chosen to foster growth. In the overall balance, the advantages and disadvantages of the two parts of Korea were roughly equal.

References

Bunge, Frederica M. (ed.). 1981. *North Korea: A Country Study*. Washington, D.C.: American University Press.

Chien, Frederick Foo. 1967. *The Opening of Korea: A Study of Chinese Diplomacy, 1876–1885*. Hamden, CT: The Shoe String Press.

Choe, Jae-Hyeon. 1986. "Strategic groups of nationalism in nineteenth-century Korea." *Journal of Contemporary Asia* 16 (2):223–36.

Cumings, Bruce. 1984. *The Two Koreas*. New York: Headline Series.

_____. 1981. *The Origins of the Korean War: Liberation and the Emergence of Separate Regimes, 1945–1947*. Princeton, N.J.: Princeton University Press.

Hatada, Takashi. 1969. *A History of Korea*. Trans. by Warren W. Smith and Benjamin H. Hazard. Santa Barbara, CA: ABC-Clio Press.

Kim, Chong Ik Eugene and Han-Kyo Kim. 1967. *Korea and the Politics of Imperialism, 1879–1910*. Berkeley: University of California Press.

Kim, Hak-Joon. 1977. *The Unification Policy of South and North Korea, 1948–1976*. Seoul: Seoul National University Press.

Kim, Key-Hiuk. 1980. *The Last Phase of the East Asian World Order: Korea, Japan, and the Chinese Empire, 1860–1882*. Berkeley: University of California Press.

Lee, Chong-sik. 1963. *The Politics of Korean Nationalism*. Berkeley: University of California Press.

Lim, Hyun-Chin. 1985. *Dependent Development in Korea, 1963–1979*. Seoul: Seoul National University Press.

National Unification Board (NUB). 1986. *A Comparative Study of South and North Korean Economies*. Seoul: NUB.

Palais, James B. 1975. *Politics and Policy in Transitional Korea*. Cambridge, Mass.: Harvard University Press.

Park, Byong-Ho. 1971. "National resources and industrial locations in South and North Korea." Pp. 476–513 in Asiatic Research Center in Korea University, *International Conference on the Problem of Korean Unification*. Seoul: Asiatic Research Center, Korean University.

Rosenberg, W. 1975. "Economic comparison of North and South Korea." *Journal of Contemporary Asia* 5:178–204.

Scalapino, Robert A. and Chong-Sik Lee. 1972. *Communism in Korea*. Part I and II. Berkeley: University of California Press.

U.S. Central Intelligence Agency (CIA). 1978. *Korea: The Economic Race Between the North and the South*. Washington, D.C.: National Foreign Assessment Center, U.S. CIA.

4

Economic Development in
South and North Korea

Economic development is normally taken to mean economic growth concerned with national product and national income. Economic development in this book refers to the growth and/or change in Gross National Product (GNP), economic structure, and foreign trade. Each indicator is structured to consider both levels of quantity and quality. The developmental outcomes of South and North Korean performance during the period of 1945–88 are assessed in this chapter by these measures.

Gross National Product and National Income

South and North Korea use different concepts to determine their aggregate national accounts. South Korea adopts gross national product (GNP) while North Korea uses gross social product (GSP). GNP and GSP are the two commonly used indicators for aggregate national accounts in world capitalist and socialist countries, respectively. GNP of South Korea refers to the total value of all end products and services in a certain period of time. GSP of North Korea represents the total value of material goods and "productive" services (freight transportation, communication, and construction) in a certain period of time, in which the values of intermediate products are included.

GNP = total amount of production in all industries including services – intermediate products.

GSP = total amount of production in all industries including intermediate products – "nonproductive" services.

Like the gross product, national income (NI) of the two Koreas differs in similar context. The NI used in South Korea represents the total of all incomes received by all factors in production and services during one year (NNP, or Net National Product at Factor Cost). Therefore, NI equals GNP less the depreciation of capital and overseas production. NI used in North Korea, as in most socialist countries, represents the sum of net material product (NMP) of all separately enumerated branches of the economy, and therefore equals GSP less all material costs including the depreciation of capital and intermediate product. This comes close to the capitalist definition of NI, though nonproductive services are still not counted in North Korean NI.

The definition of the North Korean gross product and national income basically differs from that of South Korea in two major respects: it excludes "nonproductive" services such as public administration, passenger transportation, communication, hospital services, housing, education, and so on, but it includes construction, electricity, freight transportation, and public communications; and it includes turnover taxes on transactions that are levied mainly on consumer goods (Breidenstein 1975 P. S. Lee 1972, 518–26).

Therefore, overall indicators of South and North Korean economic development cannot be directly compared unless values are adjusted. Furthermore, data on North Korea's GSP were not available after 1968. In this dissertation, the adjustments are tried in two ways: North Korean GSP is converted into GNP to be compared with that of the South; and South Korean GNP is converted into GSP to be compared with that of the North. Data on GNP and per capita GNP constructed by the first method are available directly from the several statistical sources discussed in methodology section of chapter 1. They have been reconstructed by the complement of one another as presented in chapter 1. Table 4.1 shows estimated GNP and per capita GNP in current market prices for the period of 1945–88.

Although a GNP comparison is hard to draw because of the lack of reliable data and differences in measurement, several estimates agree on the suggestion that the North had a higher per capita output than the South until at least the mid-1970s (ACDA 1988, Bridges 1986, 37, U.S. CIA 1978). It seems that per capita GNP of South Korea has surpassed that of North Korea since 1976 (*see* figure 4.1). The South's growth rate has outpaced the North's since 1966. In 1988, the size of

TABLE 4.1
Gross National Product

| | GNP (bil.$) | | GNP per capita ($) | |
	SK	NK	SK	NK
1945	.4-.8	.4	25-50	36
1949	1.4	.7	67	72
1953	1.2	.5	55	56
1960	1.8	2.2	60	208
1965	2.5	3.6	88	292
1970	8.6	4.4	264	312
1975	19.0	9.6	518	605
1980	61.8	17.9 (19.1)	1,553	1,000 (1,067)
1985	89.4	24.3	2,177	1,192
1988	164.0	27.6	3,850	1,260

Sources: EPB and BOK for SK
J.S. Chung (1974); P.S. Lee (1972) for NK
World Bank; CIA; ACDA

TABLE 4.2
Average Annual GNP Growth Rate

	SK	NK
1946–1950	—	44.4
1953–1960	4.3 (3.5)	22.1
1961–1970	8.7	7.8
1971–1980	9.1 (10.3)	6.2
1981–1988	10.0	(3.3)

Sources: EPB and BOK for SK
J.S. Chung (1974); P.S. Lee (1972) for NK
World Bank; CIA; ACDA

the South Korean economy is six times larger than that of the North, and per capita GNP of South Korea is three times higher than that of North Korea.

South Korea's GNP has increased tremendously during the post-liberation period. It has grown from far less than one billion dollars in 1945 to $164 billion in 1988. Between 1953 and 1988, GNP expanded by 141 times at an annual growth rate of 8.0 percent. The rapid growth in the South has been achieved mostly since the 1960s (table 4.2).

Until 1960 the South Korean economy could not be managed without massive foreign assistance mainly from the United Nations and the United States. National income in South Korea during 1945–49 shows only a slight increase. One estimate also shows a decrease: production in 1948 was only 20 percent of the 1940 figure (Hatada 1969, 140). The population increase due to refugees from the North aggravated the per capita GNP for the South. Per capita GNP had barely increased during the period of 1945–60. Population increase during the period was 2.1 percent annually until it rose up to 3.3 percent annually excepting the period of the Korean War.

From 1960 to 1988, GNP rose at an average annual growth rate of nearly 10 percent. While South Korea's national production was rising throughout the 1960s, 1970s, and 1980s, the annual population growth rate declined to the current 1.6 percent, resulting in a sixty seven fold increase in per capita GNP in those three decades. Per capita GNP increased from $60 in 1960 to $3,850 in 1988.

The year 1980 marked a negative growth rate of 4.8 percent in South Korea. Internal economic distortions, the political and social unrest that followed the 1979 assassination of former President Park, and the effect of world economic developments such as the drastic increase in the world oil price in 1979 triggered a severe recession in the South in 1980. The economy recovered somewhat in the following years, and trade finally marked a surplus in 1986 for the first time in South Korea's modern history.

In recent years, however, South Korea has been experiencing a series of difficulties due to the increasingly high wall of world protectionism, corruption, gradual evacuation of laborers from the Middle East and South Asia, and domestic labor strikes. In 1989, economic growth fell to around 7 percent in which exports markedly decreased due to many workers' strikes, an unfavorable exchange rate, and international protectionism. The trade surplus decreased from $10.7 billion in 1988 to $4.6 billion in 1989. The goal was $9.5 billion.

North Korea's economic performance shows that GNP increased from less than one-third billion dollars in 1946 to $27.6 billion in 1988 at the annual growth rate of 15.2 percent. As shown in table 4.2, GNP increased significantly during the early period before 1965. The average annual growth rates of GNP show 44.4 and 22.1 percent during the 1946-50 and the 1953-60 periods, respectively.

Unlike the case of South Korea, the national income of North Korea has increased considerably until the mid-1960s while, since then, it has been stagnant. In 1965 it was nearly twelve times that of 1946 and 7.2

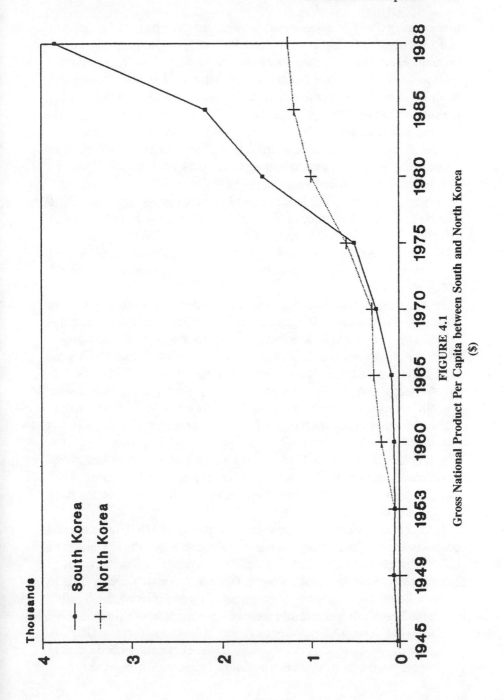

Thousands

— South Korea
+ North Korea

FIGURE 4.1

Gross National Product Per Capita between South and North Korea
($)

times that of 1953, registering an annual growth rate of 17.4 percent and 25.8 percent during 1946–65 and 1953–65, respectively. Since the population has not increased substantially owing to war losses and the outflow of refugees to the South, the growth rate in per capita national income is equally impressive, amounting to 13.7 and 19.9 percent for the two periods of 1946–65 and 1953–65, respectively.

Since entering the 1960s, the pace of overall economic progress, as measured by national income, began to drop sharply. The average annual rate of growth in national income declined from 22.1 percent during 1953–60 to 6.7 percent during 1961–65.

However, the overconfidence derived from the progress of the 1950s was dampened at the start of the 1960s. The annual growth rates of GNP declined to 7.8, 6.2, and 3.3 percent during 1960s, 1970s, and 1981–88, respectively. North Korean growth in 1988 and 1989 would be estimated about 3 percent at best and almost zero at worst (FEER 1990, 1988,161).

In April 1982, Kim Il Sung announced a new economic policy that gave priority to increased agricultural production through land reclamation, development of the country's infrastructure—especially power plants and transportation facilities—and reliance on domestically produced equipment (U.S. Department of State 1984). In 1984, the Supreme People's Assembly passed a law to permit joint ventures with foreign companies for the first time. In August 1990, North Korea allowed foreign direct investment for the first time in its history (*Chosun Ilbo*, 24 August 1990).

South Korea's GNP in 1988 was six times higher and its per capita GNP triple that of the North. It is puzzling that at least until 1975 North Korea was ahead of the South in per capita GNP, but the pace has been overturned since 1965.

In order to evaluate the "productive" aspect of GNP, net material products are compared between the two Koreas. Since the definition of the North Korean GSP excludes the "nonproductive" services, it is helpful to convert the South Korean GNP into North Korean GSP in order to compare the growth of South and North Korea by the North's concept. The NMP is a realistic indicator to which South Korean GNP is converted. The NMP of South Korea is calculated from GNP by reducing the portion of "nonproductive" development whose concept is adopted as the North Korean national income. Since there are no

TABLE 4.3
GSP Per Capita

	SK GNP p/c	%	SK's NMP p/c	NK's NMP p/c
1949	67	70.6%	47	72
1953	55	69.8%	38	56
1960	60	66.0%	40	208
1965	88	73.2%	64	292
1970	264	65.8%	174	312
1975	518	66.8%	364	605
1980	1,553	68.4%	1,062	1,000
1985	2,177	62.0%	1,349	1,192
1988	3,850	59.0%	2,272	1,260

Sources: EPB and BOK for SK
J.S. Chung (1974); P.S. Lee (1972) for NK
World Bank; CIA; ACDA

data available for North Korean NI, we apply the same technique to the the North Korea's GNP that is drawn from the statistical sources previously discussed. We simply assume the North's GNP as NMP because the portion of the service sector in North Korea is negligible (less than 5 percent of the total GNP), and some of the components in the service sector such as construction, electricity, and part of transportation and communication are even regarded as "productive."

For the construction of the South's NMP, only 15 percent out of 45 to 50 percent of total service composition in GNP, is assumed as productive service. Construction and electricity generally account for 6 percent of GNP throughout the entire period. Some of the remaining services might partially be considered "material production" in North Korea. One estimate accounted for another 9 percent as productive service (Breidenstein 1975). According to the estimate, in 1970 service industries and social overhead capital contributed 42 percent to South Korea's GNP (without construction and electricity that are included in the North Korea's National Income calculation). Considering another 9 percent as productive service, the estimate reduced South Korea's GNP by 33 percent (Breidenstein 1975,170). The estimates of NMP in South and North Korea are presented in Table 4.3.

Figure 4.2 shows that while South Korea has outperformed North Korea since 1975 in terms of GNP per capita, NMP per capita of South Korea has surpassed that of North Korea only since 1980. The most striking aspect of the North Korean economy is the continued growth

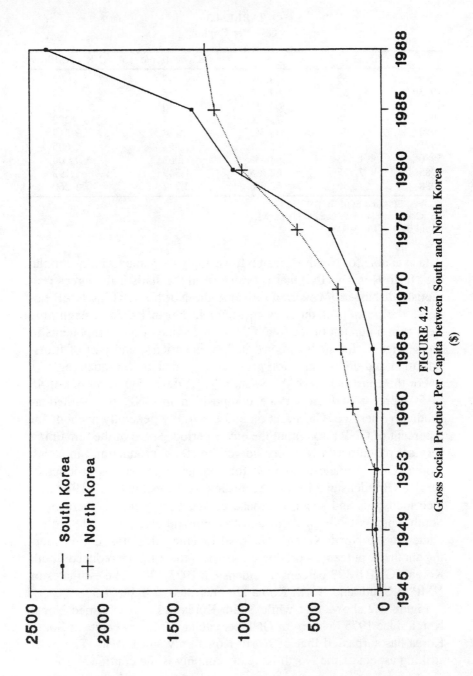

FIGURE 4.2

Gross Social Product Per Capita between South and North Korea

($)

of the machine-building and metal processing industry. Over 80 percent of industrial investment goes to heavy industry. This explains why the per capita NMP in North Korea had been higher than that of South Korea until 1979.

Economic Structure

Economic structure refers to the percentage of GNP accounted for by the products of the three general sectors of economy: first, second, and tertiary sectors. Industrialization refers to the percentage of industrial components in GNP. Quality of industrialization is analyzed by the development of the light, heavy, and high technology industries. Agricultural and rural development are compared in terms of major agricultural products. The service sector is compared by the percentage of service sector components in GNP.

One of the peculiar phenomena of the North Korean economic structure is that it has had an unbalanced development. Between 1953 and 1982, industry's share has risen from 30.7 to 70.0 percent, while the shares of agriculture and service have been reduced from 41.6 to 25.0 percent and 27.7 to 5.0 percent, respectively. Indeed, the service sectors' share of GNP has dropped to an almost negligible level (figure 4.3). At the same time, industry expanded its share of GNP remarkably. This expansion of the industry sector occurred primarily at the expense of the service sector.

In South Korea during the same period, the structure of the economy has evolved in a substantially different direction. Table 4.4 shows that the share of agriculture has dropped sharply from 45.8 to 16.2 percent; while the shares of industry and service increased from 9.8 to 30.7 percent and 44.4 to 53.1 percent, respectively. The most strikingly feature of the South Korean economy has been the large share of economic activity generated by the service sector, accounting for about 40 to 50 percent of GNP during the entire period. In the North, it has decreased to 5 percent. The service sector in South Korea has continuously increased and tends to be growing slowly in the 1980s.

Agriculture: Crops, Livestock, Fishery, and Forestry

Agricultural comparisons are made difficult by the use in North

FIGURE 4.3
Industrial Structure between South and North Korea

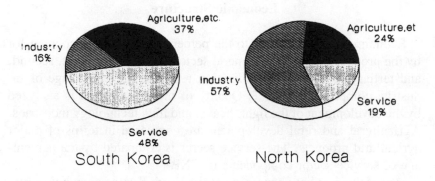

in 1960

Agriculture,etc.
37%

Industry
16%

Industry
57%

Agriculture,et
24%

Service
19%

Service
48%

South Korea   North Korea

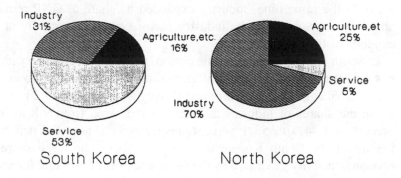

in 1982

Industry
31%

Agriculture,etc.
16%

Agriculture,et
25%

Industry
70%

Service
5%

Service
53%

South Korea   North Korea

TABLE 4.4
Composition of GNP by Industries

	1953		1956		1960		1970		1982	
	SK	NK	SK	NK	SK	NK	SK	NK	SK	NK
Agri.	45.8	41.6	47.2	26.6	36.8	23.6	28.0	20.0	16.2	25.0
Indus.	9.8	30.7	12.5	40.1	15.7	57.1	22.8	65.0	30.7	70.0
Serv.	44.4	27.7	40.3	33.3	47.5	19.3	49.2	15.0	53.1	5.0

Sources: FEER, Asia Yearbook 1984; EPB for SK.
Chung (1974), pp. 146–8, for 1950 NK.
Halliday (1987), pp. 28,33, for the year 1946, 65,70 NK.
NUB (1986), Data on NK Economy p.128 for the year 1953, 56, 60 NK.

Korea of gross tonnage rather than nutrient content of fertilizer and the reporting of crop yields in terms of unhulled rather than hulled grain. The agricultural sector comprised 18.1 and 25 percent of GNP in 1982 for South and North Korea, respectively. In general, North Korea surpasses South Korea in crops, but is inferior in livestock, fishing, and forests. North Korea claims to have the highest per capita production of rice in the world and outside observers say the North's agricultural sector is efficient, relying heavily on chemical fertilizers.

The fact that the South has a larger population and more fertile arable land than the North may be an advantage for agricultural development in South Korea. So far, however, it seems that North Korea seems to be slightly more successful in crop production than the South, but it is far below in the production of livestock and fishery. It is especially debatable regarding the real situation of food consumption because North Korea exports a considerable amount of agricultural products.

Industrialization

It is in South Korea that industrial development appears the more successful (see Table 4.6). South Korea surpasses the North in light industry. Industrial development in South Korea started with light industry, which is comparatively more advantageous and effective in the South than in the North, taking into consideration such resources as technology and the labor supply of South Korea in the 1960s, it then began to emphasize heavy industries, showing considerable progress since the beginning of the 1970s.

TABLE 4.5
Agricultural Products (1,000 metric tons)

(1)   Crops in 1987

	SK	NK
Rice	5,905	6,200
Barley	264	625
Wheat and Rye	5	893
Potatoes	450	1,950
Sweet Potatoes	542	494

Sources: FAO, *Production Yearbook, 1989.*

(2)   Livestocks Production in 1987

	SK	NK
Beef and veal	196	41
Pig Meat	368	165
Cow Milk	1,100	83
Hen Eggs	378	135
Poultry Meat	183	42

Sources: FAO, *Production Yearbook, 1989.*

(3)   Fishery and Forests in 1986

	SK	NK (1993 Target)
Total Catch in Fishery	3,660	1,700 (11,000)
Roundwood Removal	8,564	4,595

Sources: FAO, *Production Yearbook, 1988.*

In contrast, North Korea has stressed the development of heavy industry from the beginning. Moreover, accepting Stalin's concept of "socialism in one country," North Korea has been trying to build one of the most strictly closed systems even among Communist countries. Light industries are particularly poor in North Korea.

In the 1980s, "the great revolution in light industry" was stressed to improve especially the standard of the workers' material and cultural lives. Visitors to North Korea have reported that basic needs in food, clothing, housing, medical care, and education appeared to be taken care of, but that food for the ordinary person lacked variety and most consumer goods and clothes were scarce and expensive.

South Korea is in an inferior position as far as mineral and metal production are concerned. Most minerals are located in the northern

TABLE 4.6
Comparison of Selected Industrial Products
(1,000 metric tons, unless otherwise indicated)

Products	1985		1988	
	SK	NK	SK	NK
Mineral Production				
Anthracite	21,714	39,000	23,400	48,000
Iron Ore	625	3,250	565	8,500
Lead Ore	17	110		
Zinc Ore	88	160		
Energy (mil KWh)				
Electricity	58,007	48,000		52,000
Light Industry, 1984				
Textile	(1,337)	(128)	3,190	600
Shoes (mil. pairs)	(401)	(52)		
Wristwatches (1000)	(12,000)	(100)		
Syn. Fiber	667	225		218
Heavy Industry				
Metal: Pig Iron	8,833	5,800		
Crude Steel	4,885	6,500	14,200	6,730
Refined Copper		22		
Machine: Machine Tools	(50)	(30)		
Tractors	(73)	(32)		
Vehicles	333	(18)		
Ship Bldt	2,032	(210)	1,320	
Chemical: Chemicals	(174)	(20)		4,200
Cement	(20,519)	(8,000)		10,000
Fertilizer	839	765		5,200

* The numbers in parentheses refer to the year of 1984 drawn from NUB (1986).
Sources: U.N., *Industrial Statistics Yearbook*
U.S. Bureau of Mines
FEER, Asia Yearbook, 1990 for 1988.

half of the peninsula with 90 percent of the iron and 98 percent of the bituminous coal. This is the reason that energy production and consumption in North Korea are much higher than in South Korea. Per capita energy production and consumption are common indicators for measuring national development. It is said in general that the more developed the country, the higher the per capita energy, production and consumption. In the case of Korea, although the South surpasses the

TABLE 4.7
Energy Production and Consumption per Capita
and Annual Rates (kilograms of oil equivalent)

	Production		Consumption	
	SK	NK	SK	NK
1965			237	1,196
1970	292*	1,184*		
1985			1,241	2,118
1965–1980	4.1%	6.4%	12.1%	6.6%
1980–85	9.3%	2.7%	5.0%	2.9%

Sources: World Bank, *World Development Report, 1987*.
EPB, *Economic Statistics Yearbook 1976*, p. 150.
Pang, *Korean Review*, p. 115.
*Per capita output of electricity

North in general developmental results, the North exceeds the South in per capita energy consumption by five times in 1965 and two times in 1985 (see Table 4.7). Energy production in North Korea decreased sharply in the 1980's, however. The annual rates of energy production of North Korea has decreased from 6.5 to 2.7 percent between 1965–80 and 1980–85 while those of South Korea has sharply increased 4.1 to 9.3 percent between the same period. The average annual rates of energy consumption have declined both in South and North Korea. Energy consumption decreased from 12.1 to 5.0 percent in South Korea and from 6.6 to 2.9 percent in North Korea between 1965-80 and 1980-85.

South Korea surpasses North Korea in light and chemical industry. In heavy industry, the South exceeds the North considerably in transportation machinery (automobiles and shipbuilding) and in electric and electronic industries (television sets and refrigerators), but the North is stronger in some power machines, machines tools, and trucks (C.O. Kim 1981, 81-83). Despite the North's heavy industry strategy, it is in the South that heavy industry is successful.

Service Sector: Consumer Goods and Social Overhead Capital

South Korea's large investments in social overhead capital (SOC) contrast strikingly with the small amounts allotted to this sector by North Korea, which considers most SOC and consumer goods to be nonproductive. The consumer goods industry is somewhat decentral-

TABLE 4.8
Comparison of Transportation in 1988

	SK	NK
Total length of Railroads, km	6,340	4,500 (8,553)*
(Electrified railroads)	411	2,706
Automobiles		
Passenger Cars	844,350	
Freight Cars	767,025	200,000**
Trucks and Buses	746,906	24,000***
Subways, km		40
Total length of paved highway,km	1,539	
Percentage of pavement		

Sources: FEER, *Asia Yearbook* 1990, pp. 6–9.
* The number in parenthesis refers to the North Korean official source.
** The number refers to the year of 1982.
*** The number refers to the year of 1979.

ized in North Korea (Clough 1985,85). Whereas heavy industry is the domain of the central government, which also manages large factories producing consumer goods such as textile mills, most industries of consumer goods and food processing are run by local governments depending largely on local material.

The productions of television sets, refrigerators, wristwatches, clothes, and other consumer goods such as toothpaste show remarkable contrasts between the two Koreas. South Korea by far surpasses North Korea in the production of such consumer goods. In order to improve the field of consumer goods, the catch phrase of "light-industry revolution" was popularized throughout North Korea in 1990.

The paved road situation is especially poor in the North. In April 1982, Kim Il Sung announced a new economic policy that emphasized agricultural production and infrastructure—especially power plants and transportation facilities. As for international transportation, the privately owned Korea Air lines in South Korea provided worldwide service to twenty seven points internationally, carrying about 5 million passengers, while North Korea People's Airline had only 4 points internationally: Beijing, Moscow, Khabarovsk, and East Berlin.

In both South and North Korea, agriculture's share of GNP has declined sharply. Both have rapidly industrialized during the postliberation period. The North Korean economic structure shows that the service sector is underdeveloped while industry is overdeveloped. Industry in North Korea is concentrated in the machine and tractor industries supported by the relative abundance of mineral products. The South Korean economic structure seems to have been transformed into a balanced structure between sectors, although the service sector tends to have been overdeveloped since the 1980's. The production of automobiles, shipbuilding, the television/video sets is strong in South Korea.

Trade and Debt

Trade

While South Korea has been trying to expand external economic cooperation and trade as a major policy since the mid-1960s, North Korea has been acting passively in trade, clinging only to its autarky system. As a result, the South, whose trade volume was inferior to the North by five times in 1960 (J.S. Chung 1974 101–43), caught up and exceeded the North by fifteen times in 1978 and twenty times in 1986. Figures on North Korea's foreign trade are somewhat more reliable than on domestic trends because they can be obtained from the published statistics of North Korea's trading partners.

The direction of foreign trade has been diversified. Prior to the 1970s, the communist bloc countries were North Korea's only trade partners. Since around 1971, North Korea has expanded its trade ties beyond the Soviet Union and China to include Japan, Western Europe, and most recently, the nonaligned nations. South Korea depended heavily on the markets of the United States and Japan prior to 1970, but it has made some progress in diversifying its trade beyond these two countries in the 1970s.

South Korea's main trade partners are still the United States and Japan, accounting for 55 percent of the total trade volume of South Korea in 1988. South Korea's dependence on the dominant markets of Japan and the United States declined somewhat throughout the 1970s. Whereas in 1971 South Korea's imports from Japan and the United States were 40 percent and 28 percent respectively, by 1980 the share of total imports dropped to 22 and 26 percent, respectively. More dramatically, South Korea's exports to the United States decreased from 50 percent in 1971 to 26 percent of total exports in 1980, al-

TABLE 4.9
Foreign Trade of South and North Korea (mil. $)

| | South Korea | | North Korea | |
	Export	Import	Export	Import
1970	835	1,984	365	396
1975	5,081	7,274	814	1,093
1979	15,056	20,339	1,150	1,160
1985	30,283	31,136	1,380	1,720
1986	34,714	31,584	3,015	
1989	62,400	61,500		

Source: FEER, Asia Yearbook, 1990 and various years.
Bunge (1981), North Korea: A Country Study, pp. 255–56.

though since then it increased slightly to 34 percent in 1989. Its exports to Japan remained more constant: 25 percent in 1975, 17 percent in 1980, and 21 percent in 1989. South Korea is constantly trying to expand markets to European Community (E.C.) countries, the Third World, and the communist bloc. Construction contracts overseas, mainly in the Middle East, which reached a cumulative total of $21 billion in 1979, not only boosted South Korea's foreign exchange earnings, but improved the managerial and technical skills of the construction companies involved, particularly when they worked closely with more experienced U.S. or European construction companies. In the 1980s, imports from Japan increased remarkably from 26 percent in 1980 to 35 percent in 1988, while these from the United States decreased 22 to 20 percent during the same period.

Although in 1971 North Korea's trade with the Soviet Union and China accounted for 76 percent of its total imports and 61 percent of its total exports, its trade dependence on these countries declined to 44 percent and to 38 percent of total trade in 1977 and 1986, respectively. Now, the Soviet Union, Japan, and China are the three major North Korean trade partners, accounting for 80 percent of the total in 1986, which increased from 70 percent in 1978. China accounts for 19 percent of the total in 1986. Most conspicuous is the emergence of the E.C. zone as a trade partner and the decrease with Communist countries in recent years. About half (50 to 60 percent) of the total in 1988 was with Communist countries, while it was 85 percent in 1971. Its imports from Japan and its exports to Third World developing countries had increased dramatically between 1971 and 1979, to 23 percent and 34 percent respectively.

Both Korean states are actively expanding their trade ties with the outside world. Whereas South Korea adopted a policy of trade expansion around 1965, North Korea adopted a new posture of trade expansion that included some Western European countries and Japan in 1971. In 1989, South Korea's exports amounted to $62.4 billion, while North Korea's exports reached some $1.6 billion. The overall trade balance in 1989 was more favorable to South Korea than to North Korea. Whereas South Korea registered a trade surplus of $900 million in 1989, North Korea had a record trade deficit of some $960 million in that year. North Korean trade suffers from an unpaid debt to Western European and Japanese banks for the purchase of plants and equipment from these countries in the early 1970s.

The two Koreas are more dependent on Japan than on any other country. It is ironic when one considers the fact that most Koreans dislike the Japanese because they had colonized Korea in the past. Both Koreas have kept reminding their people of Japanese brutality in the colonial period. North Korea, in particular, has tried publicly to eradicate the vestiges of Japanese colonization.

The special relationship of South Korea with the U.S. is evidenced by a trade volume in 1988 accounting for 31 percent with the U.S. while only 25 percent with Japan (FEER, 1990:8). The trade pattern, moreover shows a significant variation. While South Korea maintains a trade surplus with the U.S., it suffers a trade deficit with Japan (FEER 1990). In 1987, while the United States accounted for 39 percent of total South Korean exports and 21 percent of the imports, Japan accounted for 18 percent of the exports and 34 percent of the imports (CIA 1988,131). The estimation by FEER shows that, in 1986, trade volume with Japan (34.4 percent) is even greater than that with the U.S. (20.7 percent) (FEER 1988,8). These show that dependence on Japan is a more serious problem than dependence on the U.S.

North Korean trade volume accounts for 38, 23, and 19 percent with USSR, Japan, and China, respectively. North Korea and the USSR had signed a new agreement on economic and technical cooperation in 1986, which includes nineteen new projects (The Europa World Yearbook 1988, 1615; Foster-Carter 1986 28–9). From Japan, North Korea imports an amount double of what she exports. After the Joint Venture Law in 1984, North Korea tried to attract Japanese capital, mainly from Korean Japanese.

In North Korea, arms sales abroad have become a useful new export item, to an increasing extend in recent years because of the need for foreign exchange. Zimbabwe has bought $16.5 million worth of arms from North Korea, and Iran has also become a major customer of North Korea, purchasing an estimated $800 million worth of arms, or 40 percent of its total purchase (Kerns 1984,24-25). Arms sales of both Koreas show that during 1973-83 $2.2 and $2.0 billion of arms were sold by South and North Korea, respectively (U.S. News and World Report, 13 February 1986). In 1982, North Korea had exports of $2 billion (nonmilitary exports of $1.2 billion) and imports of $1.9 billion (nonmilitary $1.78 billion).

Tourism is another means of earning foreign exchange in both Koreas. It brought nearly two million foreign visitors to South Korea and one million to North Korea in 1987. North Korea established the International Tourism Bureau and invited the president of South Korean Hyundai Incorporation and a Korean American business woman to develop a tourism program.

Foreign Loans, Investment, and Debt

In 1989 North Korea owed about $4.1 billion of which $2.23 billion to noncommunist nations and $1.83 billion to communist countries (Jeffries 1990, 269 IISS 1989,162). Between 1970 and 1974, North Korean debt was $1.7 billion, of which $710 million was owed to the USSR and $990 million to nine Western capitalist countries including Japan ($400 million). It increased to somewhere between $1.8 and $2.1 billion in 1980 (Kihl 1984, 157). North Korea's ability to repay the debt has been seriously questioned, and it was revealed at the Paris meeting of eleven creditor nations in 1975, that the total default to the eleven countries reached $430 million in 1975. North Korea suspended its repayment of debt in 1975, showing that it was suffering from a deteriorating foreign exchange position. In December 1982, North Korea had to ask Japan to reschedule payments. It is thought that North Korea paid only about 20 percent of the interest due on its foreign loans in 1982. In October 1983, after a North Korean bomb blew up many South Korean cabinet members during a visit to Burma, relations with the capitalist world worsened, and North Korea stopped paying interest on its debt. The North Korean foreign debt is a serious problem. North Korea was announced to be in default of $900 million by the consortium of Western creditors and Japan since 1976, and has been negotiating a payment schedule. North Korea is currently negotiating with Japan a colonial reparation of $5 billion (*Hankook Ilbo*, 10 April 1989). If the negotiation is successful, the debt crisis of North Korea will be lessened.

In 1989, South Korea's total external debt was about $36 billion. During the 1950s, economic development as a whole was entirely dependent on foreign aid, which financed three-quarters of total investment between 1953 and 1963. By the late 1950s the primitive import-substitution process had its limits. From the time of Park's regime, the South Korean economy was restructured toward export promotion and away from the earlier emphasis on import substitution. The 1964–66 period saw a series of major changes in economic policy. A series of export incentives and subsidies was introduced. At the same time, the normalization of relations with Japan in 1965, the passage of a new Foreign Capital Inducement Law in 1966, and government encouragement of overseas borrowing brought hundreds of millions of dollars in previously unavailable private commercial loans to the country. Similar measures were introduced by North Korea in 1984. Net indebtedness went from $301 million in 1965 to $1.57 billion in 1970. South Korean foreign debt has been decreasing since 1986 once it reached a peak in 1985 of $47 billion. It fell to $39 billion in 1988 and it is expected that it is going to be decreasing by $2 to $4 billion each year. South Korea had more credits than debts in 1989 (*Chosum Ilbo*, 22 January 1990).

In sum, an analysis of development on the two Koreas shows that South Korea outperformed North Korea during the postliberation period. The size of the South Korean economy is six times larger than that of the North, and per capita GNP of South Korea is three times larger than that of North Korea. Historically, North Korea had earned higher marks than South Korea for generating per capita economic growth until 1975 and per capita material production until 1980. In a relatively short period of time of the first ten to fifteen years, North Korea had succeeded in transforming a backward agricultural country into a rel-

atively strong industrial state. However, there had been little percep-
tible improvement in living standards, with respect to housing, public
transportation, or availability of consumer goods in the stores. Since
the mid-1960s South Korea has been successful in generating high
rates of economic growth and in transforming the economy toward an
industrial profile achieving a significantly higher standard of living for
its people. Structurally, the two Korean developments show striking
differences. The proportion of North Korean industrial production in
GNP (70.0 percent) is more than double of the South Korean's (30.7
percent) and the proportion of agricultural production in North Korean
GNP (25 percent) is fairly larger than that of South Korean's (16.2
percent), while that of North Korean service sector is only one-tenth of
the South Korea's. Trade shows far more of a contrast; it is only
one-twentieth of South Korean trade volume. And North Korea is
more vulnerable to foreign debt than South Korea.

References

Bank of Korea (BOK). 1989. *Economic Statistics Yearbook, 1989* and various years.
    Seoul: BOK.
Breidenstein, Gerhard.1975. "Economic comparison of North and South Korea."
    Journal of Contemporary Asia 5:165-78.
Bridges, Brian. 1986. *Korea and the West*. New York: Routledge & Kegan Paul.
Bunhge, Frederica M. (ed.). 1981. *North Korea: A Country Study*. Washington D.C.:
    American University Press.
Chosun Ilbo. 1990. Article on South Korea, 22 January 1990.
_____. 1990. Article on North Korea, 24 August 1990.
Chung, Joseph Sang-hoon. 1974. *The North Korean Economy: Structure and Devel-
    opment*. Stanford, CA: Hoover Institution Press.
Clough, Ralph N. 1987. *Embattled Korea: The Rivalry for International Support*.
    Boulder, CO: Westview Press.
Economic Planning Board (EPB). 1989. *Korea Statistical Yearbook* (No.35). Seoul
    National Bureau of Statistics, EPB.
_____. 1989. *Korean Economic Indicatiors*. Seoul: EPB.
_____. 1989. *Social Indicators in Korea*. Seoul: EPB.
_____. 1976. *Economic Statistics Yearbook 1976*. Seoul: EPB.
Far Eastern Economic Review (FEER). 1990. *Asia Yearbook, 1990*. Hong Kong:
    FEER.
_____. 1988. *Asia Yearbook, 1988*. Hong Kong: FEER.
_____. 1984. *Asia Yearbook, 1984*. Hong Kong: FEER.
Food and Agricultural Organization (FAO). 1988. *Production Yearbook*. Rome: FAO.
Halliday, Jon. 1987. "The economies of North and South Korea." Pp. 19–54 in
    Sullivan and Foss, *Two Koreas—One Future*? Landham, MD: University Press of
    America.
Hankook Ilbo. 1989. Article on North Korea, 10 April 1989.

Hatada, Takashi. 1969. *A History of Korea*. Trans by Warren W. Smith and Benjamin H. Hazard. Santa Barbara, CA: ABC-Clio Press.

International Institute for Strategic Studies (IISS). 1989. *The Military Balance, 1987-1988*. London: IISS.

Jeffries, Ian. 1990. "Democrative People's Republic of Korea" Pp. 261–70 in Ian Jeffries, *A Guide to the Socialist Economies*. New York: Routledge.

Kerns, Hikaru. 1984. "Trying to keep pace with a showcase state." FEER, 2 February 1984, pp.24–25.

Kihl, Young Whan. 1984. *Politics and Policies in Divided Korea: Regimes in Contest*. Boulder, CO: Westview Press.

Kim, Cae-One. 1981. "Economic interchanges between South and North Korea." *Korea & World Affairs* 5:77-106.

Lee, Pong. S. 1972. "An estimate on North Korea's National Income." *Asian Survey* 12(6):518–26.

National Unification Board (NUB). 1986. *A Comparative Study of South and North Korea*. Seoul: NUB.

Pang, Hwan Ju. 1988. *Korean Review*. Pyongyang: Foreign Language Publishing House.

United Nations (U.N.). 1989. *Industrial Statistics Yearbook, 1987*. 2 vols. New York: Statistical Office of U.N.

U.S. Arms Control and Disarmament Agency (ACDA). 1988. *World Military Expenditures and Arms Transfers, 1987*. Washington, D.C.: U.S. ACDA.

U.S. Bureau of Mines. 1988. *Mineral Facts and Problems*. Washington, D.C.: U.S. Bureau of Mines.

U.S. Central Intelligence Agency (CIA). 1988. *The World Factbook, 1988*. Washington, D.C.: U.S. CIA.

————. 1978. *Korea: The Economic Race Between the North and the South* (ER 78-10008). Washington, D.C.: National Foreign Assessment Center, U.S. CIA.

U.S. Department of State. 1984. *Background Notes*. Washington, D.C.: U.S. Department of State.

U.S. News & World Report. 1986. Article on Korea. 13 February 1986.

World Bank. 1989.*World Development Report 1989* and various years. New York: Oxford University Press.

5

Social Development in South and North Korea

Social development may be understood in a broad sense as the pattern of evolution that a society follows, resulting from factors that include changes in the pattern of demographic trends, social stratification, alteration of social and cultural values, and so on. A complex model of measuring social development needs to take all these factors into account. Social development in this book includes urbanization, education, health, labor force structure, income distribution, and significant cultural changes. Each indicator considers both levels of quantity and quality.

Urbanization, Health Care, and Education

Urbanization is evaluated by the percentage of urban population residing in cities of over 50,000 persons and by the percentage of urban population living in large cities of over 500,000 persons and of that in the largest city. Education refers to the adult literacy rate, percentage of student population, and percentage of higher education. Years of mandatory education and time spent in ideological education are also examined. Health is evaluated by life expectancy at birth, infant mortality, death rate, ratio of doctors per 1,000 inhabitants, and food consumption by calorie of per capita food consumption per day.

Despite the different economic results in the two Koreas discussed in chapter 4, South and North Korea appear to share a similar pace in many aspects of their social development, such as life expectancy, infant mortality, death rate, urbanization, and education. However, the quality of the development shows a significant difference.

TABLE 5.1
Population and Crude Birth Rate

		South Korea	North Korea
Population	1945	16.0	(9.9)
(million)	1946	19.4	9.3
	1953	21.6	8.5
	1989	43.1	21.0
Annual Growth Rate (%)	1981–88	1.3	2.4
Crude Birth Rate	1960	41	41
per 1,000	1975	24	37
	1986	20	30

Sources: World Bank, World Development Report, 1987, 1982.
U.N., Demographic Yearbook 1948.
FEER, Asia Yearbook 1990, 1988, 1982, and 1972

Some demographic characteristics require further analysis of their relation to social development. The population of South Korea is double that of the North. Since the division in 1945, the South's population has been increasing continuously, while the North's declined in early period before and during the Korean War. During the past ten years, the average annual growth of North Korea's population was 2.5 percent, while that of the South 1.4 percent. This reflects the fact that the birth rate of North Korea (30) is higher than the South's (20) in 1986. The death rate declined remarkably from 23 in 1945 to 6 and 5 in South and North Korea, respectively, in 1986. The small population of North Korea results in part from the considerable outflow to South Korea during and after the Korean division and Korean war: one million after the division and another one million during the war. The so-called "division effect" occurred: the phenomenon of population outflow from the Communist camp to the capitalist side seems endemic to the divided countries. The German case provides another example.

Simple statistics of the two Koreas show the same pace of urbanization. About 65 percent of the population live in urban areas in both Koreas in 1986. In 1960, about 28 percent of the population lived in urban areas and this rose to 47 and 43 percent in South and North Korea in 1975, respectively. Despite the same level of urbanization (around 65 percent in 1986), urbanization of the cities with a population over 500,000 shows a sharp contrast between the two countries.

Among the urban population, in table 5.2, the proportion living in large cities over 500,000 in 1988 is very high in South Korea (77 percent), while it is only 19 percent in North Korea. In 1960 it was 61 and 15 percent in South and North Korea, respectively. The population dwelling in the largest city represents 41 and 12 percent in South and North Korea in 1980, respectively, and 35 and 15 percent in 1960, respectively. Life in the largest city is very different from that in other parts of both countries. In North Korea, the gap between Pyongyang, the capital city, and the rest of the cities has been maximized. The population living in Pyongyang declined from 15 to 12 percent between 1960 and 1980. It suggests that in South Korea rapid urbanization occurred by pulling rural people into cities. In North Korea, urbanization occurred by developing the city itself, not with any significant change of residence, but with strict policy restricting the movement of the population toward the urban area. Urbanization in this case is affected by the natural birth rate of the area.

Life expectancy at birth improved from 53 years in 1960 to 69 and 68 years in South and North Korea in 1985, respectively. Life expectancy by sex resulted in the same tendency in the two Koreas, showing that females were expected to live six (in North Korea) and seven (in South Korea) years longer than males. In 1985, the life expectancies at birth for men reached 65 years in both Koreas, and for women 71 years in the North and 72 years in the South. In the period 1965–85 infant mortality dropped from 63 to 27 per 1,000 live births in both Koreas. Between 1945 and 1986, the death rate for the general population also declined from 23 to 6 in South Korea and to 5 in North Korea. Health care in both Koreas has improved markedly as the ratio of inhabitants per physician, which indicates the North's improvement. Food comsumption is higher in North Korea than in South Korea.

Formal education has expanded considerably in both Koreas since the liberation. Schooling is now mandatory for the first eleven years in North Korea, compared with six years in South Korea. The number of students suggests that North Korea is roughly equal in the enrollment of all groups in formal education with South Korea. In higher education, however, South Korea shows a somewhat more successful achievement. The enrollment ratio of higher education by the population in the 20–24 age group shows 36 percent in South Korea and 23 percent in

TABLE 5.2
Social Development

1. Urbanization

	Over 50,000		Growth Rate		Over 500,000		Largest City	
	SK	NK	SK	NK	SK	NK	SK	NK
1960	28	40	6.4	5.1 (60–70)	61	15	35	15
1975	47	43	4.6	4.3 (70–80)				
1980	56	60	5.7	4.6 (65–80)	77	19	41	12
1986	66	65	2.5	3.8 (80–85)				

2. Health

	South Korea	North Korea
Life Expectancy at Birth		
1950	50	50
1960	54	54
1965	M=55,F=58	M=55,F=58
1975	61	61
1985	M=65,F=72	M=65,F=71
1986	67	65
Infant Mortality per 1,000		
1965	63	63
1985	27	27
Crude Death Rate per 1,000		
1945	23	23
1960	13	12
1975	8	9
1986	6	5
Doctors per 1,000		
1982	.6	2.4
Hospital Beds per 1,000		
1982	1.6	12.0
Daily calorie supply per capita		
1965	2,255	2,255
1985	2,841	3,151

3. Education

	South Korea	North Korea
Literacy rate		
1988	98%	98%
Compulsory Education		
1990	6 yrs.	11 yrs.

TABLE 5.2 (continued)

Primary and Secondary (million, enrollment ratio)

1960	6.0		2.0	
1975	9.6		4.0	
1988	9.6	(96%)	4.2	(96%)

Higher Education (thousand, enrollment ratio)

1965	139	(6%)		
1988	1,340	(36%)	521	(23%)

Universities and Colleges

1988	233		175*

*One estimate shows the number as high as 708 (235U;473C).
Sources: U.S. Department of State, Background Notes, 1984
FEER, Asia Yearbook, 1990 and 1986. p. 6.
World Bank, World Development Report, 1987, 1982.
EPB (1988), Social Indicators in Korea for South Korea.
Bunge (1981), North Korea: A Country Study, pp. 84–92.
Eberstadt and Banister (1990), North Korea: Population Trends and Prospects, pp. 125–133.

North Korea in 1988. The adult literacy rates in both Koreas reached over 98 percent in 1988. North Korea spends more time in ideological education of students.

Labor Force Structure

The term labor force structure refers to the percentage of the population employed in the three industrial sectors. In 1987, a shown in table 5.3, labor force participation rates of economically active populations were 58.3 percent in the South and 78.5 percent in the North. The main reason for the higher participation in North Korea reflects the participation of women and old people (NUB 1982,ch.3). According to the study of the National Unification Board, "the old people who receive social security aid and women are forced to work" under the principle that "one who does not work should not eat." Mass movements and political campaigns are widely conducted in mobilizing all citizens for modern nation-building. The mass mobilization movement, known as the Chollima movement in the 1950s, was designed to mobilize human and material resources in agriculture. The Chongsan-ni method and Taean system in the 1960s also increased participation in the industrial labor force (I.J. Kim 1975).

Women made up 45 percent of the North Korean work force in 1981 (NUB 1982). One estimate shows a somewhat higher participation rate

TABLE 5.3
Labor Force Participation in 1987

	South Korea	North Korea
Population Age 16 and Over	67.0%	61.6%
Labor Force Participation	58.3%	78.5%

Sources: EPB (1988), Social Indicators in Korea, 1988, p . 107
Eberstadt and Banister (1990), North Korea: Population Trends and Prospects, pp. 134–46.

(48 percent) even in 1971 (Halliday 1981,898). Other estimates claim that women's participation rate in North Korea today is likely to be as high as China where it is 77 percent (Eberstadt and Banister 1990,142–43). A sizable number of women are in the armed forces and police. To facilitate such participation, there is a very extensive network of approximately 19,262 kindergartens and 28,358 nurseries (Pang 1988,162). There is also a widespread system of take-out food centers, (bapgongjang) delivering food to homes. In the South, women's participation in the labor force increased from 26.8 percent in 1960 to 38.4 and 45.0 percent in 1980 and 1987, respectively.

Different processes took place in labor force participation in the two Koreas. With higher participation of the labor force in industry (especially heavy industry), as shown in table 5.4, North Korea nevertheless retains a considerable amount of its labor force in agriculture activities: 43 percent of the total labor force in 1988 are still engaged in agriculture. The ideology of "self-reliance" makes North Korea stress agriculture seriously, despite its cost-ineffectiveness in terms of the contribution to GNP outputs of 25 percent of GNP in 1982 shown in table 4.4. This contrasts with the South where only 21 percent of the labor force are occupied in agriculture in 1988 (figure 5.1).

A recent source, however, reveals a somewhat different composition of North Korean labor force. According to Eberstadt and Banister (1990), farmers accounted for 25.3 percent of civilians at ages sixteen and above. North Korea groups its population into four occupational categories: state workers, farmers, officials, and cooperative workers. Industrial workers in state-owned units, by North Korea's estimate, accounted for 57.1 percent of the population of adult civilians in 1987. Officials accounted for 16.8 percent in 1987 and workers in cooperative industrial units was estimated at 0.9 percent. In this count, some of the agricultural population appears to be underestimated in that

TABLE 5.4
Labor Force Structure

| | 1960 | | 1970 | | 1980 | | 1980* | | 1988 | |
	SK	NK	SK	NK	SK	NK	SK	NK	SK	NK
Agriculture	66	62	51	55	34	49	36	43	21	43
Industry	9	23	14	27	29	33	27	30	28	39
Service	25	15	35	18	37	18	37	27	51	18

* World Bank, *World Development 1987.*
Sources: FEER, *Asia Yearbook, 1990* and various years. p.6.
Worldmark, *Encyclopedia of the Nations, Asia and Oceania,* 1984, p. 197.
The Europa World Yearbook, 1984, p. 1868.

farmers in state-owned agricultural units were counted as state workers rather than as farmers. Segments of the population occupied in forestry and fishing are also likely to be included among state workers. Therefore, the agricultural population including those engaged in forestry and fishing must be higher than the estimate of 25.3 percent, and it is likely to be as high as the 43 percent that is counted by the FEER estimate.

Like most communist countries, North Korea neglects the service sector, regarding it as "unproductive." It would appear that commerce and service population are virtually nonexistent. All the workers in the third sector, which accounts for 18 percent of the total work force in North Korea, are identified with those in government and public authorities (FEER 1990). The World Bank estimated that 27 percent of the North Korean work force is occupied in the service sector in 1980. It implies that about 9 percent of the North Korean work force is in service and retail occupations in the year. This figure is too high compared with the estimate of 0.9 percent by Eberstadt and Banister. Some service workers in the "non-productive sphere" (education, health care, etc.) appear to be already included among officials. The workers in government and public authorities in South Korea account for 19.8 percent. Exclusive portions of the South Korean workforce are in commerce and service occupations (25.5 percent). North Korea did not develop social overhead capital and a service sector, generally regarded as very important factors in economic development in capitalist countries. This seems to be one reason why North Korea is so slow in improving GNP in recent years.

Figure 5.1
Labor Force Structure Between South and North Korea
1960 and 1988

in 1960

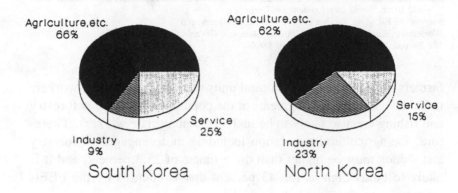

Agriculture,etc.
66%

Service
25%

Industry
9%

South Korea

Agriculture,etc.
62%

Service
15%

Industry
23%

North Korea

in 1988

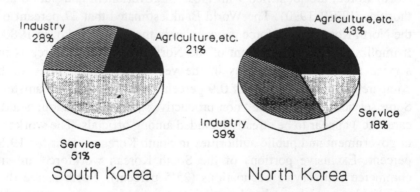

Industry
28%

Agriculture,etc.
21%

Service
51%

South Korea

Agriculture,etc.
43%

Service
18%

Industry
39%

North Korea

Income Inequality and Standard of Living

Income distribution of the two states is compared in several ways in this book. For income distribution in South Korea, average per capita income of each decile percent of the population is calculated respectively. For that of North Korea, the ranges of workers' average wage as well as that of the total population are presented and compared with South Korea's.

The numbers on North Korea in table 5.5 indicate only rough estimates. They refer neither to NIs, nor to the average income of the percentile as those of South Korea's. They refer to individual workers' income and show only the range of North Korean income in 1988. The numbers in the first five rows in the table indicate the minimum income of the decile; those in the last three rows, indicate maximum income of the decile; and those in the sixth and seventh rows indicate average income of the decile of the population. An additional consideration is required for a clear understanding of the table 5.5. For a meaningful comparison, North Korean incomes need to be converted into per capita NI as are those of South Korea's. By this method, North Korean income can be reduced by 38 percent since this portion of the population is not in the labor force. Likewise, South Korean NI should be cut down by at least 30 percent, which becomes total capital for-

TABLE 5.5
Income Distribution in 1988

% population	SK NI/pc	NK Income
0–10	648	720
10–20	1,264	900
20–30	1,684	1,000
30–40	2,010	1,100
40–50	2,349	1,200
50–60	2,755	1,300
60–70	3,211	1,400
70–80	3,818	1,500
80–90	4,850	2,000
90–100	8,897	4,200

Sources: EPB (1988), *Social Indicators in Korea, 1988*.
EPB (1989), *Korea Economic Indicator*, p. 7
Y.K. Kim (1987), "Unequal structure of class and class policy," p. 210.
An article by J.Y. Bu in *Chosun Ilbo* (16 August 1989).

mation, in order to insure proper comparison with North Korean workers' income. Yet, if these figures are to be compared with North Korean workers' incomes, the South Korean NI figures should increase by 30 percent because they have included in it those not in the labor force population. After all, it becomes meaningful to compare the separate estimates without any modification, since the figures more or less portray the average income level of the population in both societies.

Income inequality is one of the crucial issues in comparisons of capitalist and socialist development. The socialist alternative seems to be more effective in achieving income equalization. It is reported that the average income among North Korean workers in 1988 is 100 *won* a month and the range of their income is 60 to 200 *won* a month (1 *won* is equal to about $1 in domestic use and $.5 in foreign commercial exchange). This would be $720 to $2,400 at the average of $1,200 a year for domestic use. Except for selected political and administrative personnel, professors, medical doctors, military generals, and some actors, the annual incomes of the majority—maximum 95 percent— North Korean population fall in the range between $720 to $2,400 with an average of $1,200. The income range of the total population is reported to be 60 to 350 *won* a month (except for a few generals whose income is up to 490 *won*), which is equivalent to the range of $720 to $4,200 a year (Y.K. Kim 1987).

In 1988, the average South Korean per capita NIs of the lowest 40, 30, 20 and 10 percent of population were $1,392, $1,186, $956, and 648, respectively, while the per capita NIs of the highest 10 and 20 percent of population were $8,897 and $6,874, respectively. The average income of North Korean workers corresponds to the lowest 15 percent of South Korean income. If the South Korean population is posited in the continuum of per capita NI from low to high, the average per capita NIs of the population between 10 to 20, 20 to 30, and 30 to 40, are $1,264, $1,648, and $2,010, respectively (Table 5.5). The average per capita NIs of the population between 90 to 100, 80 to 90, and 70 to 80 percent are $8,897; $4,850; and $3,818, respectively. The average per capita NI in South Korea ($3,145) is located at 68 percent in the continuum. The highest income level in North Korea would be located at the highest 80 percent of the South Korean income level. However, extrapolation indicates that the majority of North Korean incomes fall below the lowest 50 percent of South Korean income level, and that the average income of North Korean workers would be located at the lowest 15 percent of that of South Korea. It also indicates that the lowest 7 percent of South Korean population falls into the level below the lowest of North Korea (Figure 5.2). This portion of population is identified with those in extreme poverty by the South Korean government in 1988.

Although no further specific data on income distribution are available for North Korea, it should be mentioned by way of Table 5.5's rough calculation that there is apparently a much greater disparity of income distribution in South Korea than in North Korea. Yet, North Korea's relatively equal distribution of income reveals that the level of income is very low: the income level of ninety-five percent of North Korean population ranges from 7 to 50 percent of that of South Korea.

Due to the allocation of high rates of national investment in capital goods production, the standard of living has improved only slowly in North Korea. Such planned targets for retail sales, housing construction, and the provision of services to the population have been consistently unfulfilled while industrial production targets have consistently been overfulfilled.

Since military spending is not directly related to private consumption, the standard of living in the South is much higher than in the North if the share of military spending is subtracted from the GNP. The per capita GNP of North Korea is thus reduced from $1,260 to $960 in 1988 while that of South Korea drops from $3,850 to only $3,650 in the same year. Time series analysis shows that, subtracting the share of defense from GNP, per capita GNP in South Korea has surpassed that of North Korea since 1970 ($252 versus $238 in 1970). This shows that the actual standard of living in North Korea had been higher than that of South Korea only until 1969. Concerning the ability of the system to meet basic human needs and improve living standards, capitalist South Korea has achieved success.

The South Korean government allots a larger portion of national budget to social and cultural welfare than North Korea. In 1979, social and cultural welfare expenditures accounted for 32.4 percent of South Korean national budget compared to only 23.0 percent of North Korean budget (T.W. Lee 1988,174, NUB 1986,36–38). One significant trend that emerged in the official government budget is increased

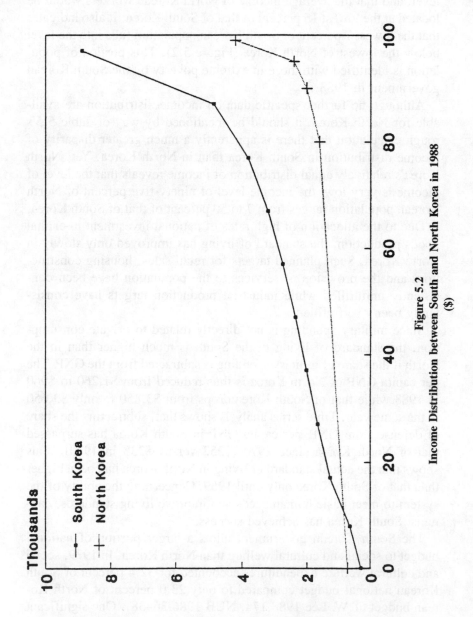

Figure 5.2

Income Distribution between South and North Korea in 1988

($)

TABLE 5.6
Composition of Household Consumption Expenditures

	SK	NK
Food & Drink	36.0	44.0
Clothing & Footwear	7.6	33.0
Housing	20.0	.7
Fuel and Power	6.5	4.0
Household Equipment	4.2	2.4
Health, Education, etc.	25.7	15.9
	100.0%	100.0%

Sources: EPB (1988), Social Indicators in Korea for South Korea in 1980; Y.K. Kim (1987: 212) for North Korea in 1970.

national economy spending in North Korea and decreased spending in South Korea. In order to fund the national economy, national defense spending is being cut. This is consistent with the announced intentions of the North Korean state to stimulate the growth of consumer-oriented industries and services, but there is no way of knowing the specific breakdown of expenditures across the various industries. Much of the expenditure on general economic development could still be diverted to heavy and defense-oriented industries.

Some may question whether the cost of housing and rent is so high in capitalist countries that the real living standard is not as high as that in Communist countries, withholding the cost of housing. This is not true of the two Koreas. Although housing expenditures in South Korea take up a much larger portion of household income than in North Korea (table 5.6), the South Korean income level remains higher than North Korea's. Since North Korea's defense burden comprises about 20 percent of the national income, the effect of excluding housing costs from total South Korean income is very similar to that of excluding defense costs in North Korea.

In addition, the exclusion of the housing cost from total South Korean income would not be meaningful unless the quality of houses were the same between the two countries. The quality of houses in North Korea is far lower than that of South Korea. According to a video tape report, the two-bedroom apartment of one upper middle class family was strikingly small and eight family members including four relatives lived there (S.S. Lee 1988). Moreover, the cost of food and clothes in North Korea is so expensive that 73 percent of house-

TABLE 5.7
Consumer Goods (1,000)

	SK		NK
	1982	1988	1982
Radio receivers	15,000		4,000
TV Receivers	5,390	7,846	250

FEER, *Asia Yearbook, 1990* and 1984.

hold income in North Korea is spend on these necessities (table 5.6). An interview with a North Korean also reveals that the cost of clothing is beyond the means of ordinary people (S.S. Lee 1988).

Although energy consumption is a well-recognized measure for comparing national development cross-nationally, this indicator is deceptive in comparing the development of different social systems, particularly those of Korea. The energy industry in North Korea has been given primary emphasis to support its independent economy. North Korea exceeded South Korea in per capita energy consumption by five times in 1965 and two times in 1985 (see table 4.7 in chapter 4). However, the average annual rates of energy consumption have declined in both South and North Korea. They decreased from 12.1 to 5.0 percent in South Korea and from 6.6 to 2.9 percent in North Korea between 1965–80 and 1980–85.

The numbers of radio and television owners and telephone users are quite different in South and North Korea. The numbers are much larger in South Korea (table 5.7). The number of radio owners in South Korea is four times larger than that in North Korea in 1982, and that of television owners twenty-two times larger in South Korea than in North Korea in the same year. In cultural living standards, South Korea is in advance of North Korea.

Political and Cultural Indoctrination

The most significant area that differentiates the two Koreas over the past forty-five years is culture and values. North Korea actively tried to transform people into new communist men by intensifying the ideological revolution based on *juche* ideology. In 1967 the Supreme People's Assembly (SPA) said that in strengthening the ideological revolution, North Korea should eradicate all the old bourgeois ideological debris remaining in the people's consciousness. The communist regime in North Korea criticized and rejected all kinds of traditional family ties and social organizations, accusing them of being "feudalist" and "imperialist" remnants. In their place, North Korea established a "Communist culture" that highly valued a collectivist spirit placing the interest of the group above that of the individual. In practice, the collectivist spirit finds expression in loyalty to the Party and the Great Leader, Kim Il Sung. The country is comparable to the medieval church-state.

By contrast, South Korea has been overwhelmingly "westernized" in its culture although with some disparity between urban and rural regions. The social values of education are conceived in terms of moral cultivation and the ideal of the man of virtue as well as the acquiring of wealth.

North Korea revised Korean history emphasizing the history of revolutionary struggle on the premise that the creators of history are the people or masses. Ironically, at the same time, Kim Il Sung is lionized as a revolutionary hero and his lineage is idolized.

The two Koreas vary also in language usage. Language is the most important of the many factors that determine a nation. It is a medium of cultural transmission. In Asian society, in particular, people with different languages are rarely regarded as one nation, even if they have the same lineage and live in the same land. North Korea has enacted several language reforms. North Korea refers to their language as "cultural language" as against the "standard language" of the South.

Significant language reforms carried out in North Korea include the elimination of Chinese characters in the written language in 1949, the reduction in the number of foreign loanwords, and the reduction in the number of "levels of politeness" from five to three (Bunge 1981,102). And the elimination of Chinese characters resulted in the change in the writing system: e.g., horizontal rather than vertical in daily newspapers. North Korea tried to "equalize" the language hierarchy in early period. North Korea has rejected almost all the foreign loanwords that are increasingly used in the South, purposely adopting many words that enhance Communist ideology. Simultaneously, South Korea has reflectively avoided these words. North Korea uses the word "revolution" for reform and improvement, which is exactly opposite in the South. The North uses the word "class" rather than "strata," "struggle" versus "conflict," "labor" versus "work," "laborer" versus "worker," "comrade" versus "friend," "capital" versus "wealth," "accumulation of capital" versus "growth of wealth," and so on.

North Korean culture is characterized by the absence of any significant religion, an overflowing phenomenon by contrast in South Korea. Instead, Kim-worship has taken on a religious fervor and in some homes his picture stands on the altar where tablets of ancestors once stood. Numerous statues and structures have been dedicated to Kim. The Korean Revolution Museum, opened in 1972, has over ninety rooms filled with objects glorifying his revolutionary exploits. The International Friendship Exhibition Hall, established in 1978, displays thousands of gifts to Kim from all over the world, aimed at convincing the streams of Korean visitors that their leaders is universally admired. Placing himself in charge of preparations for the celebration of Kim Il-Sung's seventieth birthday in April 1982, he supervised the construction of a massive Arch of Triumph (larger than the French) and a 552–foot Tower of the Juche Idea, said to be the tallest stone tower in the world. Kim's boyhood home at Mangyungdae has become a shrine visited by hundreds of Koreans daily and is a required stop on tours of the capital by foreign visitors. The entrance to every public building has a large painting, mural, or mosaic of the leader, as do the subway stations. All citizens wear Kim buttons on the left breast. Every room visited by Kim on one of his continual on-the-spot guidance tours is marked by a red plaque with gold letters giving the date of his visit. Glorification of Kim is the main theme of dances, songs, operas, and films. Everyone is expected to devote some amount of time daily to the study of Kim's works.

North Korea opened two Christian churches in 1988 and one in 1989, presently, the only churches in the North. The estimates on the number of Christians in North Korea have varied widely from some seven hundred to ten thousand. It is reported that there are only seven theology students. In South Korea, in extreme contrast, about 24 percent of population is Christian and 27 percent Buddhist.

Two-generation families are common in South Korea, while three-generation families are as common in North Korea. The status of women has improved moderately in both Koreas. In both, filial piety and the continuation of the male line are still considered to be very important in family life, and there still is a tendency to prefer male children over female children.

In South Korea, the nuclear family is increasing as the dominant type of family. During the 1975–80 period one- and two-generation families increased by 47.2 and 19.1 percent, respectively. On the other hand, three-generation families increased only 2.7 percent during the same period. Although extended families increased slightly in absolute terms, the extended family decreased substantially in relative terms against the nuclear family.

North Korea introduced laws mandating equality of the sexes, a labor law in 1946, and the collectivization of the farms called cooperatives in 1953. By these measures the traditional structure of the three-generation family was reported to be transformed into a two-generation family (NUB 1982). Nevertheless, there are still many three-generation families due to the shortage of housing (Lee 1988). North Korea also established a so-called "communist morality," which highly values a collectivist spirit placing the interest of the group above the individual. In Article 68 of the Socialist Constitution established in 1972, collectivist spirit calls for self-sacrifice, rigidly organized life, and strict discipline in the interest of the whole. Ideological education is practiced under the guidance of family elders in a manner comparable to religious worship.

In sum, labor force and social structure in the two Koreas show striking differences. The agricultural population in North Korea still represents a large portion: 43 percent in 1987, while that in South Korea stands at 21 percent. As for the service population, which includes the public administrative population, the North Korean share is only 18 percent of the population while in South Korea it is 51 percent. There is apparently a much greater disparity of income distribution in South Korea than in North Korea, but the level of income in North Korea is very low: the income level of most North Koreans ranges from a low of 7 to a high of 50 percent of that of South Korea; the average income of North Korean workers equals the lowest 15 percent of South Korean income; and only 7 percent of South Korean poverty falls below the lowest of North Korean income. As for whether the system is able to meet basic human needs and improve living standards, capitalist South Korea is far more successful. Development in urbanization, health care, and education is unequal in part, but there is a higher standard of living in South Korea than in North Korea.

On the socioeconomic development of South and North Korea, one must conclude that South Korea has outperformed North Korea by three times in per capita GNP output, exceeding it in per capita GNP since 1976, in per capita NMP since 1980, and in standard of living since 1970. Except for the machine-tool industry and crop agriculture, South Korea is far ahead of North Korea in industrial and agricultural production and trade. Urbanization has been achieved through the development of large cities in South Korea as compared to many medium-sized cities in North Korea. In terms of health-related criteria, both Koreas have achieved comparable levels, although South Korea has achieved lower standards in food consumption and the ratio of doctors to inhabitants. With respect to education, South Korea has been more successful in achieving higher education. Income distribution suggests that on the average South Korean citizens enjoy a higher average individual standard of living than North Korea, despite the fact that income is more evenly distributed in the North than in the South.

References

Bunge, Frederica M. (ed.). 1981. *North Korea: A Country Study*. Washington, D.C.: American University Press.

Chosun Ilbo. 1989. An article by J.Y. Bu on North Korea, 16 August 1989.

Eberstadt, Nicholas and Judith Banister. 1990. *North Korea: Population Trends and Prospects*. Washington: U.S. Bureau of the Census.

Economic Planning Board (EPB). 1989. *Korea Economic Indicators*. Seoul: EPB
_____. 1988. *Social Indicators in Korea, 1988*. Seoul: EPB.

Europa World Yearbook, The. 1984. *The Europa World Yearbook, 1984*. London: Europa Publications.

Far Eastern Economic Review (FEER). 1990. *Asia Yearbook, 1990* and various years. Hong Kong: FEER.

Kim, Il-pyong J. 1975. *Communist Politics in North Korea*. New York: Praeger.

Kim, Yong-Kee. 1987. "Kaekeup eui boolpyungdeung kujo wa kaekeup jungchaek," (Unequal structure of class and class policy). Pp. 187–218 in Hong-Chul Yum et al., *Bookhan sahoe eui goojo wa byunhwa*, (Structure and change of North Korean society). Seoul: Institute of Far East Asian Studies, Kyungnam University.

Lee, Seung-Sang. 1989. *Bukhan bukhan saramdul*. Video tapes on North Korea and North Korean People.

Lee, Tae Wook. 1988. "Kyungjae: jaryuk gaengsaeng jungchaek eui ijum kwa han-guae," (Economy: advantage and limitation of the policy of self-reliance.), Pp. 111–227 in S.W. Lee et al., *Bookhan sasipnyun* (Forty years of North Korea). Seoul: Eulyoo Moonhwa Press.

National Unification Board (NUB). 1982. *A Comparative Study of South and North Korea*. Seoul: NUB.

_____. 1986. *A Comparative Study of the South and North Korean Economies*. Seoul: NUB.

Pang, Hwan Ju. 1988. *Korean Review*. Pyongyang, Korea: Foreign Language Publishing House.

United Nations (U.N.) 1948. *Demographic Yearbook, 1948*. New York: U.N.

U.S. Department of State. 1984. *Background Notes*. Washington, D.C.: U.S. Department of State.

World Bank. 1987. *World Development Report, 1987*. New York: Oxford University Press.

———. 1982. *World Development Report, 1982*. New York: Oxford University Press.

Worldmark. 1984. *Worldmark Encyclopedia of the Nations*: Asia and Oceania. New York: Worldmark Press.

6

Political and Institutional Mechanisms of the Development of South and North Korea

The different results and patterns of development in South and North Korea can be explained *prima facie* by the political and institutional changes of the two states. Considering that social and cultural factors could safely be assumed to be fundamentally identical throughout Korea at the onset of national division, the development during the early period, in particular, may be largely attributed to political factors and institutional transformations initiated by extremist political leaderships and state ideologies. In particular, the very early success of North Korean development vis-à-vis South Korean (1945–65) is understandable mainly as a result of the radical transformations of the traditional and colonial political economy by the North Korean state into a fairly industrialized structure with equal income distribution. The later success of South Korean development vis-à-vis North Korea (1965–89) is also traceable to the guardianship of the South Korean state, not of its free markets.

The Taking of Power and Extremist Ideology

Korean society right after liberation was about to be newly "restructurated" from the chaos when the Japanese-controlled infrastructure suddenly disintegrated. Political competition was honed by new ideologies drawn from Soviet, U.S., Chinese and Japanese sources. Thousands demonstrated. Hundreds of social and political groups, parties, unions, committees, and federations were started. Local people's committees, unions, and peasant organizations, with "peace preservation corps" replacing Japanese police, were formed all over the peninsula. The Korean People's Republic (KPR), an outgrowth of Lyuh Woon-Hyung's "preparatory committee," was established in Seoul under moderate leftists and communists claiming jurisdiction over the people's committees (J.A. Kim 1975, 48–53). In an effort to dilute somewhat its strongly leftist composition, the KPR named several well-known rightists, including Syngman Rhee, Kim Ku, and Kim Kyu-Sik. All were members of the Korean Provisional Government (KPG) long in exile abroad. But, Hu Hun took the position of premier, which put him in effective control of the new government, when Lyuh was attacked by a terrorist. Conservative and gradualist landowners and businessmen, worried by the Communists' radical policies within KPR, banded together in an opposition movement under the name of the Korean Democratic Party (KDP). They backed the KPG as the legitimate government of Korea and named as leaders two of the same politicians chosen by KPR—Syngman Rhee and Kim Ku, both then in exile.

In the South, the American Military Government (AMG) was established after U.S. troops under General John R. Hodge arrived three weeks after the liberation. The rule of the AMG (1945–48) was direct and undiluted. It refused to recognize the Korean people's committees, particularly the KPR (J.A. Kim 1975, 57). As rapidly as they were able, they countered and abolished the local committees. Instead, the AMG tried to build a new state restoring the power of Japanese-trained police, and favoring the gradualist KDP. A constitution modelled broadly on the American system with separation of powers was adopted by a National Assembly created by a U.N.-supervised election in May 1948. South Korea became the independent Republic of Korea (ROK) in August 1948, with Dr. Syngman Rhee, leader of the National Society (N.S.) and later the Liberal Party (L.P.) as the country's first president. The KDP was the strongest opposition party and was subsequently transformed into the Democratic Nationalist Party (DNP) through merging with the KPG group and then developed into the Democratic Party (D.P.) merging finally with those who abandoned the L.P. The AMG and Syngman Rhee regime vetted candidates and prevented left-wing individuals from standing for office. In general, the scrutiny of candidates has been an important element of electoral control since 1948. Before the new state could even attempt to cope with the insurmountable political and economic difficulties, it was faced with a civil war (1950–53) instigated by North Korea.

Rhee was forced to resign in April 1960 when electoral corruption reached a peak in the 1960 elections and led to massive demonstrations spearheaded by students. A cabinet system was attempted by Chang Myon of the Democratic Party, but this government was deposed in May 1961 by a military coup, led by General Park Chung Hee. Power was assumed by a Supreme Council for National Reconstruction (SCNR), which dissolved the National Assembly, suspended the constitution and disbanded all existing political parties. In 1963 the military leadership formed the Democratic Republican Party (DRP) that was patterned after the KWP of North Korea (J.A. Kim 1975, 237), and General Park became President of the Third Republic in December. The fairly strong opposition party, the New Democratic Party (NDP), was erected from the merger of the two major opposition parties, Yun Bo-Sun's New Korea Party (NKP) and Park Soon-Chun's People's Party (P.P.). The slim victories of Park Chung Hee in presidential elections held in 1963, 1967, 1971 made him and DRP introduce a more authoritarian "Yushin" (revitalizing) constitution that was at last adopted in 1972. The direct election of the president ceased and the new assembly, the National Conference for Unification (NCU), was created to elect the President.

President Park was assassinated in 1979 and power was seized by General Chun Doo-hwan and his close colleagues, removing the army chief of staff. After putting down a week-long revolt by students and citizens in Kwangju-City in May 1980, General Chun created the Committee of Emergency Measures for National Security. He was elected president by the NCU and created the Democratic Justice Party (DJP), which became the majority party in his reign.

A presidential election was held in December 1987, which former General Roh Tae-woo won by receiving only about 36 percent of the vote, the result of a split in the major opposition party. He was followed by Kim Young-sam and Kim Dae-jung receiving about 27 percent each. In a general election held in April 1988, the DJP of Rho remained the majority party followed by the three major opposition parties: the Peace Democratic Party (PDP) of Kim Dae-Jung, the Reunification Democratic Party (RDP) of Kim Young-Sam, and the New Democratic Republic Party (NDRP) of Kim Jong-Pil. The last two opposition parties, however, dissolved in order to unite with the ruling party in February 1990 creating a conservative Democratic Liberal Party (DLP) whose economic program marks a revival of the growth-first policy rather than one of more equal distribution.

In the North, the Soviet military entered a few days before the liberation. Unlike the AMG in the South where the people's committees were abolished, the Soviets in the North generally did not try to dissolve them. Rather, the Soviets soon recognized the people's committees and used them as the united front organizations through which the Communists took power. The Soviets brought with them a group of Koreans who had been born and raised in the Soviet Union and whose numbers varied from several hundred to several thousand (Henderson 1987, 99). To a great extent these Koreans effectively diluted the Soviet presence. About one hundred Korean Soviet military officers were supported in their bid to take power by the Soviet Army (Do 1988, 257). Among them, Kim Il Sung and his small group of partisans, later to be known as the "Kapsan" faction, were particularly favored by the Soviets. The Russians had been training Soviet Koreans in separate military units for some time, apparently with the thought of using them as a "liberating" force in Korea (J.A. Kim 1975, 30).

While no political organization was allowed in the South, an embryonic government was created in the North in October 1945 in the form of a Five Provinces Administration Bureau (FPAB). The Soviets originally installed as chairman Cho Man-sik, a Christian and the most popular noncommunist political leader in North Korea. He was soon replaced after being accused of opposing trusteeship like all noncommunists in the South and the North. Then, the name was changed to the North Korean Provisional People's Committee. All the Communist groups, including domestic Communists, those working with Mao in Yenan, those who had been in exile in the Soviet Union, and those born and raised in the USSR, founded the North Korean bureau of the Korean Communist Party (KCP) and joined the Korean Provisional People's Committee (KPPC). In October 1945, the Soviets introduced Kim Il Sung who was a onetime anti-Japanese guerrilla leader and a former Soviet Army major. He became the head of the northern branch of KCP in December 1945 and soon became chairman, with Kim Tu-Bong, a leader of the Yenan faction, as vice chairman, of the North Korean Provisional People's Committee (KPPC), the first separate Northern regime.

A Supreme People's Assembly (SPA) was created by the KPC in 1947 and Kim Il Sung became premier. A new assembly was elected in August 1948 and the Democratic People's Republic of Korea (DPRK) was proclaimed in September 1948. A North Korean Workers Party (NKWP) was formed from the merger of Kim's KCP and the Yenan group's old Korean Independence League which established the New People's Party (NPP) led by Kim Du-Bong in August 1946. Kim Du-Bong was elected as chairman with Stalin as honorary president (Scalapino and Lee 1972, 356). A further merger of the NKWP in 1949 with the old South Korean Labor Party (SKLP) created the supreme Korean Workers Party (KWP), bringing the political base of rival Communist leaders firmly under Kim Il Sung and creating today's monolithic political system. Since then political leadership in North Korea has remained unchanged under Kim Il Sung except for two incidents: an open challenge from the Soviet and Yenan faction in 1956 and an abortive coup in 1967 caused by the conflict among the Kapsan group, both results of the growing Sino-Soviet conflict.

At the Sixth KWP Party Congress in 1980 Kim Jung-il, son of Kim Il Sung, was listed fourth in the KWP Politburo and second in the KWP Secretariat. In 1984 it was finally announced that the son was the sole successor to the father, but there were reports of domestic opposition to the son, particularly among older members of the KWP. Criticism of the hereditary succession was deleted in the North Korean political dictionary since 1972 (An 1983, 150–51). The "Three Revolution Squads," which aims at ideology, technology, and culture in development, has given the son some support among the new generations. In 1984 Kim Il Sung undertook a six-week foreign tour, including his first visit to Moscow in seventeen years, and a tour of seven other Eastern bloc states in order to receive Soviet approval of the succession of Kim Jongil, as well as renewed economic aid. He also visited the People's Republic of China, in line with his policy of maintaining a balance between Moscow and Beijing. The *juche* ideology was further stressed in the 1980s superceding Marxism-Leninism. After the fall of East European communism, North Korea has strengthened the maxim of North Korean state communism even more: "*juche* in ideology."

The military occupation of both Koreas by the U.S. and the USSR (1945–48) laid a significant base for their national development to be undertaken and confined within its own system. The states of both

South and North Korea were not autonomous; the power of Rhee and Kim was built by the U.S. and USSR respectively. All the domestic centralists including central-leftists or central-rightists were excluded by the U.S. and Soviet military in the process of state-building on both sides, not to mention that extreme left and right political organizations were abolished by the AMG and the Soviets, respectively. Many centralists were either purged as in the case of nationalist leader Cho Man-Sik of North Korea, or bypassed and excluded from political participation, as with nationalist leaders Kim Ku and Kim Kyu-Sik of South Korea (Kihl 1984, 32–33). In their place, extremely conservative and extremely radical leaderships were chosen by the superpowers.

The AMG needed a leadership to encounter communism in the North. Syngman Rhee was born to an upper-class family in the southern part of Korea. He was seventy years old, an American-educated anti-Japanese activist and extreme anti-communist. Arrested and tortured in 1897, Rhee spent seven years in jail and emigrated to the United States on his release in 1904. By 1919 he was well known and was elected president of the Korean Provisional Government established by a small group of Korean exiles in Shanghai.

Kim Il Sung was an anti-Japanese guerrilla leader and a former Soviet Army major. He was born to a lower middle-class family near Pyongyang (D.S. Suh 1988, 3–5; Scalapino and Lee 1972, 203–4) and was only thirty-three years old when he returned to Korea from the Soviet Union. His family moved to Manchuria in 1919 and he came back to his home town for a few years. Then, he emigrated with his family to Manchuria in 1926, where he remained until 1941, when he went to the Soviet union to stay until 1945. He advanced through the ranks of the Chinese Communist military organization to the position of division commander. He had been closely associated with the Chinese Communists in Manchuria and had developed relationships with the Soviets during his sojourn in the Soviet Union. The army was the backbone of Kim's dominance and its leaders were hardbitten guerrillas with as much as twenty years' experience. Unlike the USSR and China, where an autonomous and violent revolution and internal civil war were the routes to power (Jameson and Wilber 1981, 805), North Korean state power was built under the tutelage of the Soviet military which imposed the extremely radical regime of Kim Il Sung. He strongly advocates the Stalinist autarkic system of "socialism in one state" that admonishes "each state to establish its own integrated industrial base."

The fact that extremely conservative and extremely radical leaderships had been chosen by the U.S. and USSR military forces, respectively, played an important role in producing different patterns of development later on. The political ideology of North Korean communism was announced by Kim Il Sung as following the pattern of autarkic Stalinism. The ideology of *juche* (self-reliance) was developed later on as an application of the theory of Marxism-Leninism to the Korean experience. The extremely radical North Korean state has latched on to a Marxist concept of national development in which material growth is valued. In the North Korean concept, development is synonymous with material productivity. Therefore, the industrial sector of the economy is more valued than the service sector, especially, the "nonproductive" services such as public administration, housing, and so on. Full employment is sought by the state, even at the cost of considerable inefficiency.

The official ideology guides its political life, and the KWP applies this ideology in developing workable policies and programs. With about 2.5 million members (11 percent of the total North Korean population), the KWP leaders and cadres are entrenched in key positions of power in North Korea. Like other Communist systems, the ruling party in North Korea controls the state through a system of lateral controls such as the overlapping of key positions in the party and government agencies at the center and the periphery.

The ideology of South Korea was both anticommunist and procapitalist. Expression of sympathy with communist or even socialist ideas was vigorously suppressed. During the 1970s, in response to the shift toward a multipolar world, the South Korean state eased restrictions on contacts with communist states for practical reasons, without softening ideological opposition to the political philosophies of those states. At the same time, it proclaims constitutional democracy with a multiparty system and market economy, although strong authoritarian rule has been practiced in both politics and economy. Under the capitalist system, parliamentary republics have existed throughout the regimes in postliberation South Korea, from the civil regimes of Rhee (1948–60) and Chang (1960–61) to the military-turned-civil regimes of Park (1961–79), Chun (1980–1987), and the present Roh since 1988. Notwithstanding these changes, each phase has been consistent in terms of preserving the predominance of private ownership, private enterprises, and market mechanisms. The means of production and distribution are privately owned and operated, at least in theory although this aspect of the South Korean state has been changed since the 1960s.

The extremist political ideologies were transplanted in each side by foreign powers. Extremism was significantly expedited by the tradition of the strong state inherited from the Yi dynasty and Japanese military rule. The extremist nature of political leadership in each state was to dominate the system.

Institutional Changes and the Growth of Economy

Under the AMG, South Korea was transformed into a market economy under the capitalist mode of production. Nationalization and redistribution of colonial properties were slowly implemented in South Korea. The AMG initiated limited programs such as land reform and education reform. An effective national educational system was established, which was one of the more effective forms of aid from this time on. And, through land reform, about one third of all arable land that was owned by the Japanese in 1945 was redistributed to the cultivators by the AMG in 1948, but only 16.5 percent of all farmers in South Korea became full owners of the land they farmed (Gregor 1990, 26). This stage turned out to be only a moderate success. The AMG did not introduce basic reforms as the basis for later development. For the AMG, economic development was left to the operation of the market system through aid and development programs. Political democracy was rather the primary goal to precede economic development.

Legislation to redistribute the rest of the land was at an advanced state when the Korean War broke out. This reform did not produce an early increase in productivity, for the distribution of land was not accompanied by other measures to extend irrigation and give farmers access to credit, improved seed, cheap fertilizer, and extension services (Clough 1987, 70). This stage was moderately successful in that the immediate result of the land reform was to increase the income of the mass of farmers and eliminate large disparities in income throughout the countryside. The pattern of small owner-operated farms, one hectare or less in size, established at that time has continued to the present. After the completion of land reform in 1952, 71 percent of all farmers owned the land they tilled. As a consequence, there was a dramatic reduction in outlays for rent and a corresponding escalation in disposable family income. Family income also burgeoned because of increases in production that followed land reform (Mason et al. 1980, 237–243). Through land reform, the state could lessen the power of landowners, redirecting idle capital away from land speculation and into manufacturing.

The state of South Korea, however, did not destroy the existing class structure in the process of early accumulation. The First Republic headed by Syngman Rhee did not liquidate the old remnants of the Yi Dynasty and colonial past. Many of the dominant elites were of past *yangban* landlord background and included even collaborators from the colonial period. They worked through Japanese-trained Korean officials and policemen. Throughout the 1950s the United States advised that the fundamental strategy must be stabilization of prices, whereas the preoccupation of the South Korean state was to reduce the gap between imports and exports and to build up national resources. When an American team produced in 1954 the first long-term economic plans known as the Nathan Report, they were largely sidetracked mainly by the lack of requisite political leadership (Lim 1985, 49). The government was authoritarian in nature but incapable of achieving development; it aimed at the long-term exercise of power rather than the mobilization of manpower and resources for development.

Between 1945 and 1961 the main goal of the South Korean state was to create a stable, viable economy out of what was successively a divided economy, a war-ravaged economy, and a stagnant economy with imports running at 20 times more than exports. Years before and after 1960, the growth of national output in per capita terms declined to nearly zero. Dwindling foreign aid and import levels acted as a brake on production and investment; all this was accompanied by political unrest.

The early failure of South Korea is attributed, in part, to the AMG whose economic policy attempted only limited reforms and a maximum market economy. Before the Korean War, there had been gradual improvement in the economy with substantial foreign aid from the United States. Various institutional reforms such as land reform and the creation of a new central bank had been introduced. With respect to development planning, in the early years substantial guidance was provided by U.S. experts under the auspices of several development projects. In its early development, the state of South Korea depended largely on foreign aid for several years after the war. Grant aid that South Korea received under various programs directly or indirectly from the United States between 1946 and 1962 amounted to $3.4 billion. Between 1946 and 1952, South Korea received $679 million of economic and military aid from the U.S. (Mason et al. 1980, 1982). UNKRA, Public Law 480, and AID amounted to $2.78 billion for the years 1951–62.

Since 1962, the role of the South Korean government in advancing economic development has been radically changed by the military leadership, with the state exercising enormous influence in the economic area. The power of the South Korean state in the 1960s and 1970s was comparable to the very early North Korean socialist transformation in terms of initiating state enterprises and regulating financial institutions. The state has introduced consecutive five-year plans. The Park regime introduced the "indicative" capitalist planning method and launched a series of five-year economic development plans unprecedented in Korean history, the First (1962–66) and Second (1967–71) Five-Year Plans with emphasis on industrial growth. The Third Five-Year Plan (1972–76) emphasized balanced growth between industrial and agricultural sectors, introducing the mass mobilization measure of the New Community Movement; and the Fourth Five-Year Plan (1977–81) focused on sustained economic growth and equity. Of particular importance, South Korea began to develop an extensive relationship with Japan centering on mutual beneficial economic activity, following the ratification in 1965 of a treaty normalizing relations between the two countries. A year later a Foreign Capital Inducement Law was enacted to attract foreign investment, especially that of Japan. The state of the Third Republic concentrated its attention on the goal of economic development from the very moment of its assumption of power. Economic development was the sacred national goal during the period of the Third Republic.

The Fifth Plan (1982–86) and the Sixth Plan (1987–91) were implemented by the new military-turned civil leadership. The target of these plans was extended to the area of social development. South

TABLE 6.1
Economic Planning of South and North Korea

	South Korea	North Korea
1947		One-Year, 1947
1948		One-Year, 1948
1949		Two-Year, 1949–50
1954		Three Year, 1954–56
1957		Five-Year, 1957–61(60)
1962	First 5-year, 1962–66	Seven-Year, 1961–67(70)
1967	Second 5-year, 1967–71	
1972	Third 5-year, 1972–76	Six-Year, 1971–76(77)
1977	Fourth 5-year, 1977–81	Seven-Year, 1978–84(86)
1982	Fifth 5-year, 1982–86	
1987	Sixth 5-year, 1987–91	Seven-Year, 1987–93

Korea continued to invite more international capital in the 1980s. South Korea held a series of international events, including the 1985 IMF and World Bank annual conference, the 1986 Asian Games and the 1988 Summer Olympics.

The political and social unrest that followed the 1979 assassination triggered a severe recession in South Korea in 1980. The recession was worsened by the drastic increase in world oil prices in 1979. The economy has slowly recovered since then. In 1986, South Korea achieved surpluses in the trade balance for the first time in its recent history.

It is debatable, however, that only military leadership could produce extensive development programs. The initial plan was drawn up by the short-lived Chang government, which did not survive to implement the plan because of the military interruption. Drawing upon this aborted plan, the new junta regime finalized the program and actually embarked on active economic growth policies. Export drive development had been already discussed by the Rhee state in 1957 and 1958.

Economic plans at present are formulated largely by the Economic Planning Board (EPB). The organization spans a broad range of activities: overall planning, infrastructure development, social development, current economic research, external relations planning, and financial planning. Moreover, the EPB utilizes the private planning of the large corporations (Kang 1989, 30). When a private sector company is successful in a particular industry or product area, the EPB planners write up the success formula and implement it. Most of the environmental input to the plans come from the private companies.

Although South Korea's "indicative" plan since the 1960s does not directly compel the enterprises to adhere strictly to the specific and general targets set forth as does the North Korean "imperative" plan, it does attempt to exert broad indirect pressure through market mechanisms. Private enterprises are asked to conform to the basic objectives of the plan, and the state resorts to fiscal, monetary, and other policies to achieve the planned goals. Reliance on the market, private initiative, and pecuniary incentives remain the basic tenets of the system. The state's influence is used to change the parameters of the market and provide incentives in order to achieve the desired economic and social goals.

The crisis in this system occurs with, on the one hand, the external situation of the world market, and the rise of an industrial working class after developmental takeoff, on the other. The state plays an unusually strong role in mobilizing resources and manpower and controls social and political tensions. Crisis seems to come from domestic conflicts including working-class strikes and student demonstrations. Crisis also comes from the change of external market situations. The disadvantage of this model is greater monopoly of business, such as the *chaebol* (industrial conglomerate) phenomenon, which results in an inequality problem. Small- and medium-sized industry (SMI) cannot be developed because large conglomerates dominate all industries from manufacture and technology to consumer goods. Social wealth is distributed into the upper half of the population, and social inequality in the process of development increases.

In North Korea, in contrast to the reluctant nationalization and slow redistribution in South Korea, the rapid transformation of the national economy took place upon the Communist takeover. The economy was radically transformed according to Soviet prototypes and directions within a few years. The state forcibly decoupled (or, rather, was decoupled) from the capitalist world economy from the start. The state kept all foreign capital out and foreign trade low and, especially, subordinate to the interests of a comprehensive domestically oriented economy.

Between March and October 1946 the Provisional People's Committee promulgated a land reform act, a labor law, laws on equality of the sexes, and a law nationalizing key industries. The state nationalized major industries that comprised 90 percent of all North Korean industry. The takeover was made easier by the withdrawal of the Japanese, who formerly owned and controlled almost all the key industrial enterprises. Land formerly owned by the Japanese and all owner's land exceeding 5 hectares was allocated free to landless peasants, creating for a few years a rural economy of small, owner-operated farms. Land reform was completed in less than one month, affecting 54 percent of total cultivated land (Chung 1974, 5–10).

The state of North Korea instituted distinct economic plans from the beginning of its development. After two one-year plans for 1947 and 1948 respectively, Two-Year (1949–50), Three-Year (1954–56), and Five-Year (1957–61) Plans followed. Then, long-term plans followed: Seven-Year (1961–67), Six-Year (1971–76), Second Seven-Year (1978–84), and Third Seven-Year (1987–93). North Korea has strengthened the role of central planning. The state introduced what it calls the "united planning system" and the "detailed planning system." Under "united planning," introduced in 1962, regional planning commissions were created in cities, counties, and provinces under the direct control of the State Planning Commission (SPC), while at the same time SPC branches were also established at each enterprise.

The early institutional change brought about the rapid mobilization of the North Korean population into industrial buildups. Most of the abrupt changes occurred during the 1950s. These political and institutional changes, however, could not create other social improvements such as education, birth and death rates, urbanization, and health care. Social development in North Korea has been achieved at a similar pace with that in South Korea (as discussed in chapter 5), while rapid economic growth occurred only during an early period in North Korea.

Complete socialization of the economy was accomplished by 1958 when private ownership of productive means, land, and commercial enterprises was replaced by state and cooperative (collective) ownership and control. In 1953, North Korea introduced collectivization of the farms into "cooperatives." Collectivization (1954–58) totally abolished private farming as a type of agricultural organization and as a way of life, transforming it into either a collective or state farm. The individual farms were combined into agricultural cooperatives averaging about 300 households. As the work was done by work teams, the members of the work teams earn wages in cash or kind for work done. The cooperatives became a basic social unit and a basic form of state

power for the rural area. By these measures the base of political opposition in urban and rural areas was broken down, while increasing
farm productivity to the maximum (Chung 1974, 9).

In the early 1960s the state brought the cooperatives under more
centralized control by establishing county farm management committees to establish production targets, allocate resources, and supervise
the financial operations of the cooperatives in each county. At about
the same time, the state adopted a variety of material incentives to
stimulate production, such as paid vacations and bonuses. Families
were allowed private plots on which to produce foodstuffs for their
own use or for sale at open markets. In 1977, the state reduced the
authorized size of private plots from 50 *pyong* (160 square meters) to
twenty to thirty *pyong* (66 to 99 square meters) (Bunge 1983, 146).

Increased state investment in agriculture during the 1960s indicates
that grain production increased slowly during the 1970s. In the early
1960s Kim Il Sung introduced the "Chongsan-ni method" in agriculture, requiring administrative personnel to emulate Kim's example by
going to the fields to talk over problems with farmworkers. As a result,
according to an estimate by the U.N. Food and Agriculture Organization (FAO), rice production increased at 7 percent annually during this
period. The production of corn, barley, wheat, and other cereals rose
at less than one-third this pace, suggesting a shift of acreage to rice at
the expense of other grains (Bunge 1981, 138, 253, J.S. Chung 1974,
50–54).

Communist allies provided considerable amounts of funds, supplies,
and technical personnel to aid the reconstruction. The long-range recovery and development plan launched in 1953 was greatly helped by
this assistance. Data on the amount of aid received by North Korea
varied greatly. North Korea announced a figure of 500 million rubles
or 550 million dollars in postwar assistance (Breidenstein 1975, 168).
Western sources estimate Soviet, Chinese, and East European aid to
North Korea between 1946 and 1960 at over $1.8 billion (Kihl 1984,
154–55).

North Korea did not waste any time in implementing state and
cooperative ownership of production, an organizational objective of
the Communist economic policy. Key industrial enterprises came first
under the control of the state (People's Committee) then under the
tutelage of the Soviet occupation force. As a result, industrial firms are

today either state-owned or in the form of cooperatives, the former contributing significant shares of the total industrial output, more than 90 percent since the 1960s. The state uniformly controls the economy including the price system through a centralized plan. The income tax system was abolished in North Korea in April 1974. By this measure, transactional revenues and profits from state-run industries account for about 92 percent of national revenues, and 8 percent of total revenue is turned over to the central government from the provinces. The state accumulates capital through forced savings from domestic agriculture. The state destroyed the landed class and national capitalists and expropriated all foreign investments. They substituted for capitalists by taking over all major economic tasks and mobilizing the working class and peasants for development. The rapid development during 1946–1960 in North Korea was mainly the result of these political measures.

Kim Il Sung began to emphasize *juche* ideology as the creative application of Marxism-Leninism to the concrete conditions of the North Korean situation from 1955. Along with the ideology, the mass mobilization scheme was introduced, known as the Chollima Work Team Movement, patterned on the Stakhanovite Movement in the Soviet Union and the Great Leap Forward Movement in the People's Republic of China. One can hardly understand North Korea's development in the 1950s and the early 1960s without a knowledge of the Chollima Movement. With the help of this movement, the average growth rate in industry was 41.7 and 36.6 percent during the Three-Year and the Five-Year Plans, respectively.

Slowdowns in economic growth in North Korea in the 1960s set off a chain of organization reform movements, such as the Chongsan-ni method for the solution of organizational problems in the agricultural cooperatives and the Taean Work Team System for the solution of management problems in the industrial plants. They enhanced communication between workers and farmers on the one hand and the managerial staff on the other. They required the mobilization of administrative personnel in "on-the-spot" guidance. However, the dispute between China and the Soviet Union slowed down the pace of North Korean development in the late 1960s.

The early ideology of participating in the world socialist economy changed since the *juche* ideology was stressed in the early 1970s. The state began to accumulate capital through "selective participation" in the world capitalist and socialist economy. The capitalist world economy, which was radically rejected during the early period, attracted the stagnant North Korea. The state joined the capitalist and socialist world economy only on the basis of selective participation. The state embraced publicly the "ideology" of the Third World, that is, nonalignment and neutrality.

In a striking departure from past practice, North Korea decided to import large quantities of plants and machinery from West European countries and Japan in the early 1970s. North Korea was probably disturbed by the accumulating evidence in the late 1960s that industrial growth in South Korea had begun to outstrip its own. North Korea could not increase its exports rapidly enough to meet the payments due on the sudden surge in imports, especially when the prices of some of its chief export products such as metals and minerals dropped during the recession following the unexpected jump in world oil prices in 1973. For this reason, in the 1970s, while South Korea's economic growth averaged close to 10 percent annually, North Korea's averaged 6.2 percent.

North Korea enacted a joint venture law in 1984, designed to attract foreign investment aiming primarily at European companies. However, only two joint ventures have been arranged in the few months after the announcement, one Japanese project for a department store (backed mainly by Koreans in Japan) and a French project to construct a hotel. The number of joint ventures in operation increased to about fifty in 1987, forty-four in which Korean Japanese invested (*The Europa World Yearbook* 1988, 1615). North Korea continues to attempt to borrow foreign capital to upgrade technology. A government reshuffle in February 1988 included the appointment of a new Chairman of the State Planning Commission and new ministers to supervise construction, light industry, and chemicals.

The North Korean command and closed economy was not merely less harmful but positively advantageous during the early period of economic development for the first seven to fifteen years. These advantages of political and institutional transformations were gradually and increasingly dwarfed by shortcomings as the economy grew.

The economic bureaucracies in both Korean states—the Economic Planning Board (EPB) in the South and the State Planning Commission (SPC) in the North—are working closely with other agencies in mobilizing energy and resources. Central planning was highly effective and capable of developing the North Korean economy at the beginning stage—the first seven or fifteen years—relying on mobilization measures. As the size of the economy grew, the complexity of planning and choice-making multiplied, making the central decision-making process more inefficient and wasteful than in the formative and reconstruction period.

Both South and North Korea experienced an authoritarian transformation of the constitutions and states in 1972. In South Korea, a popular referendum approved the Yushin (revitalizing) constitution that greatly strengthened presidential power. Key provisions included indirect election of the president through a new body, the National Conference for Unification (NCU); presidential appointment of one-third of the National Assembly; and presidential authority to issue decrees to restrict civil liberties in times of national emergency. President Park was reelected by the NCU and the DRP obtained a decisive majority in elections for the new National Assembly. In North Korea, a new "socialist" constitution was promulgated. The new constitution declared Kim's political thought, *juche*, to be the ideology of the state.

The formal authoritarian adaptation of both Korean states in 1972 was the result not only of the economic situation per se of each side in the late 1960s, but of the "comparison effect" formed by the awareness of each other through the Red Cross Conference in 1972. In South Korea, economic development was on the rise and it needed social security to attract more and more international capital when it entered a deeper level of expansive development; this necessitated a more authoritarian state. Moreover, the South Korean state introduced the *Saemaeul* (New Community) Movement, a mass mobilization measure, in 1972 that took aim at rural development encouraging self-help by villages with small government grants. This was probably stimulated by the nature of the early success of North Korea. In addition to the mass mobilization of the rural population, the state adopted a policy to increase prices paid by the government for grain to be sold at a lower price to the urban population, despite the resulting increase in the budget deficit and inflationary pressures. (The North Korean state purchases rice from the farmers for 60 *chon* per kilogram and supplies it to workers for 8 *chon*.)

Also, the ever-growing threat from North Korea peaked at the end of the 1960s. A commando squad of thirty-one armed guerrillas infiltrated South Korea near Blue House in an attempt to assassinate President Park Chung Hee. Some 120 guerrillas were reported to have landed from October to November 1968 in the eastern coastal areas, and more than two hundred incidents had been reported in South Korea (D.S. Suh 1988, 231–32). North Korea publicly called for the revolution in South Korea toward the end of the 1960s. These threats stimulated South Korea to introduce a tightly controlled authoritarian state to deter the proclaimed threat.

North Korea contrasts with South Korea in that economic growth slowed down in the late 1960s. Economic activity, which depended on only mass mobilization, needed to be revitalized by introducing Western capital, which led to a more authoritarian transformation of and surveillance within North Korea so as not to be exposed to the external world. Together with such changes and probably noting the more rapid economic development of the South in the late 1960s, North Korea attempted a large-scale development program through the importation of Western technology from Japan, France, and West Germany. The drastic change in the international environment resulting from Sino-American detente also challenged North Korea in the 1970s and seemed to aid the liberal climate. The importation, however, resulted in default on its loans from free market countries at the end of 1976.

The basic pattern of capital accumulation differs in South and North Korea. The South Korean state has actively sought foreign capital; not only is the role of foreign capital important, but the state's role is also important in South Korean development. South Korean state accumulates capital in three ways. First, it accumulates through establishing state enterprises including a social infrastructure, banks, and financial institutions. Second, it also stimulates and supports the private investment of national capitalists, and, finally, it seeks foreign investment and loans.

The South Korean state did not operate as in a free market system. It assumed an "entrepreneurial role" in the process of development (Evans 1979, 214). The state is expected to invest not only in the "social overhead" necessary to make private economic activity productive but also to undertake production and service activities. The state has run many important state enterprises, which are the foundation of the infrastructure, energy, raw materials, and heavy industries.

Such an enterprise is usually found in public utilities or in strongly monopolistic industries such as railroads, electricity, the telephone system, cigarettes, and steel mills. Moreover, the state is also a stockholder in more than thirty state-invested corporations, most of which also have private stockholders. These provided the industrial base and inputs for the manufacturing sector.

State enterprises were also engaged in banking and other services in the financial sector. The state directly owns or controls nearly all the financial institutions including the Bank of Korea. Except for local banks, branches of foreign banks, life insurance companies, and merchant banking organizations, every commercial institution was either partly owned by the state, or was a state agency. Hence in 1970, the state directly controlled 96.4 percent of financial assets; this proportion decreased to 82 percent in 1980. Of the remaining 18 percent, only the foreign banks were not exposed to direct state pressure. Thus, the state can directly determine the interest rates and other quantitative and qualitative lending policies. And also the state exerts direct and powerful control over the foreign sector through its monopoly of foreign exchange, preferential tariffs and interest rates, and direct or indirect subsidies. The government allocated public loans to the social infrastructure (72.9 percent), such as banking and insurance, energy sources, transportation and storage, and so on. (Lim 1985, 93, 95). And the government constructed various industrial estates operated by the state-owned Export Industry Public Corporation in order to facilitate the export promotion of manufactured goods. The state control of financial institutions has been slightly deregulated throughout the 1980s, however.

The state invited the multinationals mainly to use them as the mediating agents of technology transfers for the purpose of reinforcing export promotion of manufactured goods. So, the priority of the Foreign Capital Inducement Law was given to those industries that were capital- and technology-intensive, export-oriented, and located in the heavy-chemical sectors. Foreign capital was concentrated in a few sectors that contribute to export promotion. Multinational-direct investment was directed to the expansion of manufacturing industries, such as chemicals, textiles, and electronics.

The state effectively took advantage of the national capitalists as major agents of development. Reliance of loan capital has strengthened the hand of the Korean state in relation to the local bourgeoisie (Evans 1987, 216). The most potent instrument for influencing national capitalists was control of bank credit and foreign borrowing. National capitalists were created through political connections after 1945 (Jones and Sakong 1980, 258–85). Although there had been some national capitalists such as Sam Yang and Whashin, and ex-Japanese firms such as Oriental Brewery, Sunkyung, and Korea Explosives, most national capitalists that became major participants in export promotion later emerged after the liberation. They developed into large conglomerates known as *chaebol*. *Chaebol* refers to a system of highly centralized family-based industrial and business conglomerates. Samsug, Lucky-Goldstar, and Ssangyong which survived from the fifties are called the first generation of *chaebols*. They were the major agents of import substitution in the 1950s. Twenty *chaebols* accounted for about fifty percent of the total South Korean GNP in 1987.

There emerged a second generation of *chaebol* under the Park regime, which grew rapidly during the phase of outward-looking development. Hyundai, Daewoo, and Hanjin were among them. Their formation as large conglomerates depended not only on entrepreneurial talents but also on full state support, including privileged access to domestic lending and foreign borrowing, bargain-price acquisition of public properties, noncompetitive awarding of government contract, and so on. The national capitalists become economically dominant but remain politically subordinate to the state bureaucracy, for the capitalists have been unable to represent or promote their class interests as the general interests of society.

Despite domination of national capitalists, the state prefers the national capitalists to the multinationals as its main partner. However, the state favors multinationals against workers, trying to keep wages low in order to provide an attractive investment climate for multinationals who have an interest in cheap labor. Unions are weak and exist as no more than an arm of the state; labor unrest is severely punished (H. Koo 1987, 174). An abrupt and intense proletarianization and lack of strong collective response to it are the unique characteristics of South Korean development (H. Koo 1990, 669-81).

The North Korean state accumulates capital through state enterprises in industry and cooperatives in agriculture. With the elimination of private industry, all industrial establishments in North Korea today fall under two categories: state enterprises and industrial cooperatives.

State enterprises contribute an overwhelming portion of the total industrial ouput—over 90 percent. The state-appointed manager assumes responsibility for the productive activities of the enterprises and is assisted in his task by the chief engineer, vice managers, second engineer, and supervisors.

The vast majority of agricultural production takes place in rural cooperatives. State farms account for only 9 percent of the total agricultural land and for a small share of the agricultural population, but are ideologically the most advanced type of agricultural organization. Both the means of production and the output are state owned, and farmers receive standardized monetary wages on the basis of an eight-hour work day rather than shares of the farm's production. State farms are often model farms that experimented with new cropping methods, or specialized in livestock or fruit production. State farms are often coterminous with a county, and their larger scale allows room for greater mechanization. State farms attempt to integrate all the agricultural and industrial activities of the county into one complementary and integrated management system. Private lands are allowed only for plots under 20 to 30 *pyong* (66 to 99 square meters).

The state controls all the financial institutions including the Central Bank, the Industrial Bank, and the Foreign Trade Bank. Through the Central Bank, the state regulates the supply of money and credit to state enterprises, government institutions, and individuals. The Industrial Bank lends funds to agricultural cooperatives and local industries, and the Foreign Trade Bank controls all foreign transactions, letters of credit, and balance of payment adjustments for the Central Bank.

The state mobilizes industrial workers and farmers toward national development. The state employed such mobilization systems as the *Taean* industrial management system, the Juche ideology, the *Chollima* movement, the *Chongsan-ni* spirit. And mass-production campaigns such as "Pyongyang Speed," "Kangsun Speed" "Carrying One More Load," "100-Day Speed Battle," "200-Day Speed Battle," and the like, were imposed on the workers and farmers by the state.

Adaptation to Environment

The development of both Koreas has been to a great extent advantaged or disadvantaged by the two world systems into which each Korea was incorporated. At the beginning, South and North Korea cut off all relations with world socialist and capitalist countries, respectively. The U.S. and the USSR presided over Korea's national division in 1945 and colonialized their ideological systems, but Japan and China have been equal, or probably a greater influences on the later developmental course as they were incorporated into the system.

The economic and military aid from each political sphere was great. After the war, both sides received considerable amounts of economic and technical aid from their allies. Data on the amount of aid received by North Korea varied greatly. North Korea has announced a figure of 500 million rubles or 550 million dollars of postwar assistance (Breidenstein 1975, 168). Western sources estimate Soviet, Chinese, and East European aid to North Korea between 1946 and 1978 at $2.8 billion of which $2.0 billion was in the form of economic assistance and $800 million in the form of military assistance (Kihl 1984, 154–55). Between 1946 and 1960, North Korea received $1.8 billion of which $700 million came from the Soviet Union, $600 million from China, and $500 million from Eastern European countries. During 1961–78, North Korea received another $1.0 billion of which $700 million came from the Soviet Union and $300 from China. In 1984, North Korea received U.N. aid of $18.4 million.

Aid to South Korea was much greater. According to South Korean sources, grant aid that South Korea received under various programs directly or indirectly from the United States amounted to $15.4 billion dollars for the years 1946–75, of which $12.6 billion came from the U.S. (military and economic aids are half and half), and $2.8 billion from Japan ($1.0 billion), and other countries ($1.8 billion) (Kihl 1984, 154–56).

South Korea began to develop an extensive relationship with Japan centering on mutually beneficial economic activity, following the ratification in 1965 of a treaty normalizing relations between the two countries. A year later in 1966 the Foreign Capital Inducement Law was enacted to attract foreign investment.

China came into North Korea through the Korean War. The measures of mass mobilization in the late 1950s and the policy of equally emphasizing agriculture appear to be related to Chinese influence. The *Chollima* campaign was clearly inspired by Mao's Great Leap Forward.

The Stalinist system had reigned uncontested in a "monolithic" socialist world before the death of Stalin. With Stalin's death, the Yugoslav and Chinese schisms in the 1950s, Cuba's entrance into the socialist world, the Eastern European reforms, and the Chinese, Yugoslav, and Czechoslovakia experiments in the 1960s, there has been increasing pluralism in the field. The death of Stalin and the subsequent de-Stalinization movement had sparked a major political crisis in North Korea in 1956, when challenges from the Soviet and Yenan factions publicly criticized Kim's personality cult while Kim was visiting Western European countries.

As the confrontation between the Soviet Union and China after 1957 grew, North Korea refused to take sides in the dispute until 1962. North Korea's neutral stance in the Sino-Soviet dispute had resulted in increased aid from the competing power between 1957–61, but North Korea's decision to side with China in 1962 incurred the stoppage of military aid from the Soviet Union between 1962–64. As a result, the Seven-Year Plan was extended for three more years. North Korea stood firmly on the side of China in 1963–64. Only after the fall of Khrushchev in October 1964 and the visit of Premier Aleksei Kosygin in 1965 did relations improve. On the other hand, in early 1967, as China was experiencing the initial stage of its Cultural Revolution, Mao Zedong began to attack North Korea as a "fat revisionist." In this situation, there was an abortive coup in 1967 among the Kapsan members in North Korea (Rinser 1988, 52–3; Scalapino and Lee 1972, 614–15). Both Soviet- and China-connected groups attempted a joint conspiracy but failed. Since then, North Korea has maintained balance in the struggle between the two.

North Korea placed increased emphasis on its links with the USSR in 1985, culminating in a new arrangement for the supply of Soviet aircraft to North Korea, and an exchange visit by senior officials from each government. This trend continued in 1986, when North Korea granted the USSR the use of its naval port at Nampo, indicating growing military links between the two states. Since early 1990, however, being pressed by the Soviet Union to open and liberalize the economy, North Korea has attempted to effect close ties with China when Kim Il Sung visited Deng Xiaoping in September 1990.

While Western powers established the two Korean states, it seems to be Eastern powers that played a decisive role in shaping the developmental course, as they did in similar roles at the time of Korea's opening. South Korea had adopted the United States' model of development during the late 1940s and 1950s. Since the 1960s, South Korea has modeled itself after the Japanese. Similarly, North Korea had modeled itself after the Stalinist development during the early period of the late 1940s and the 1950s. North Korea was probably most deeply influenced by the Chinese Communist model (Cumings 1984, 51–52). Now, the structure of North Korean development is more like the Chinese who emphasize ideology over pragmatism and hold significant portions of the population in agriculture (Mesa-Largo 1975, 97). Kim Il Sung is very much a "mass line" leader like Mao, making frequent visits to factories and the countrysides, sending cadres "down" to local levels to help policy implementation and to solicit local opinion, requiring small-group political study and so-called criticism and self-criticism, using periodic campaigns to mobilize people for production or education, and encouraging soldiers to engage in production in good "people's army" fashion. North Korea, like China but unlike the USSR, maintains a "united front" policy toward non-Communist groups, so that in addition to the ruling KWP there are much smaller parties that have mainly symbolic functions. This may prove that both Koreas have a cultured "Asian" way of development despite the fact that they were transplanted initially by the "Western" developers.

In conclusion, both Korean states have played significant roles not only in their adoption of specific economic plans but also in the sense of implementing these development plans and programs rigorously. South Korea does not practice pure capitalism in that some key enterprises such as financial institutions, utilities, rail transportation, and steel mills (Pohang Steel Mills), are government owned and operated. The economic system can be called state capitalism. State capitalism here means direct and/or indirect state intervention in production through commercial enterprises operating in profitable sectors of the economy and through various agencies of controlling the process. In the communist system of North Korea, the means of production and distribution are state-or collectively owned and controlled by the people, and the state administers the people's property. Power has been dominated by the Communist Korean Workers party. State communism refers to the economic order in which the means of production is formally nationalized in the hands of the state.

North Korea had an energetic start with great help from the Soviet forces, nationalizing all industries, collectivizing land, and launching a series of development plans. South Korea could not begin any major development plans, as it was tied up in political struggles. The political insecurity in South Korea during the early period is attributed partly to the AMG's direct control. After fifteen years passed, the ideology of *juche* in North Korea developed as surviving measures from the dispute between China and USSR impeded further structural development. North Korea has been seeking possible breakthroughs for further development, keeping a back and forth balance between the *juche* ideology and importation of foreign capitals. On the other hand, South Korea launched late the major development programs after spending several years in continued political conflict. South Korea effectively used private entrepreneurs, strictly controlling national financial mechanisms and foreign investment. The South Korean state engaged in pragmatic planning. At the same time, South Korea upgraded its structure, which can sustain high growth, and has been expanding its economy by breaking more and more into world markets for more advanced industrial products.

References

An, Tai Sung. 1983. *North Korea in Transition: From Dictatorship to Dynasty.* Westport, CT: Greenwood Press.

Breidenstein, Gerhard. 1975. "Economic comparison of North and South Korea." *Journal of Contemporary Asia* 5:165–78.

Bunge, Frederica M. (ed). 1981. *North Korea: A Country Study.* Washington, D.C.: Foreign Area Studies, The American University.

Choi, Yearn Hong and Dong Hyun Kim. 1990. "Korea-U.S. trade friction: Content analysis of the *Chosun Ilbo, Korea Times, Washington Post,* and *New York Times.*" *Korea Observer* 20(4):507–35.

Chung, Joseph Sang-hoon. 1974. *The North Korean Economy: Structure and Development.* Stanford, CA: Hoover Institution Press.

Clough, Ralph N. 1987. *Embattled Korea: The Rivalry for International Support.* Boulder, CO: Westview Press.

Cumings, Bruce. 1984. *The Two Koreas.* Foreign Policy Association. No. 269. New York: Headline Series.

Do, Heung-Ryul. 1988. "Bookhan sasipnyun: toji kaehyuk aesu saeseup chaejae gkaji" (Forty years of North Korea: From land reform to the father-son succession). *Shin Dong-A,* 9/88:256–266.

Europe World Yearbook, The. 1988. *The Europa World Yearbook, 1988.* London: Europa Publications.

Evans, Peter. 1987. "Class, state, and dependence in East Asia: Lessons for Latin Americanists." Pp. 203–26 in F. Deyo (ed.), *The Political Economy of the New Asian Industrialism*. New York: Cornell University Press.

———. 1979. *Dependent Development: The Alliance of Multinational, State, and Local Capital in Brazil*. Princeton, N.J.: Princeton University Press.

Gregor, A. James. 1990. *Land of the Morning Calm: Korea and American Security*. Washington, D.C.: Ethics and Public Policy Center.

Henderson, Gregory. 1987. "The politics of Korea." Pp. 95–118 in Sullivan and Foss (eds.), *Two Koreas—One Future?* Lanham, MD: University Press of America.

James, Kenneth P. and Charles K. Wilber. 1981. "Socialism and Development: Editor's Introduction." *World Development* 9(9/10):803–11.

Jones, Leroy P. and Il Sakong. 1980. *Government, Business, and Entrepreneurship in Economic Development: The Korean Case*. Cambridge, Mass.: Harvard University Press.

Kang, Jeong-Koo. 1988. *Rethinking South Korean Land Reform: Fousing on U.S. Occupation as a Struggle against History*. Ph.D. Diss. Department of Sociology, The University of Wisconsin-Madison.

Kang, T.W. 1989. *Is Korea the Next Japan?: Understanding the Structure, Strategy, and Tactics of America's Next Competitor*. New York: The Free Press.

Kihl, Young Whan. 1984. *Politics and Policies in Divided Korea: Regimes in Contest*. Boulder, CO: Westview Press.

Kim, Joung-won Alexander. 1975. *Divided Korea: The Politics of Development, 1945–1972*. Cambridge, Mass.: East Asian Research Center, Harvard University.

Koo, Hagen. 1990. "From farm to factory: Proletarianization in Korea," *American Sociological Review* 55(5):669–81.

———. 1987. "The interplay of states, social class, and world system in East Asian development: The case of South Korea and Taiwan." in F. Deyo (ed.), *The Political Economy of the New Asian Industrialism*. New York: Cornell University Press.

Lim, Hyun-Chin. 1985. *Dependent Development in Korea, 1963–1979*. Seoul: Seoul National University Press.

Mason, Edward S. et al. 1980. *The Economic and Social Modernization of the Republic of Korea*. Cambridge, Mass.: Harvard University Council on East Asian Studies.

Mesa-Lago, Carmelo. 1975. "A Continuum Model for Global Comparison." Pp. 92–120 in Mesa-Lago and Beck (eds.), *Comparative Socialist Systems: Essays on Politics and Economics*. Pittsburgh: UCIS Publications.

Rinser, Louise. 1988. *Bookhan Iyagi*. (Stories on North Korea.) Seoul: Hyungsung Press.

Scalapino, Robert A. and Chong-Sik Lee. 1972. *Communism in Korea*. Part I and II. Berkeley: University of California Press.

Suh, Dae-Sook. 1988 *Kim Il Sung: The North Korean Leader*. New York: Columbia University Press.

7

Strategy of Development in South and North Korea

Both South and North Korea are committed to rapid economic growth through industrialization and have enjoyed a high rate of growth, at least for one period in their history, undergoing fundamental structural changes from predominantly agricultural to industrial economies. However, certain structural aspects, such as heavy-light industry, service sectors, trade, foreign capital, and moral-pecuniary incentives, have differed with the South's outward- versus the North's inward-orientation, and the South's *imitation* versus the North's *juche*, or self-reliant strategies of development. While the early success of North Korea versus the failure of South Korea is primarily the result of political factors, the structural factors seem to be a convincing explanation of the later success of South Korean development and the failure of North Korean development. In this chapter, the success of South Korea's imitation vis-à-vis the failure of North Korea's self-reliance particularly after 1962, are examined through the structural factors transformed by conflicting strategies.

The principle of the South Korean strategy for development is characterized by its *imitation* of the advanced countries, particularly Japan. The principle has been "Do what the Japanese have done, but do it cheaper and faster" (Kang 1989,23). South Korea has imitated whatever can produced at a cheap price. The principle of "imitation" has been driven by the Korean spirit of "that's good enough" policy and by the aggressiveness of "first start and then let's see" practices (Kang 1989).

The principle of the North Korean strategy for development has stubbornly been guided by, what it calls, *juche sasang*, or the ideology of self-identity, creativity, and autonomy. This thought system encompasses the idea of *juche* in ideology, the idea of *chaju* (independence) in political work, the idea of *charip* (self-sustenance) in economic endeavors, and the idea of *chawi* (self-defense) in military affairs (Suh 1988,302). *Juche* was first used by Kim Il Sung when he addressed the propaganda and agitation workers of the Party around the end of 1955, stressing "*juche* in ideology." *Juche* meant self-reliance in the economic area. Kim Il Sung said:

> Building an independent national economy is an embodiment of the *juche* idea in the field of economic construction. . . . Economic independence is the material foundation for political independence. A country which is economically dependent on outside forces becomes a political satellite of other countries; an economically subjected nation cannot free itself from colonial slavery politically. (FLPH 1975,2; Kim Il Sung 1960, vol. 4: 557)

The North Korean strategy of self-reliance is defined as a line of economic construction for meeting by home production the needs for manufactured goods and farm produce necessary to build one's country with one's own people's labor and one's own national resources. In Kim Il Sung's words:

> Building an independent national economy means building a diversified economy, equipping it with up-to-date technology and creating our own solid basis of raw materials, thereby building up an all embracing economic system in which every branch of the economy is structually interrelated, so as to produce domestically most of the products of heavy and light industry and the agricultural produce needed to make the country wealthy and powerful and to improve the people's living conditions. (Kim Il Sung, 1960, vol. 3: 399)

The basic strategy of self-reliance calls for the economy to rely, when it can, on domestic resources in all sectors for 60 to 70 percent of supplies. When key raw materials are not available, the strategy is to substitute domestic resources and to minimize dependency on a structural, long-term basis. This line expresses the essential requirements of the *juche* idea to build one's country with one's people's labor and one's own national resources. Without building an independent national economy, according to this line, it is impossible to establish the material and technological foundations for socialism, and build socialism and communism successfully. The old Korean exclusionism, and flunkyism were revived as the guiding spirit of national development in the North and South, respectively.

Patterns of Industrialization

The South Korean outward-oriented strategy has evolved through a two-stage principle of "imitation": the first was the semiconscious or unconscious stage of "import substitution" strategy; the second was the conscious and well-planned stage of export-promotion strategy. The South Korean model usually refers only to the planned export promotion stage. In contrast, North Korea has stuck to the "self-reliance" strategy. Only during wartime, did North Korea practice the "import substitution" strategy.

Until 1962, import substitution constituted the main strategy of the development of South Korea. Import substitution industrialization is defined as the expansion of industrial production to supply a domestic market previously supplied by import goods. In this strategy, the rapid expansion of consumer goods production may occur when this production is aimed at satisfying an already existing domestic market that is newly protected by the imposition of tariffs or import controls and/or by the collapse of foreign trade (Collier 1979, 400–1). It was not implemented by a deliberate state strategy of capital accumulation. Faced with war and reconstruction, South Korea initiated import substitution industrialization in the early 1950s financed largely by U.S. aid. Import substitution emphasized the local production of consumer nondurables of textiles and foods. Those industries were protected by and matured behind a wall of tariffs, overvalued exchange rates, and other obstacles to foreign entry (Cumings 1987,68).

There was virtually no conspicuous economic growth and structural change in South Korea during this period. It has been estimated that the direct contribution of import substitution to industrial growth accounted for 24.2 percent, while that of export promotion was only 5.1 percent (Frank, Kim, and Westphal 1975,92). U.S. aid, however, provided a major source for the financing of the import substitution. As much as 90 percent of the import bill was paid for with American aid and local military procurement (Krueger 1979). Indications are that the volume of trade was very small and dependence on export and imports was almost negligible although imports exceeded exports twenty times.

The next stage extending from 1963 to the present in South Korea was conscious and well-planned export-led development. In fact, this export-led development had been discussed since 1957 by the government of the First Republic. The import-substitution strategy, which had been attempted mainly by U.S. experts in the early 1950s, began to be opposed by the South Korean state in 1957. With the strong military regime of Park, the state did carry out the plan and began to actively seek foreign investment. In this sense, among three strategies suggested by Wallerstein, South Korea pursued "the strategy of promotion by invitation" moving out of the "import-substitution strategy," while North Korea followed "the strategy of self-reliance breaking away from the world capitalist economy" (Wallerstein 1979,76–83). In the process of courting foreign capital, the state of South Korea gave priority to indirect (loan) over direct foreign investment (Lim 1985,90–98).

Exports have been the engine of the South Korean economy and the hallmark of its economic model. Since the mid-1960s exports have accounted for 20 to 50 percent of the increased in GDP (World Bank 1987). Export growth averaged 34 percent in real terms in the 1960s, 25 percent in the 1970s, and 15 percent in the 1980s. Between 1985 and 1986, for example, the rate of the consumption growth increased only slightly from 4.8 to 6.3 percent, but GDP growth more than doubled (from 5.2 to 12.0 percent) due to a sharp increase in exports and an associated investment boom. Furthermore, export growth has stimulated the influx of technology and the acquisition of know how (Westphal 1984) and helped to raise South Korea's total productivity growth to unusually high levels (Nishimizu and Page 1987).

The gist of the export promotion development strategy of South Korea has been to export manufactured goods, first through labor-intensive (1960s) and next through capital-intensive (1970s), and finally through the technology-intensive (1980s) industrialization. This timely change of export product and markets based on pragmatic planning is highly valued as one of the important factors in South Korean success; compared with North Korea in which change is blocked by the ideology of self-reliance. The export promotion of the 1960s first led to a very sharp increase in the share of light manufactures in total exports such as clothing, luggage, textiles, human hair wigs, and so on. Then, as the heavy and chemical industries drive took hold in the 1970s, the proportion of machinery and intermediate goods increased, including such items as steel, ships, automobiles, cement, tubes, and so on. Finally, in the 1980s, there has been an accelerated expansion of consumer electronics and automobiles along with somewhat limited growth in heavy intermediate goods.

The shift of exporting products over time is paralleled by important export market changes (Petri 1988). The labor-intensive product boom in the 1960s occurred at the same time that U.S. demand expanded due to the Vietnam War. The expansion of intermediate-product exports in the 1970s in turn reflected the growth of developing country markets and European Community markets as well. The needs in heavy construction from the Middle East and South East expedited exports in the 1970s. Finally, the strong growth of consumer goods in the 1980s was associated with a new spurt of American import expansion.

Not only did exports play an important role in overall growth and external balance, but they had a significant effect on the structure of South Korean industry. The change of major trade products created quite a balanced development among industrial sectors.

The centerpiece of the North Korean self-reliant strategy is to build self-sufficient agriculture, on the one hand, and to drive industrialization through heavy-industry-first development, on the other. To achieve self-reliance, agriculture must produce the surplus for other sectors. Agriculture was designed to increase output sufficiently to sustain the rapid development of heavy industry. The agricultural sector has been expected not only to feed the entire population, but also to provide some of the raw materials for heavy industry and to produce an exportable surplus for the purpose of earning foreign exchange. North Korea aimed at self-sufficiency in agriculture and seems to be entirely self-sufficient in food, under the guidance of state control.

This method of self-reliance is problematic for long-term development for several reasons. It leads to unbalanced growth between light and heavy industries, and to underdevelopment of the trade and service industries. The most conspicuous example of the ineffective aspects of the self-reliance strategy is the building of the most coal-dependent industrial economy in the world. The CIA estimated that in 1976 coal accounted for 77 percent of primary energy consumption in North Korea, with hydroelectric power accounting for 18 percent and oil for only 5 percent, with 35, 2 and 63 percent, accounting respectively for the same in South Korea (Halliday, 1980:129).

Much of the large labor input into agriculture in North Korea seems inefficient. Although agriculture has progressed through large labor input and use of technology as well, North Korea still retains a considerable amount of its labor force in an agricultural sector: 43 percent of the total labor force in 1987 are still engaged in agriculture. The policy of "self-reliance" makes North Korea stress agriculture, despite its cost-ineffectiveness in terms of the contribution on GNP outputs of 25 percent in 1982. The large labor input includes forty days work per year by state functionaries and labor by the armed forces. On the other hand, agriculture received a lot of technical assistance, including high mechanization, the high use of fertilizers, and a nationwide irrigation system. Rice and vegetables are the main items to be considered, and they are exported, too. There also has been extensive terracing of hillsides, especially for growing fruit.

The heavy-industry-first strategy in North Korea has caused several problems. The highest priority was allotted to investment in heavy industry and the production of means of production (and armaments). The heavy-industry-first strategy relies on domestic natural resources, but depends heavily on the USSR for capital and technical assistance. Self-reliance was accomplished only at the low level of technology, such as cement and marine production. Social overhead capital, facilities, and light industries were set aside in the heavy-industry-first strategy of development. The North Korean state has consistently affirmed that the development of heavy industry, with the machine-building industry at its core, gives the best guarantee for equipping light industry, agriculture, transport, and all the other branches of the national economy with modern technology and for effecting a steady technological progress.

> The keystone of socialist industrialization lies in the priority development of heavy industry. Only with the establishment of a powerful heavy industry is it possible to ensure the development of all industries, transport and agriculture, and the victory of the socialist system. (Kim Il Sung 1960, vol. 1, 510).

The machine industry is the sector in which North Korea has been applying its most strenuous efforts in accordance with its heavy-industry-first strategy centered on defense industries. "The next important thing in our Party's basic policy for the building of an independent national economy" a Party document declared "is the acceleration of the technical revolution to put all branches of the national economy on the social basis of modern technology (FLPH 1975, 25)." The development of a comprehensive machine-tool sector, in which 98 percent self-sufficiency is claimed, is central to this strategy (Halliday 1987, 29–30). Success is apparent in the building of power generating machinery—much more so than in the South (NUB 1986, 67)—and of ships, farm machinery (power cultivators and tractors), and trucks developed mainly for domestic use. There has been rapid expansion in investment in "human capital," especially technical education, because the emphasis on heavy industry (in particular, machine-building industry) required technical reforms, but the reforms have been confined to the agricultural area and to low levels of technology (I.J. Kim 1975, 14–15).

The North Korean heavy-industry-first policy has been closely linked to a military buildup and increased munitions production. Although some see the positive sides of military buildup in the process of development, general opinion contends it is inefficient in national development. North Korea launched large-scale construction projects, and these efforts have brought about imbalances among its industrial sectors, stagnation in scientific and technological evolution, high production costs, and other problems. The development of the economic structure lacked balance. Industry in North Korea in 1982 accounts for 70 percent of the GNP, while that of the South accounts for only 35 percent. Light industrial and electronic goods are in short supply. Consumer goods are not supplied to the people. This explains the fact that while material production had been higher than in South Korea until 1980, the living standard has not been higher since 1970.

The role of the service sector must be seen as a significant factor in the development of the two Koreas. In 1987, only 18 percent of the North Korean labor force is engaged in services, compared to 46 percent of the South's. The North Korean policy of self-reliance neglects the service sector, which is not willingly developed by most communist countries which regard it as "unproductive." North Korea did not develop social overhead capital, which is generally regarded as a very important factor in economic development by capitalist countries. Poor transportation has imposed limitations on the supply of materials required by industry, and increases in cargo capacity and the electrification of railway lines are seen as key targets of the current Seven-Year

Plan. This seems to be one reason why North Korea has been so slow in improving its economy in recent years.

The self-reliance-based industrial growth has been affected by the inability of the energy and mining industries to supply the power and raw materials as fast as the manufacturing industry has needed them. Since the heavy industry of North Korea has been developed on the basis of domestic raw materials and labor, it mainly depends on raw material deposits. Although Korea is generally a resource-scarce area, the domestic production of iron, steel, and nonferrous metal (zinc, lead, and copper) seems to be enough to provide for the development of heavy industry in North Korea (NUB 1986, 58). Where domestic raw materials are not available, substitution is a key component of self-reliance. About three-quarters of its energy is produced from coal, and the rest comes from hydroelectric sources. Transformation was made possible by building a high-technology chemical industry. The best-known case of substitution is that of vinalon, a synthetic textile produced from limestone. Synthetic rubber is produced from carbide, and fertilizer from coal. Coal has been crucial, since more than two-thirds of the electric power is generated by coal-fired power stations. Soviet and Polish technicians have been involved in a major development of the Anju coalfield (Bridges 1986, 40). Significantly, electric power, together with steel and nonferrous metals, was among the three industries not mentioned as having achieved their targets under the Second Seven-Year Plan.

Yet, North Korea appears to depend on the USSR for finance and technology. It was necessary that North Korea change the labor-intensive policy of the 1950s and 1960s to technology-intensive programs in the 1970s. The technology-intensive policy of the 1970s introduced a large-scale program for purchasing advanced Western plants and technology and expanding foreign trade. But it turned out to be unsuccessful.

The role of foreign trade in the strategies of the two Koreas' development has been conspicuous. In North Korean development, it has been static and unimportant—as is usually assumed in Central Planned Economies (CPEs); in the South, it is exploited extensively. The nature of the two Koreas' development in this respect can be captured by the North's autarky versus the South's dependence until the 1970s and interdependence since the 1980s (Clough 1987, 67–93). Exports have been the engine of South Korea's success. Since the mid-1960s exports have contributed 20 to 50 percent to the increase in the GDP. Export growth has also stimulated the inflow of technology and acquisitions to raise South Korea's total factor productivity.

Imports are still important in the export-driven strategy of South Korea. Since South Korea started to export to the world market without a well-established domestic economy, relying on substantial imports of machinery, components, and technology, trade potential and technology inflow tended to determine the structure of output. Felix (1965) explains that the import-substitution industrialization generally paralleled industrial development. He says that opening the model to include the capacity to import makes it more realistic, since underdeveloped economies depend on imports for some of their consumer goods, including food, much of their industrial materials and fuels, and most of their capital goods (Felix 1965, 142). In South Korea, export helped to import and import helped to export. Hamilton (1986) has shown that imports are still important for South Korean development. He claims that exporting was not an end in itself and, in fact, was often unprofitable. Instead, the state strongly encouraged the export sector in order to gain the foreign exchange needed to buy the imports on which growth depended.

South Korea did not, however, experience the extension of imports substitution when the export-promotion strategy was launched. Rather, export-promotion industrialization was vigorously launched without a strong base of import substitution and agricultural substructure. In this sense, South Korean export-promotion strategy since the 1960s deserves to be considered rather than as an extension of import substitution strategy.

Recently, competition for South Korea has come from the East Asian NICs and Japan. South Korea could surpass the NICs by emphasizing heavy industry, including various types of steel, metal products, and basic textile fabrics (but not clothing). On the other hand, South Korea's success vis-à-vis Japan at least in some areas has been mainly due to environmental advantages. With such products as color television sets, steel, automobiles, and semiconductors, the protection aimed at Japan has often accelerated the South Korean entry into the markets of Canada, America, and other countries (Petri 1988, 60–1). Another strategy to "defeat" Japan is, first, to make the product popular by putting the price of the export product at the low end of the market; and next, to introduce a new model of the product, moving out of the low end of the market into the middle range of the market. This is illustrated by the Hyundai's strategy of having Sonata start selling at the medium price in the U.S. market in 1989, after the Excell made a big splash with a price at the low end of the market (Holusha 1988). But this strategy turned out to be far less successful than early ones because of the low quality of technology.

The future growth of export promotion will be determined by the evolution of protectionism and the capacity of technological development. In the past the impact of international protectionism on trade has been more positive than negative for South Korea, since in a number of important cases foreign protection restrained Korea's competitors more than Korean exports themselves. South Korea did escape the detrimental effect of protectionism, being situated between other NICs and Japan. Although nearly 40 percent of its exports are currently subject to quantitative barriers, South Korea was not affected by protectionism, while other NICs were (Petri 1988, 59). This was because most of the barriers were targeted at labor-intensive items, such as clothing, textiles, and footwear. But, South Korea already changed the products of exports from labor-intensive to capital- and technology-intensive ones, which have benefited from the protection against Japan. It is not clear, however, whether South Korea will continue to receive these benefits in the future.

In international relations for development, the main elements in the self-reliance of North Korea are to withdraw from the world capitalist economy and to selectively participate in the socialist world economy—manufacturing tractors for example, rather than importing them from the USSR, even if this is not "cost beneficial." Also, North Korea rejects full membership in CMEA, even though North Korea did join (as a founding member) the three suborganizations. The selective participation in the international economy and organization is the strategy of self-reliance.

In keeping with this strategy, North Korea has taken a passive attitude, toward international trade. North Korea regards foreign trade as a means supplementary to its self-sufficient economy. The external trade of North Korea is planned and regulated by the state under the Ministry of Foreign Trade. A trade policy of strict self-reliance changed

into one of expanding foreign trade in the early 1970s. The change
seemed to have beneficial effects on industrial productivity at the
beginning, and the average annual growth rate of industrial output
reached 16 percent in the first half of the 1970s. But after it caused a
balance-of-payment problem, North Korea has been faced with a reluctant trading environment.

The self-reliant strategy of North Korea brought about an underdeveloped structure in a trade pattern that exports raw materials and
agricultural products and imports manufactured commodities. The main
items North Korea exported to the Soviet Union and Japan in 1984 are
metals, iron and steel products, iron ore, magnesium clinker, coals,
and cement; agricultural and marine products and textiles were minor
items. On the other hand, 57 percent of North Korea's imports were
manufactured goods, including electrical appliances, chemicals, metals, and sundry goods, while 36.6 percent were raw materials and 6.4
percent were agricultural products (NUB 1986, 75).

The size of industry has been emphasized both in South and North
Korea. It is generally accepted that the socialist countries stress the
size of the economy more than do capitalist countries, and that the
bigger industries produce the more effective products and results (Ehrlich 1985). There are a few big plants and corporations in North
Korea. However, there has been a spatial decentralization, partly related to a strategic-military concept of local self-reliance and controlled urbanization. Each province is relatively self-reliant, and the
county government has now become the basic-level government. In
spite of that, economic planning remains rigidly centered. In general,
the size of industries remains medium in North Korea. South Korean
development was accomplished by several business conglomerates and
huge industrial complexes. In the case of Korea, it seems that in South
Korea more than in North Korea, efficient sizable industrial complexes
are the norm.

Role of Foreign Capital

Closely related to foreign trade, the role of foreign capital is crucial
in the two Koreas' development. While Soviet and Western capital is
sought by North Korea, no communist country's capital is invested in
South Korea, where U.S. and Japanese capital plays a dominant role.

The unavailability of Western capital has been the most critical factor in North Korean stagnation; active and efficient use of it has created South Korea's sustained growth for the past three decades.

Seeking to attract foreign capital, the South Korean government gave priority to indirect over direct investment. Given the assumption that multinational activities would be disruptive to the nationalistic logic of capital accumulation, the state tried to exercise control over the foreign presence by favoring loans over direct investment, since loans do not entail foreign control of local firms. It resulted in huge indebtedness. The state was reluctant to cooperate with multinationals until domestic industries reached a competitive stance in technological and capital capabilities. It was only after 1980 that South Korea's FDI was increased quickly in relative terms. The 1980s saw an increase in South Korea's foreign direct investment (FDI), most of which was invested in service industries (E.M. Kim 1989, 24–45). The sharp increase of the service sector portion in GNP during 1980s is due to the increase of FDI.

The South Korean foreign debt has been decreasing since 1986; it reached its peak in 1985, recording $47 billion. It decreased to $39 billion in 1988, and it is expected that it will decrease by $2 to $4 billion each year.

The self-reliant strategy of North Korea is economically dependent on extensive Soviet financial and technical aid (*The Europa World Yearbook 1988*, 1615; Foster-Carter 1985, 28–29). The role of Soviet capital in North Korean development is not clear enough to be assessed. North Korea owed $710 million to the USSR in 1974, but it is doubtful whether this represented economic aid or a loan. Some Soviet sources and Soviet Koreans have recently given many details of very extensive Soviet aid (Halliday 1987, 31). These Soviet accounts indicate that Soviet loans were rescheduled over very long periods, up to thirty-five years. According to the accounts, the projects built with Soviet assistance comprise the backbone of the North Korean national economy and encompass practically all its major branches. North Korea and the USSR had signed a new agreement on economic and technical cooperation in November 1986. According to the agreement, the USSR would contribute nineteen new projects in North Korea, including the construction of a nuclear power station with a generation capacity of 1.76 million kw. And the trade volume of North Korea with the USSR has also been overwhelmingly high. This is quite a different picture from the one presented by North Korea. The official North Korean version of events is thus not of much use, since it fails either to confront the hard facts or to spell out how well North Korea has been able to use Soviet aid. In general, the Soviet and Chinese system that surround North Korea are far less favorable for providing capital and advanced technology than the U.S. and Japan are in the case of South Korea.

Unavailability of a steady flow of Western capital has been one of the critical factors in the stagnation of North Korean development. After North Korea had changed the labor-intensive policy of the 1960s to a technology-intensive policy in the 1970s, large-scale programs for purchasing advanced Western plants and technology and expanding foreign trade were attempted. These changes seemed to have beneficial effects on industrial productivity at the beginning, and the average annual growth rate of industrial output reached 16 percent in the first half of the 1970s. However, the self-reliant economy could not absorb the new external inputs. The introduction of foreign capital and technology must be supported by the capability of repaying the influx. North Korean trade volume is too small to absorb the influx in a short-term period. Furthermore, the external environment that brought benefits also caused rising prices of some raw materials and a drop in the nonferrous metal exports, which brought about a balance of payments problem (Bridges 1986, 37–42). North Korea failed to pay its trade bills, and the consequent attempts to reschedule its debts have remained a continuing irritant in its trade with the capitalist world economy.

The North Korean foreign debt is a serious problem. North Korea was announced to be in default by the consortium of Western creditors since 1976 and has been negotiating a payment schedule. The shortage of foreign currency, with Western credit virtually drying up after 1976 and a continuing balance of payment deficit, has restricted the import of Western technology and plants. After an agreement was reached with Japan, its largest foreign creditor, in 1979, North Korea began repayment of its debts, but from 1983 payments again began to drop behind schedule. According to Japanese calculations, North Korea has an average annual trade deficit of $250 million from 1980 to 1984, $465 million in 1985, and $960 million in 1989 (JETRO 1990).

Toward the late 1980s, North Korea returned to the labor-intensive policy again, because it could not take advantage of a technology-intensive policy due to an unfavorable world economy. The country has been plagued by the reassertion of hard-line orthodoxy in domestic economic planning because of the early bitter experience during 1973-74 and the largely unsuccessful experiments in liberalization undertaken in 1984-85 (FEER 1988, 161–2). Moreover, the recent breakdown of Eastern European communism makes North Korea hesitate to adopt a liberal economic policy. Industrial growth has been affected by the inability of the energy and mining industry to supply the power and raw materials as fast as the manufacturing industry has needed them. Steel production has sharply decreased. Depending on the USSR, North Korea has tried to find a breakthrough to enhance its economy. Soviet and Polish technicians were involved in major development of the Anju coalfield (Bridges 1986, 40). New cooperative projects with the USSR were launched in 1987. Japan and South Korea appear to be the last available sources of Western capital for North Korea.

North Korea takes a delicate position between the two goals of self-reliance and glasnost. The latter must be accompanied by modern technology from abroad. In recent years, there have been occasional signs that the self-reliance policy has displayed a certain amount of flexibility. This has been the case not only in relation to the Soviet Union, which assisted the opening of the Kimchaek Iron Works in 1983; it has been even more pronounced in relation to the West and international organizations. In 1980, North Korea received nearly $9 million from the United Nations Development Program. Of more significance was the announcement in September 1984 of a joint-venture law, which drew inspiration from similar legislation in China. Although North Korean officials initially implied that the new law was aimed primarily at European companies, the main emphasis recently has been on encouraging Japanese companies to invest. However, Western companies have remained unenthusiastic about joint ventures, while the problem of outstanding debts from the 1970s remains unresolved.

No Western company is interested in investment in North Korea. North Korea is currently suffering under the default of a $900 million Western loan. The international isolation from Western capitalist countries has encouraged North Korea to approach Japan, attempting to solve the problem by borrowing Japanese capital. North Korea had already defaulted on a Japanese loan in 1976 and rescheduled it in 1979. The secret negotiation of colonial reparations of $8 billion will be a crucial factor for the revitalization of the North Korean economy in the 1990s. Japan already accounts for 23 percent of North Korea's total trade, only behind the USSR and exceeding China. The role of Japan will be critical to the North Korean development for the 1990s. The economic stagnation in North Korea necessitates negotiation of economic exchanges with Japan and even with South Korea.

North Korea recently established a Free Economic Zone (FEZ) in Habsando Island in order to promote trade with the Soviet Union and China and to attract Western investment (*Chosun Ilbo*, 31 March 1990). In August 1990, North Korea allowed foreign direct investment (FDI) for the first time in its history (*Chosun Ilbo* 24 August 1990). This measure may stimulate her neighbors, but it will not attract any Western capital except Japanese unless North Korea makes up her mind to restructure and open its economy.

Mobilization and Incentive Policy

In order to enact their strategies, each Korea resorts to different mobilization incentives. To effectively implement export promotion, the South Korean government introduced various kinds of incentives, such as tax exemption, tariff exemption, financing, waiver insurance for shipping, and so on (Jones and Sakong 1980, 94–5). Most South Korean companies provide their workers with bonuses. The bonuses well exceed 400 percent of a worker's one-month salary. Sometimes, workers are paid bonuses of up to 1,000 percent. The government has also guaranteed the cheap price of labor, which was very attractive to many multinationals. The maintenance of the cheap labor price served as an important factor for the continued export promotion.

One of the important factors in South Korean success is the introduction of the mass mobilization movement in the 1970s, which South Korea probably borrowed from the successful experience of the North Korean mass movement during the 1950s. This moral incentive worked quite well because it was practiced for a relatively short period of time. Through the measure, the gap between urban and rural income narrowed. Both Korean experiences suggest that a mass mobilization technique based on moral incentive can be a successful measure, as long as it is only implemented for about seven to ten years. The idea is that in human nature any firm determination cannot last for too long a time. This accords with Comte's concept of ennui, or boredom, which he said resides in human nature, because of which the moral incentive cannot be successful for long-term development.

The North Korean state basically mobilized the population relying on moral incentives. Mass movements, moral exhortations, and political campaigns have been widely and consistently relied upon as substitutes for pecuniary incentives. Live band music as well as radio are utilized to encourage workers (Perry 1990, 177). People are mobilized to make superhuman efforts by working 480 minutes rather than by eight hours per day (D.S. Suh 1988, 296). Farmers do not take a day off per week. Instead, they take one-day holiday every ten days, what they call Farmers' Holiday, so that only three days (1,11,21) per month, not four or five, are holidays for North Korean farmers. Emulating Mao's Great Leap Forward, the mass mobilization movement in the late 1950s known as the Chollima Work Team Movement was designed to mobilize human and material resources in agriculture for the priority development of heavy industry. The labor force was exhorted to surpass goals and to work ceaselessly and selflessly for nonmaterial rewards in the service of socialism. According to Kim Il Sung, the *Chollima* Movement was an all-people's movement for continuous innovations in all spheres—economy, culture, ideology, and morality— and for expediting socialist construction to the maximum (I.S. Kim 1960, vol. 4, 121–2). The primary goal of the movement was to combine the programs of ideological indoctrination and agricultural reform. It was based on a general-line policy with moralistic fervor and ideological appeal to increase maximum productivity and to maintain maximum savings.

The tax system does not work as a material incentive in North Korea any more. North Korea abolished a direct income tax system in 1974. All income from productive activities becomes government revenue, which comprises about 76 percent of the GNP (NUB 1986, 40). The revenue consists of the turnover taxes on the income of collective farms, cooperatives, and other sources. Basically, North Korea uses material incentives far less than South Korea.

The mobilization movement also reshaped the organization techniques in agricultural cooperatives (known as the Chongsan-ni method) and management in the industrial plants (known as Taean Work Team System) (I.J. Kim 1975, 211). The Chongsan-ni method and Taean system were a combination of ideological indoctrination and material incentives to stimulate the peasant and the worker population to increase productivity. The material incentives consisted of awarding prizes, paid vacations, and honorific titles to the work teams that surpassed production quotas (I.J. Kim 1975, 83). Those material measures do not seem to be enough to provide people with work incentives. The Three Revolution Team Movement was begun in 1973 to address this matter. The state sent groups of upper-level party cadres, technicians, and students to factories all over the country to attack conservatism, bureaucratism, and other ills. Right before the World Student and Youth Festival in July 1989, North Koreans were paid a bonus of one extra month's salary as a reward for Two Hundred Days Battle for the preparation of the festival. Yet, moral and ideological motivations still dominate. Overtime in general and during frequent special campaigns is not paid. The army functions as a mobile labor force. Prison labor and student workers (e.g., on roads every ten days and on production in schools) are also mobilized.

Mobilization of the general populace, even if successful for a short period, has economic limitations in the long run. It proves to be more advantageous at the early stage of development where development can be achieved by expansion in the utilization of natural resources and unemployed labor. Except in the areas of such highly labor-intensive projects as food processing, irrigation facilities, and construction of unpaved roads, continued substitution of labor for capital will produce, after a point, very small or near-zero marginal output, so that it seems to fall behind in productivity and efficiency at the later stage of intensive development where productivity must be raised through more advanced technology (Chung 1980, 286). Eventually, expansion in labor must be accompanied by an increased supply of capital or other inputs, such as advanced technology.

Problem of Dependency

Let us look at the deeper structure of the two Korean developments. The initial result of such an exercise is, paradoxically, almost to reverse the images of dependency arguments. The South Korean economy seems to be more dependent on the external environment than the North because the portion of South Korean foreign trade in GNP is very high (74 percent), while that of North Korea was only 12 percent in 1988. This self-reliant orientation of North Korea makes its economy less vulnerable, at least in theory, to fluctuations in the world economy. However, the trade dependence itself is certainly no dependency. In general, the amount of trade of a country can produce economic growth. The pattern of trade seems more important. The trade pattern reveals that North Korea has more dependent structures than the South showing that North Korea retains traditional patterns of trade, characterized by mining and agricultural exports and industrial imports, while South Korea shows the opposite. South Korea exports manufactured goods and imports raw materials, while North Korea exports raw materials and imports manufactured goods. According to dependency theory, the country that has a traditional pattern of trade is not able to have good long-term prospects of development.

South Korea, at first glance, presents a highly dependent picture. So far from proclaiming autarky, South Korea emphasized the advantages of international economic integration. It has entailed ever-increasing integration into the global market. South Korea is open about the depth of its economic links to its own two powerful sponsors, the U.S. and Japan. Politically and strategically, the role of South Korean troops in Vietnam in the 1960s, and the continued presence in Korea itself of some 40,000 U.S. troops also serve to underline the dependent image of South Korea in wider networks. Yet, appearances may be deceptive. South Korea has become somewhat independent within the world economy. For a resource-poor South Korea, a quarter century ago, the best route to economic strength and industrialization was to carve out a niche in the world market—with all the risks that dependency entailed. Export-oriented industrialization, never an end in itself, proved an effective means.

The South Korean state has persistently intervened in every way and at every level in the economy. The state command of investment funds (state owned all major banks until 1980) has been reckoned to be comparable only with Communist countries. It is not foreign capital but Korean firms such as Hyundai, Daewoo, Samsung and Goldstar that have been the beneficiaries of crucial state support. In South Korea, at least, capitalist development has not denationalized the economy, as is often claimed by dependency theory. South Korea has been fairly unfriendly to foreign capital, preferring to borrow internationally wherever possible rather than permit direct foreign investment. Hence, of course, the huge debts, but South Korea's debt service ratio remains low, and so far there are no signs of any difficulty in keeping up the payments.

South Korean foreign debt has been decreasing since 1986 once it reached a peak of $47 billion in 1985. It came down to $39 billion in 1988 and it is expected that it is going to be decreasing by $2 to $4 billion each year. On the other hand, North Korean foreign debt is a serious problem. North Korea was announced to be in default by the consortium of Western creditors since 1976, and has been negotiating a payment schedule.

North Korea is conspicuous as an autarkic economy. Economically, North Korea has gotten away all along with not joining CMEA participating only in such areas as it found useful. Internally, North Korea successfully ignored initial Soviet advice to stick with raw materials and light industry, and instead emulated what the USSR itself had practiced rather than what it was now preaching; namely, classic heavy industrialization, based on indigenous raw materials, and centered on home market demand. The fact that all the signs suggest that in the 1980s this inward-looking model is running out of steam by no means implies that in the 1950s it was the wrong choice.

For starters, in spite of its claim of self-reliance, North Korea would not have existed in the first place in 1945 without the Soviet Army, nor would it have survived in 1950 without the Chinese. South Korea, equally, would neither have come into existence in 1945 nor been saved from extinction in 1950 without U.S. military force. Economically, too, North Korea has always been more involved in the socialist international division of labor than it lets on, and to a degree in fairly traditional ways: as a consistent exporter of minerals and increasingly metals, and a consistent importer of capital goods. Above all, just how much North Korea owes both literally and figuratively to the USSR in economic terms has been stressed in considerable detail, in recent years, by the Soviet Union itself (*Chosun Ilbo*, 23 April 1990). Both in Korean-language broadcasts from Moscow, and in scholarly projects, past and present, North Korea turns out to owe much to Soviet finance and technology (Foster-Carter 1987).

Despite North Korea's stress on self-reliance, imports of plants and machinery were crucial to its industrial growth. Plants built with Soviet assistance accounted for 60 percent of North Korea's output of electricity, 45 percent of its oil products, 40 percent of its iron ore, 34 percent of its rolled steel, 30 percent of raw steel, and 20 percent of fabrics (Richardson 1982, 96–97). China assisted in the construction of power plants, a petroleum refinery, textile mills, and factories producing consumer goods. Large quantities of machinery, including whole plants, were imported from Japan and Eastern Europe in the early 1970s until the flow was choked off by the inability to pay. North Korea is also totally dependent on imported oil and coking coal, which come mainly from the Soviet Union and China. Clearly, self-reliance has its limits. In the case of such a small state as North Korea, a self-reliant strategy may not be beneficial for national development.

Such economic achievements are intimately linked to external politics and internal psychology. Considering the origins of the regimes—and indeed Kim Il Sung's and Syngman Rhee's own immediate backgrounds—in 1945, these are remarkable accomplishments. In a basic sense, both South and North Korea depend on the United States and the Soviet Union, respectively, though in different contexts. Of course, in one sense the Sino-Soviet dispute was a godsend, in that it permitted North Korea a degree of leeway that it would not otherwise have had. The image of the South's dependency and the North's independence are largely political and psychological phenomena. No Soviet troops are on North Korean soil whereas some 40,000 U.S. forces are stationed in the South; the number of Korean military trained in the Soviet Union was far smaller than the number of South Koreans trained in the United States; and no joint maneuvers of Soviet and North Korean forces took place in North Korea, while the U.S.-South Korea joint military maneuver, called Team Spirit, are exercised every year in South Korea.

Both Koreas are more dependent on Japan than on any other country. In contrast to the appearance of South Korean dependency on the U.S., the South Korean trade volume with Japan is 1.7 times larger than that with the U.S. The volume of North Korean trade with Japan marks the second largest partner next to the Soviet Union, larger than China. The trade patterns are in a more serious condition. Both Koreas suffer a trade deficit with Japan. This indicates that dependency of the two Koreas on Japan is a more serious problem than dependence on any other country.

There are certain problems hampering the pace of North Korean economic development. Although population growth is averaging around 2.2 percent annually, North Korea is a relatively labor-scarce country. The substantial diversion of manpower into the armed forces does not help. Difficulties in both the quantity and quality of workers were clearly behind the endeavors to improve the comprehensive eleven-year compulsory education system and to train more technicians and specialists, particularly in engineering.

In conclusion, the development of the two Koreas is bound or fostered by the structural aspects of the strategies: the self-reliance of North Korea and the imitation of South Korea. The self-reliance development in North Korea led to the extremely unbalanced growth of heavy industries and to extreme underdevelopment of service industries and trade. Heavy industries require more and more energy and raw materials that cannot be supplied with domestic resources. Poor transportation imposed limitations on supply of materials required by industry. South Korea, on the other hand, has developed balance, moving from light industries in the 1960s through heavy industries in the 1970s, to technology industries in the 1980s. South Korea has also taken advantage of foreign capital, technology, and foreign markets, whereas North Korea failed to use them actively. Underdevelopment in foreign trade limits the North Korean economy in introducing foreign capital and advanced technology. Exhortations based only on moral incentives in North Korea became exhausted after the early fifteen years or so, while South Korea not only relies on pecuniary incentives, but also introduced the timely mass mobilization movement based on moral incentives in the 1970s. More serious problems of dependency are involved in North Korea than in South Korea, regardless of appearances, and propaganda.

Owing to the continued confrontation between the two, both models are comparable in their high defense expenditures, especially the North's. We will see this in the next chapter.

Reference

Bridges, Brian. 1986. *Korea and the West*. New York: Routledge & Kegan Paul.

Chosun Ilbo. 1990. Articles on North Korea, 31 March 1990, 23 April 1990, and 24 August 1990.

Chung, Joseph Sanghoon. 1980. "The Economic System." Pp. 274-300 in Kim and Park, *Studies on Korea: A Scholar's Guide*. Honolulu: University Press of Hawaii.

Clough, Ralph N. 1987. *Embattled Korea: The Rivalry for International Support*. Boulder, CO: Westview Press.

Collier, David (ed.). 1979. *The New Authoritarianism in Latin America*. Princeton, NJ: Princeton University Press.

Cumings, Bruce. 1987. "The origins and development of the Northeast Asian political economy: Industrial sectors, product cycles, and political consequences." Pp. 44-83 in Frederic Deyo (ed.), *The Political Economy of the New Asian Industrialism*. New York: Cornell University Press.

Ehrlich, Eva. 1985. "The size structure of manufacturing establishments and enterprises: An international comparison." *Journal of Comparative Economics* 9:267-95.

Europa World Yearbook, The. 1988. *The Europa World Yearbook, 1988*. London: Europa Publications.

Far Eastern Economic Review (FEER). 1988. *Asia Yearbook, 1988*. Hong Kong: FEER.

Felix, David. 1965. "Monetarists, structuralists, and import-substituting industrialization: A critical appraisal." *Studies in Comparative International Development* 1:137-53.

Foreign Language Publishing House (FLPH). 1977. *The International Seminar on the Juche Idea*. Pyongyang, Korea: FLPH.

_____. 1975. *Our Party's Policy for the Building of an Independent National Economy*. Pyongyang, Korea: FLPH.

Foster-Carter, Aidan. 1985. "Korea and dependency theory." *Monthly Review* 37:(5):27-34.

Frank, Charles R., Jr., Kwang Suk Kim, and Larry Westphal. 1975. *Foreign Trade Regimes and Economic Development: South Korea*. New York: National Bureau of Economic Research.

Halliday, Jon. 1987. "The economies of North and South Korea." Pp.19–54 in Sullivan and Foss, *Two Koreas—One Future?* Lanham, MD: University Press of America.

_____. 1983. "The North Korean enigma." Pp. 114–54 in White, Murray and White (eds.), *Revolutionary Socialist Development in the Third World*. Lexington: The University Press of Kentucky.

Hamilton, Clive. 1986. *Capitalist Industrialization in Korea*. Boulder, CO: Westview Press.

Holusha, John. 1989. "Hyundai's bid to move up in class." *The New York Times*, 2 November 1988:D1, D9.

Japanese Economic and Trade Research Organization (JETRO). 1990. *The North Korean Economic and Trade Status, 1989*. Tokyo, Japan: JETRO.

Jones, Leroy P. and Il Sakong. 1980. *Government, Business, and Entrepreneurship in Economic Development: The Korean Case*. Cambridge, Mass.: Harvard University Press.

Kang, T.W. 1989. *Is Korea the Next Japan?: Understanding the Structure, Strategy, and Tactics of America's Next Competitor*. New York: The Free Press.

Kim, Eun Mee. 1989. "Foreign capital in Korea's economic development, 1960-1985." *Studies in Comparative International Development* 24(4):24-45.

Kim, Il-pyong J. 1975. *Communist Politics in North Korea* New York: Praeger Publishers.

Kim, Il Sung. 1960. *Selected Works*. Pyongyang, Korea: Korean Workers Party Press.

Kreuger, Anne O. 1979. *The Developmental Role of the Foreign Sector and Aid*. Cambridge, Mass.: Harvard University Press.

Kristof, Nicholas D. 1989. "Great Leader to Dear Leader." *The New York Times Magazine*, 20 August 1989.

Lim, Hyun-Chin. 1985. *Dependent Development in Korea, 1963-1979*. Seoul: Seoul National University Press.

National Unification Board (NUB). 1986. *A Comparative Study of South and North Korean Economies*. Seoul: NUB.

Perry, John Curtis. 1990. "Dateline North Korea: A communist holdout." *Foreign Policy* 80:172-91.

Petri, Peter A. 1988. "Korea's export niche: Origins and prospects." *World Development* 16(1):47-63.

Richardson, Ron. 1982. "Big brother barks: North Korea's proclaimed self-reliance is undercut by detailed evidence published in a Soviet journal." FEER, 3 December 1982: 96-97.

Suh, Dae Sook. 1988. *Kim Il Sung: The North Korean Leader*. New York: Columbia University Press.

Wallerstein, Immanuel. 1979. *The Capitalist World-Economy*. Cambrige: Cambridge University Press.

Westphal, Larry. 1984. *Export of Capital goods and Related Services from the Republic of Korea*. Washington, D.C.: World Bank.

World Bank. 1987. *World Development Report, 1987*. New York: Oxford University Press.

8

War, the Military, and Militarization in the Development of South and North Korea

The growth of military spending and militarization is one of the most salient phenomena in the development of divided Korea. South and North Korea have developed into two of the most militarized societies in the world today by any measurement—per capita military spending, military spending as a percent of government spending, or incorporation of the "civilian" population into the military structure. There are about 1.7 million soldiers—highly trained and maintained in a perpetual state of war readiness—with a combined total of some 5,000 tanks and 1,100 combat aircraft, facing off in the peninsula. And, most of the forces and equipment on both sides are deployed forward, close to the Demilitarized Zone (DMZ), only 155 miles long. While much of the rest of the world has been slowing down its military spending and rate of armaments procurement, both South and North Korea have continued to invest more into preparations for war, or measures to prevent war. Considering that North Korea has only one-sixth of the GNP and one-half of the population of South Korea, the military burden for North Korea is even more serious. North Korea's overriding commitment of resources to military expansion at the expense of the civilian economy is a key reason why South Korea has moved ahead of North Korea in development since the 1970s.

Both Korean societies have been profoundly affected by the trauma of the division of war. Born in an atmosphere of confrontation and conflict, the Korean states place a high value on military preparedness and domestic security control. Military concerns and the existence of large military establishments have shaped social and economic development of South and North Korea in important respects.

Military Spending

Since 1975, South Korea's military spending has outstripped that of North Korea, growing in a steady fashion. South Korea doubled its outlay on defense during the period between 1977–81 in the face of a North Korean military buildup. According to the U.S. Arms Control and Disarmament Agency (ACDA), North Korea's defense budget increased ten-fold from $576 million in 1970 to $5.8 billion in 1987, while South Korea's increased nearly eleven-fold from $491 million to $5.6 billion during the same period. North Korea invested heavily in the military in the first half of the 1970s, but since then spending has been erratic. North Korea declared in 1962 an all-out drive to improve military preparedness, pouring one third of its national income into strengthening the armed forces and building extensive underground military installations.

The recent situation of North Korean military spending is not clear. North Korean official figures are that defense spending accounted for 12.1 percent of the 1989 government budget and that the armed forces totaled between 350,000 and 400,000 in 1980. Western sources claim that the defense budget accounts for anything between 10.2 and 25 percent of the GNP, and that the armed forces total up to one million people. There is a wide variance between estimates offered by the U.S. Government, primarily found in the ACDA annual publication, and those of respected private groups such as the International Institutes for Strategic Studies (IISS), which publish an annual entitled *The Military Balance*. According to ACDA, in 1987, North Korea outspent South Korea by $5.8 billion to $5.6 billion. IISS and SIPRI seem to follow the North Korean official data. The IISS shows South Korean spending $7 billion and North Korean spending just $4.2 billion in 1987. Moreover, it shows North Korean spending decreasing to $4.07 billion in 1988, while South Korean spending leaps to $8.51 billion. Thus, IISS shows the South spending two times as much as the North in 1988. SIPRI estimates North Korean military spending at $1.8 billion in 1985 and $1.9 billion in 1987, which accounts for 10 percent of GNP in respective years.

ACDA began to reevaluate North Korean defense expenditures since 1984. The 1983 ACDA edition listed North Korean spending in 1980 at $1.3 billion; the 1984 edition boosted it to $3 billion; and the 1988

TABLE 8.1
Military Spending Between South and North Korea
(million dollars)

Year	ACDA Data (current price)		SIPRI Data (constant,1986*)		IISS (constant,1980)	
	SK	NK	SK	NK	SK	NK
1965	113	175	311	429		
1970	491	576	617	878	753(3.7)	936(11)
1975	1,461	1,080	1,271	909	1,286(3.4)	878(11)
1980	3,515	3,000E	2,990	1,337	3,309(4.3)	1,337(10)
1985	4,891	5,400E	4,439	1,765	4,621(5.2)	1,924(10)
1987	5,600	5,800E	5,310	1,876		

* At 1986 constant prices for 1985–87, and at 1980 constant prices for 1965–80.

edition estimated it at $3.5 billion. Its estimation goes far beyond the North Korean official figures. But, the IISS and SIPRI have not followed it. As a result, ACDA maintains that North Korea has consistently outspent South Korea for the past two decades, while IISS and SIPRI maintain the opposite. Some official Korean sources, focusing on quantitative as opposed to qualitative measures, established that at present South Korean capabilities are 60 percent of the North's and would, at current rates of growth, reach the 80 percent level in the mid-1990s or toward the end of this century. And, from visible evidence, it is clear that the armed forces in North Korea are extremely numerous. While North Korea does enjoy numerical superiority in most manpower and weapons categories, that advantage is offset by other factors, most notably the superior quality and greater sophistication of South Korean weapons.

A large percent of GNP spent on the military by North Korea indicates that North Korea carries a heavy military burden in the process of development. About 6 to 7 percent of the GNP, on average, is spent for military defense by South Korea; some 15 to 20 percent of the GNP is believed to go to defense in North Korea. For 1987, ACDA estimates that North Korea spent over twenty percent of its GNP (22.22 percent) on the military, while South Korea spent only six percent (6.3 percent). The Far Eastern Economic Review estimates that in 1988 North Korea spent 23.8 percent of its GDP on military, while South Korea spent only 4.7 percent of it. The IISS and SIPRI call into question the high figures cited by the U.S. government on

North Korea's percentage of the GNP spent on the military. The IISS estimates the North Korean percentage in 1984 at 10.2 percent, the South Korean at 5.4 percent. The 1988 SIPRI's estimates are 12.3 percent for North Korea in 1984 and 5.0 percent for South Korea in 1986. The wide speculation implies that North Korea manipulates figures, particularly those related to military spending, by ensconcing part of them elsewhere in the budget.

The spending suggests a much higher burden in Central Government Expenditure (CGE). According to ACDA, during the past ten years (1976–85) South Korea spent an average of 29 percent of its CGE on the military compared to 23 percent for North Korea. The CIA estimated that South Korea spent 32.8 percent of its central government budget on the military in 1988 and that North Korea spent over 40 percent in 1985 (CIA 1988, 132).

As for per capita military spending, ACDA's estimates show the North Korean expenditure significantly larger ($115 versus $257 in 1985). The IISS data shows South Korea exceeding North Korea for the first time in 1978, with the gap growing to $110 versus $100 in 1983 and $126 versus $88 in 1987, respectively.

This pattern of military spending in South and North Korea reflects the changes in the defense policy orientation and posture of the Korean regimes (Kihl 1984, 147). North Korea has pursued a parallel policy of military preparedness and economic development, which "might affect to a certain degree the development of the national economy" (Scalapino and Lee 1972, 594). The "Four Great Military Policylines" adopted at the Fourth KWP Congress in 1962 articulated the goal. The widening rift between China and USSR, the Cuban missile crisis, increasing U.S. involvement in Vietnam, U.S. support of India in the Sino-Indian border clash, and the Park Chung-Hee's military coup in South Korea seemed to create an atmosphere of growing threat.

South Korea's increase in military spending was stimulated by the 1960 Nixon Doctrine of gradual U.S. military disengagement from Asia and by the withdrawal of the U.S. Seventh Infantry Division from South Korea in 1971–72.

North Korea's large investment in the military machine-building industry since the 1960s has diverted considerable capital equipment and manpower from other more productive sectors of the economy.

The heavy defense burden constrains the allocation of scarce capital for economic development. It would be four to five times harder for North than for South Korea to produce similar achievements under the condition of North Korea's heavy defense burden. A long-term program of building underground industrial and military facilities is a heavy resource drain on North Korea. Underground construction is three to four times more expensive than similar aboveground construction and much more time consuming. The fourth underground tunnel constructed by North Korea to infiltrate South Korea, for example, has been found recently.

On the other hand, South Korea enjoys the advantage of being on the edge of the U.S. security umbrella. U.S. military assistance greatly helped to lessen South Korea's heavy defense burden. Since the 1960s, the ratio of defense expenditures to GNP amounted to around 5 percent every year. Even though U.S. economic aid decreased sharply after the mid-1960s, its continued military aid had helped reduce South Korea's defense burden. A ball park percentage of what South Korea might have to spend were the U.S. not playing the defense roles would be approximately 10 to 11 percent of its GNP.

South Korea's military ties with the U.S. also led it to participate in the Vietnam War between 1964 and 1973. During this period, South Korea earned at least $1 billion in net economic gain in current prices from participation in the war (Lim 1985, 84–88). These earnings were very important in financing the rapid expansion of export promotion in the early seventies, a critical stage of South Korea's outward-oriented development phase (S.J. Han 1978, 898).

It has now become a dilemma for both South Korea and the U.S. military forces to decide whether the U.S. military forces should stay or leave South Korea in view of the North's strong position. The American military withdrawal from South Korea will certainly entail a significant military burden for South Korea. Although it will promote democratic systems in both South and North Korea, it also involves dangers and the difficulties of premature judgments. The Carter administration promised as an election pledge to withdraw U.S. forces from South Korea, but found it could not and withdrew the pledge. By 1992, seven thousand soldiers will be withdrawn. Together with the climate of a changing Sino-Soviet world, the policy on the part of the

U.S. to promote direct dialogue with North Korea will be an incentive for a new North Korea under Kim Jong-Il, which will be significantly beneficial for the sustained development of South Korea.

Militarized Society

Today North Korea maintains a military force larger in manpower than South Korea's despite having only one-half of South Korea's population. South Korean military forces increased rapidly right after the Korean War. By 1954 the army numbered nearly 600,000 in sixteen divisions stationed along three-fourths of the front. The army was cut back to 520,000, but improved greatly with rigorous training and a steady influx of U.S. equipment. South Korea's armed forces followed the U.S. pattern closely in organization, equipment, and training (Clough 1987). There are also three backup forces in South Korea: the Homeland Reserve Force, the Civil Defense Corps, and the Student National Defense Corps.

North Korean military manpower well exceeded one million in 1990 (U.S. Department of Defense 1990), having begun a significant military buildup in 1969–70. Estimates of the size of North Korea's armed forces in 1953 vary widely from a low of 257,000 to a high of 410,000. Early rapid development of North Korea during the 1950s had been greatly helped by the low defense burden of military personnel.

North Korea's regular armed forces now number 1,040,000 compared to 650,000 for South Korea. South Korea's regular armed forces outnumbered North Korea's until 1978, but North Korean troops have expanded considerably since then, while South Korean troops number about the same. North Korea's numerical superiority is mostly in ground forces, where it has an advantage of 930,000 to 550,000. North Korea also has a manpower advantage in air forces of 70,000 to 40,000, but a disadvantage in naval forces of 40,000 to 60,000.

The military portion of the regular armed services in 1988 accounts for 13.7 percent of North Korea's working age males, compared to only 4.7 percent in South Korea. The huge drain of labor force into the military partly explains the chronic labor shortages in North Korea. Because of labor force shortages, the North Korean Army participates

TABLE 8.2
Comparison of Militarization between
South Korea and North Korea, 1990

	South Korea	North Korea
Population (million)	43.1	21.4
Total Armed Forces:		
Total Active	650,000 (1.5%)	1,040,000 (4.8%)
Ground Forces	550,000	930,000
Air Force	40,000	70,000
Navy	60,000	40,000
Reserves	4,840,000(11.4%)	5,540,000(25.3%)
Military Spending, 1987		
% of GNP	5.2	25 (12.3)('83)
% of Public Budget	32.8	40 (12.2)
$ per person		
% of GNP in 1970 (FEER)	5.6	25.0
Military Service	2.5 years	5 years
Tanks	1,500	3,500
Armored Personnel Carriers	1,500	1,940
Artillery	4,000	7,200
Multiple Rocket Launchers	37	2,500
Anticraft Artillery	600	8,000
Jet Fighters	480	750
Bombers	0	80
Helicopters	280	280
Attack Submarines	0	23
Torpedo Craft	173	0

Sources: U.S. Dept. of Defense, "A Strategic Framework for the Asia Pacific Rim: Looking Toward the 21st Century." April 1990; ACDA (1989), *World Military Expenditures and Arms Transfers* 1990.

in harvesting crops and constructing many civilian projects. The West Sea Berrage is known to have been constructed by military manpower, involving as many as two divisions for five years.

The heavily armed society of both Koreas has naturally caused a heightened concern about security on the part of Koreans. It has also led to an enhanced role of the military in the civil affairs of the state. Military security has become the number one preoccupation of the ruling elites in both Korean states. The heavily fortified garrison states of divided Korea in the postwar period are ironically in sharp contrast with the civilian society that prevailed for more than 500 years during the Yi dynasty (Kihl 1984, 145–6).

The armed forces are a major instrument of socialization, along with the family and the educational system. At no other time in the history of Korea has military organization become such an influential institution in determining the direction of national development in both Koreas, and the presence of the military has had an enormous effect upon socialization. Every male must by law serve in the military approximately two and one-half years in the South and five years in the North. During this duty some experience the tension of the demilitarized zone. After their mandatory military duty, they are sent to the reserve army. This, combined with the all-encompassing military requirement, makes for a society that operates well with top-down leadership. Not only is there the guerilla background of some of the country's (now aged) top leaders, but also the war of 1950–53. The confrontation between the heavily armed condition of both countries has kept them in a state of permanent militarization.

North Korea probably has more of its citizens under arms than any other country in the world, except Iraq and Israel. In North Korea, life in the armed forces may not be particularly different from that in civil society, in which nearly all able-bodied men and women were organized into a "people's militia" (Scalapino and Lee 1972, 594–96). There is also a militia of perhaps six million people. North Korean society is thoroughly regimented and the entire country is organized like military units. Work teams are divided into platoon, company, and so on. Leaders in the work teams are called platoon leader, company leader, and so on. The North Korea government still keeps reminding people of the morale of anti-Japanese guerrillas in the every workplace. Life has been likened to a military campaign with people urged to set new records in production through ceaseless "speed battles." Under the social system, North Korea has been portrayed to its people as engaged in a continuing war with imperialism that requires a wartime spirit of dedication and sacrifice. This type of behavior often manifests itself in the industrial arena. They command speed and aggressiveness.

Military readiness continues to be the principal preoccupation of the two Korean developments. Modernization of South Korean armed forces proceeded steadily during the 1980s, giving South Korea a qualitative edge in certain weapons systems, particularly in aircraft, but leaving North Korea well ahead in numbers of weapons. In early 1990 North

Korea still had a quantitative advantage of two to one in tanks, assault guns, personnel carriers, artillery, and combat aircraft (table 8.2).

South Korea is disturbed, not only by North Korea's growing quantitative edge over South Korea in weapons and equipment, but also by other military preparations. North Korea has continued to construct underground factories and hangars for aircraft, as well as adding to its underground fortifications along the DMZ. It converted several infantry divisions into mechanized or motorized divisions. North Korea continues intensive training for special forces numbering 100,000 men, some of whom could rapidly infiltrate South Korean lines by numerous fast patrol crafts or by 250 slow, low-flying AN-2 aircraft, capable of ducking beneath radar detection but also noisy and vulnerable to ground fire.

North Korea does indeed have very large, very capable armed forces. The size and strength of North Korea's forces cannot be denied. South Korean forces are also strong enough to deter and if necessary defeat a North Korean invasion force. However, the two forces are roughly equivalent so that neither is capable of a successful major offensive against the other without significant foreign assistance.

Military Trade

Both South and North Korea have emerged as important weapons exporters in recent years. ACDA ranked South and North Korea as the second and third largest arms exporters in the Third World for the period 1979–83, with $2 billion and $1.8 billion in military exports respectively. Arms sales of both Koreas show that during 1973–83 $2.2 and $2.0 billion of arms were sold by South and North Korea, respectively (*U.S. News & World Report,* 13 February 1986).

For North Korea, arms sales abroad have become a useful new export item, to an increasing extent in recent years, a source of much needed foreign exchange. Thanks to the heavy investment in the military, North Korea is capable of producing a wide variety of military equipment. Current military production capacity is sufficient to equip the armed forces with all but the most sophisticated equipment. North Korea was ranked number one by ACDA for the rate of arms sale from total exports in 1985 (27.54 percent). North Korea has sold $16.5 million worth of arms to Zimbabwe, and Iran also has become a major customer of North Korea, purchasing an estimated $800 million worth of arms, or 40 percent of its total purchase (Kerns 1984, 24–25). The shortage of foreign currency is helped by these arms sales.

South Korea, in comparison, has a fledgling defense industry and is heavily dependent on imports for its military hardware. The major systems that South Korea exports are naval vessels, especially fast attack craft. South Korea has sold PSMM–5 type fast attack craft to Indonesia and the Philippines, as well as amphibious craft to Venezuela and Argentina, and patrol craft to Malaysia (IISS, 1986).

Weapons imports have played an important role in building the military establishments of South and North Koreas. Until the 1970s, when North and South Korea began to develop an indigenous military industry, both countries had to rely entirely on weapons from other countries. According to ACDA, during the decade 1978–87, North Korea imported $2.4 billion worth of arms, South Korea $4.6 billion. According to the Department of Defense, the U.S. delivered $4.4 billion worth of weapons and equipment to South Korea from 1979 to 1988. South Korea's weapons have come almost exclusively from the U.S. South Korea has continued to look to the U.S. for over ninety percent of its imported weapons. For the 1983–87 period, the U.S. accounted for 98 percent of the value of arms delivered to South Korea. More than 25 percent of the South Korean military budget is spent in the United States.

Until the early 1970s, North Korea imported nearly all the arms from the Soviet Union. During the next decade, however, it imported few weapons (as its domestic production capabilities grew) and looked mainly to China as its supplier. China accounted for 27 percent of the weapons delivered to North Korea from 1979 to 1983, compared to 25 percent for the Soviet Union (ACDA 1985, 132). North Korea seems to be returning to its policy of seeking support from both the USSR and China since 1984 when Kim Il Sung visited Moscow in 1984. The turn to the Soviet Union may be a reaction to China's improved ties to the United States and South Korea and certainly reflects North Korea's recognition that the USSR is better able than China to provide the type of modern weaponry needed to match the South's systems such as the F–16.

It has been demonstrated that South Korea spends more on its military buildup than North Korea in absolute terms. South Korea has a superior domestic military production capability and it imports more weapons, while North Korea exports more weapons. The North Korean economy in recent years is somewhat dependent on the export of armaments. The huge amount of North Korean armaments is being sought for more export these days, which certainly aims at restoring its stagnant economy.

The Korean War (1950–53)

The Korean War (1950–53) left deep scars on the process of both Koreas' development, physically and psychologically, especially North Korea. The war provided North Korea with the sociological and psychological foundation of *juche* ideology. It is reported that the North was more devastated than the South (Halliday and Cumings 1988). Most destructive was the one-sided bombing that the U.S. Air Force inflicted on the cities and industrial centers of the North. Damage to industrial installations in the South was not as devastating as in the North although Seoul, which underwent four military occupations, was heavily damaged. Human casualties were heavy on both sides. Although neither North Korea nor China reported the number of dead, one estimate is that over 2 million North Korean civilians and about 500,000 North Korean soldiers died (Halliday and Cumings 1988, 200). Material damage has been estimated at 420 billion *won*.

South Korean civilian deaths were about 1 million, and the soldiers' deaths were more than 47,000. The physical loss of South Korean industries and infrastructure amounted to 400 billion *whan* ($ 2 billion; $5 bil. by KDI), comparable to the South's GNP in 1953 (Kuznets 1977, 37–8). South Korea had received a great amount of U.S. economic and military assistance.

Population growth significantly affected the two Korean developments. One cannot underestimate the importance of this factor to economic development. It is closely related to the supply and demand for food, urban planning, infrastructural planning, and so on. The human casualties in South Korea were estimated at one million, and those in the North 2.5 million. The human loss in South Korea was set off by a large influx from abroad (1.8 million) and refugees from North Korea (1.8 million) in 1945 (Henderson 1987). The population growth of South Korea during the 1949–55 period was .7 percent. North

Korea, however, lost three and one-half million people, 35 percent of population. In 1946, around one million people left for the South and two and one-half million were lost in the Korean War. The so-called "division effect" brought about an acute labor shortage in North Korea. This is the main factor explaining why birth rates in North Korea have not decreased. There was a mass migration of one to two million people from the North to the South during and after the war. Some 1.8 million North Koreans, about 17 percent of the population, fled to South Korea, including the bulk of the political opposition (Henderson 1987, 100). Approximately another 1.2 million fled during the Korean War. It seems that the Communist system loses its population in one way or another. It is true in the cases of such divided countries as Germany and Vietnam. It caused an acute labor shortage in the North and an immense refugee problem in the South.

In October 1950, North Korea began to receive support from the People's Republic of China. Peace talks began in July 1951 and an armistice agreement was made in July 1953 between North Korea, China and the U.N. Command. The ceasefire line, roughly following the 38th Parallel, remains the frontier between North and South Korea.

The Korean War also caused social problems of widows, separated families, orphans, and the disabled. The war produced almost 300,000 widows, 100,000 orphans, and 330,000 injured in South Korea (H.J. Lee 1985, 6). The statistics in North Korea are undoubtedly much higher. According to the Korean Red Cross, ten million people in both Koreas (half in the South and half in the North) have been separated from their families (H.J. Lee 1985, 5). Around half of the separated are brothers and sisters, parents are 15 percent and spouses are 1 percent (H.J. Lee 1985). The separation statistically explains about 13 percent of South Korean and 25 percent of North Korean population. But if we take those who died during the war into account, the statistics of separated families would be much higher.

The effect of the Korean War on the mentality and the developmental principles in the two Koreas is significant. The war started by North Korea left a deep feeling of defensiveness in South Korea, but of loss and failure in North Korea. The negative effect of the war stimulated North Korea to stick to a self-reliant strategy in development, a revival of the old Korean exclusionism. The war, on the other hand, affected South Korea positively and encouraged it to adopt an outward-oriented policy, leading to a revival of the old flunkyism in South Korea.

One can hardly ignore the social psychological impact of the fear of North Korean communism in South Korea and fear of South Korean capitalism in North Korea on development. Extremist ideologies of capitalism and communism have not been changed. Fear of the other side occupies people's minds.

The experience of the Korean War had the effect of drawing social classes together, and people who lived through their experience stress the nature of the transformation that greatly assisted in producing "the will to develop" in the early 1960s. A widespread symptom of this will was the rise in demand for education at all levels. The fear of communist threat from North Korea is relieved by the military assistance of the United States to South Korea regardless of the fact that it promoted a South Korean dependent mentality toward a big nation. The Korean War left a great fear of North Korea and the American military presence continues to strengthen xenophobic hard-liners in North Korea.

To Koreans from each side with bitter memories of the brutality they experienced during the war, their lives are faced with constant anxieties over the threat posed by the other side. One can hardly ignore the psychological impact of the U.S. security commitment to South Korea on the minds of the people. The U.S. presence goes far toward reliving the constant anxieties of South Koreans. In this way, however, such a psychological configuration tends to penetrate, rather than eliminate, the dependence mentality toward a big and strong nation that was deeply rooted in the idea of *sadae* in the Yi dynasty.

The ideology of self-reliance in North Korea appears to have easily been strengthened by the extreme trauma of U.S. bombing which destroyed 99 percent of all above-ground structures in two and one-half years (Henderson 1987, 101). More bombs were unleashed than on all of Europe in World War II. Through the experience of the war, North Korea became a xenophobic, perhaps paranoid, nation. North Korea evolved into a notoriously suspicious state toward all foreigners. It works very hard to maintain a policy of maximum insulation from the outside world. The war also intensified the fear that openness to foreign ideas may subvert the country's official ideology and transform the North Korean people's attitudes and life-styles.

The admiration of Kim's composure under bombardment and of his determined planning was accelerated by the result of the war. The fact that the war left a significant amount of orphans and broken families would foster an acceptance and admiration of Kim among the North Koreans. Among the 10 million of North Korean population in 1950, 2.5 million died and the casualties probably doubled the number of deaths. These statistics indicate that almost 75 percent of North Koreans were either killed or injured. This provided the sociological base for the acceptance of the *juche* ideology by the majority of North Korean people. For them, it would be easy to praise Kim Il Sung for their lives.

In conclusion, both Korean developments have been significantly affected by the military situation. The heavy defense burden for North Korea since the 1960s is an important reason why North Korean development is lagging behind that of South Korea since the 1960s. The North Korean defense burden, which is estimated at 10 to 30 percent of its GNP, is far greater than that of South Korea, which accounts for only 5 percent of its GNP. The diversion of a huge labor force into military personnel in North Korea, accounting for 5 percent of the total North Korean population, is another reason for North Korea's failure. The Korean War momentarily shaped the passive psychology of the North Korean self-reliant strategy toward the capitalist world, particularly toward the United States, while it offers South Korea positive spirit toward the outside world. South Korean development received many benefits from the favorable environment.

References

Clough, Ralph N. 1987. *Embattled Korea: The Rivalry for International Support*. Boulder, CO: Westview Press.

Halliday, Jon and Bruce Cumings. 1988. *Korea: The Unknown War*. New York: Pantheon Books.

Han, Sungjoo. 1978. "South Korea's participation in the Vietnam conflict: An analysis of the U.S.-Korean alliance," *Orbis*, 21:893–912.

Henderson, Gregory. 1987. "The politics of Korea," pp. 95–118 in Sullivan and Foss (eds.), *Two Koreas—One Future?* Lanham, MD: University Press of America.

International Institute for Strategic Studies (IISS). 1989. *Military Balance 1987–1988*. London: IISS.

_____. 1986. *Military Balance 1986*. London: IISS.

Kerns, Hikaru. 1984. "Trying to keep pace with a showcase state," FEER 2 February 1984 pp. 24–25.

Kihl, Young Whan. 1984. *Politics and Policies in Divided Korea: Regimes in Contest*. Boulder, CO: Westview Press.

Kuznets, Paul W. 1977. *Economic Growth and Structure in the Republic of Korea*. New Haven: Yale University Press.

Lee, Hyo-Jae. 1985. "National division and family problems," *Korea Journal* 25(8):4–18.

Lim, Hyun-Chin. 1985. *Dependent Development in Korea*, 1963–1979. Seoul: Seoul National University Press.

Scalapino, Robert A. and Chong-Sik Lee. 1972. *Communism in Korea*. Part I and II. Berkeley: University of California Press.

U.S. Arms Control and Disarmament Agency (ACDA). 1988. *World Military Expenditures and Arms Transfers 1987*. Washington, D.C.: U.S. ACDA.

_____. 1985. *World Military Expenditures and Arms Transfers 1985*. Washington, D.C.: U.S. ACDA.

U.S. Central Intelligence Agency (CIA). 1988. *World Factbook 1988*. Washington, DC: U.S. CIA.

U.S. Department of Defense. 1990. "A strategic framework for the Asia Pacific rim: Looking toward the 21st century." April 1990.

US News & World Report. 1986. Article on Military Trade, 13 February 1986.

9

Democracy, Social Structure, and Development

Social structure and sociopolitical culture in both Koreas have been transformed by political and institutional changes, the level and structure of economic development, and the military situation of the two states. The different sociopolitical forces have a significant influence on national development. If state power, economic structure, and the military are necessary conditions for development, they are not sufficient. Social and political factors will be critical in the 1990s development.

Democracy and Development

Most studies on the successful development of South Korea with respect to other developing countries have often pointed out the strong or authoritarian nature of its political system, Confucianism, and the "relatively equal" distribution of income. From the Western point of view, the South Korean political system is, in fact, highly nondemocratic and strictly authoritarian in character. Human rights seriously deteriorated in the process of past development. The Korean Central Intelligence Agency (KCIA) has taken ruthless measures to minimize political competition not only by eliminating communists but by tightly controlling opposition leaders. Torture, including sexual abuse, and terrorism are exercised by the government.

But when South Korea is compared with North Korea, the latter reveals a much higher level of authoritarian control in guiding national development. Anyone aware of the situation of political and individual freedom in North Korea readily concludes that South Korea is a far

173

freer country than North Korea. Of all the Marxist-Leninist states, North Korea is one of the most traditional and rigid, a tightly controlled totalitarian society. The commitment to "democratic centralism," by which all subordinate bodies submit to the decisions rendered by the Standing Committee of the party's Central Committee, insures a unity and homogeneity deemed essential to a "socialist society." North Korea has become a garrison state with all the restrictions and austerity that this term implies (An 1983). North Korea is highly bureaucratized, and this bureaucracy is one of the most politicized in the modern world. It seeks to unite the twin priorities of being both "Red" and "expert" in every individual, that is, both politically and ideologically loyal and technically competent.

A vast apparatus is structured to control the thoughts and behavior of the entire populace. The North Korean people are subjected to rigid measures of control, notwithstanding the fact that dissidence seems minimal. Every day North Korean people are subjected to intensive indoctrination on Kim Il Sung's political ideology of *juche* that interferes with their private leisure. Persons who fail to cooperate with the regime face imprisonment, confiscation of property, or enforced removal to remote villages. The limits on personal freedom—to travel, to choose one's place of work, and to venture to a big city from the countryside to improve one's life—are severe. There is no choice in listening to radio programs because the radio is tuned only to government broadcasts (An 1983, 23). Almost all movement is under surveillance. Travel requires police documents and government permission. Trips to foreign countries, even communist allies, are prohibited for the common citizens but are reserved only for trustworthy officials. Emigration is illegal.

Everything is planned and organized in North Korea. Everyone is disciplined, obedient, and "happy" under the wing of the "beloved" and "respected" leader who has a panacea for all ills and problems. The intended result is the creation of a citizenry animated by devoted fidelity to their leader, party, state, and system. Whatever nominal rights are accorded them, the North Korean constitution obliges all citizens to observe the socialist norm of life and the socialist rules of conduct. Citizens are also required to heighten their revolutionary vigilance against all maneuvers of those hostile elements who are opposed to the socialist system, a system identified without equivocation as the dictatorship of the proletariat. In the tightly controlled and highly bureaucratized society, innovations, creative ideas, and individual motivation are not encouraged.

The South Korean situation is enormously complicated because democratic characteristics are evident when in comparison to North Korean society. The first South Korean constitution, promulgated in 1948, was essentially democratic in character. Its catalog of political and civil liberties were typical of democratic practice. The potential restrictions on liberties were no more severe, in principle, than those found in the French or Italian constitutions (Gregor 1990, 54). The increasingly authoritarian character of the South Korean state was largely due to the "legitimate" fear of attack from the North, as well as concern for the political future of the leaders, Rhee and Park. Even under the authoritarian rule of Rhee, a formal political opposition not only survived but prevailed in South Korea. Park Chung Hee, in the elections of 1963, 1967, and 1971, could prevail only with narrow victories. No one could possibly suggest that an organized political opposition could have existed in post-1950 North Korea.

Democratic practices continued to be present in South Korea in the 1980s. Three major opposition parties opposed the Chun Doo Hwan regime, and achieved considerable success throughout the Fifth Republic. In the March 1981 general elections, the government party won only 35 percent of the popular vote, and in the February 1985 elections, the three opposition parties received 58 percent of the popular vote to the ruling party's 35 percent. In the April 1988 election, the government party won only 34 percent of the popular vote (C.W. Park 1988, 59–76). Unlike the North, the ultimate legitimation for political rule in the South is through elections. The employment of emergency powers remains precisely a temporary reaction to a crisis.

The democratic potential of South Korea in terms of national development seems great, and the flaws of authoritarianism are correctable, in principle, within the system. Although workers have been given limited opportunity to organize formally, their influence in the political arena has become much greater. The students are a critical social force in the democratic process in South Korea. The churches and Christians (22 percent of the total population) tend to be more sensitive to human rights problems. Many church-based organizations were established with political concerns and most political dissidents against authoritarian government are Christians and ministers. The growth of the middle class is certainly a source of democratic potential in South Korea. These intermediary groups are growing forces for pluralism and tend to foster democratization (Steinberg 1988, 19–34).

The different attitudes toward freedom that characterize South and North Korea are derived from the conflicting ideological convictions that animate each polity. They originated in the early twentieth century when Koreans were facing the challenges of the new epoch. As early as the eighteenth century, *sohak* (Western learning) had begun to influence some of Korea's leading intellectuals. By the end of the century, Korean reformers including Suh Che Pil were advocating the rational administration of public affairs at the expense of the "irrationalities" of traditional feudal institutions.

Of particular importance for South Korea were the works of those who had been educated in the United States during the early part of this century such as An Chang Ho and Syngman Rhee. They became advocates of civil and political rights, mass education, and economic development. They were committed to the rehabilitation of a decadent Korea through democratic practice and institutions. These ideas made up the intellectual substance of the noncommunist Korean nationalist movement in the early history of South Korea.

In contrast, North Korea has followed the traditional "exclusionism" and *tonghak* (Eastern learning) at the time of Korea's opening in the nineteenth century. The political development of North Korea has conformed to the self-reliant industrialization model first contrived by Stalin in the 1930s. Of all neo-Stalinist systems, North Korea is perhaps most faithful to the original.

The two Koreas have developed politically in distinctive fashions. North Korea has created a system to assure material adequacy to its population. It possesses an institutional stability unmatched almost anywhere in the world. But in the process, democratic measures have been impaired, and freedom and opportunity have been sacrificed. The rights of voluntary association, expression, conviction, choice, and personal security are nonexistent. South Korea, for its part, has built a system of remarkable efficiency and differentiation. The derogation of civil and political rights has been serious, but it is less systematic, extensive, and protracted than that in North Korea. South Korean development is supported by creative minds and individual freedom while North Korean stagnation is abetted by its totalitarian rigidity.

Confucianism and Political Indoctrination

The Confucian culture has been credited with the remarkable success of South Korean development. How does the same Confucian culture that is practiced in both Koreas yield such different results? Confucianism as a religion is not actively practiced in both Koreas today. North Korea has certainly banned any religion including Confucianism until three Christian churches were recently allowed to open for reasons of political expediency. Confucianism and Buddhism as well are no long practiced as religions in North Korea. In South Korea in 1985, about 20.2 percent (8.2 million) of the population are Buddhist and about 20.7 percent (8.3 million) are Christian.

Confucianism as a moral principle in both Koreas have flourished in conjunction with a strong centralized government. Although the North Korean state explicitly suppresses Confucianism and denies any feudal characteristics in their society, it would appear nevertheless that it is practiced more rigidly in the North than in the South. Given the centralized structure of the state, the values of Confucianism operate with fair consistency. The concept of the family is relevant to the organizational philosophy of corporations and cooperatives and is probably the origin of the paternalistic aspects of many corporations in both Koreas. The familial structure has a clear pecking order. The father is the head of the household, as the president of the company is of the firm. The first son is clearly next in line; the people higher on the totem pole and higher in age deserve respect. The value placed on experience and job titles in both Koreas reflects this tendency. The principle is hierarchy within a reciprocal web of duties and obligations. The Confucian culture of the family hierarchy—that is, higher position and experience command respect—and the militaristic aspect of two Korean societies contribute to a top-down mode of operation.

One aspect of Confucianism pertinent to development is scholarship. Traditionally highly valued by Korean Confucianism, tertiary professional and technical education is a major concern both of the state, in pursuit of economic growth and national strength, and of individual families, seeking the relative economic security and status afforded by higher education. In Confucianism, being a scholar entails a rather prestigious status. Compared with the Japanese emphasis on applied knowledge, the value Koreans place on the Ph.D. shows a stronger Korean emphasis on pure scholarship. Sixty percent of the students learn English while only forty percent learn Russian in North Korea despite the fact that North Korea has closer relationships with the Soviet Union, and hardly any with the United States (Zweig 1988, 72). Intellectuals are a leading force in both Korean societies.

In North Korea, as demonstrated by the North Korea's symbol—a hammer and sickle intersected by a Chinese writing brush—state intellectuals are well treated. This attitude toward intellectuals reflects the national emphasis on education. North Korea has compulsory high school education, and through collective agriculture the government of North Korea implements this policy in the countryside. North Korea has 266 universities and colleges. Final grades in school are still publicly displayed (in some cases, including failing grades), which had been practiced in South Korea during 60s and 70s. Not only the grades, but students' pictures are displayed as well.

Education is a large investment area in which the two Koreas have concentrated much of their resources. Education yields "production benefits" through the knowledge and skills acquired through schooling. The quality of society and government is determined by education. It is a commonplace idea of modernization that a stable and democratic society is impossible without a minimum degree of literacy, knowledge, and acceptance of a common set of values and that for all these purposes formal schooling plays a major role.

On the basis of classical doctrines, Marxists would predict that total educational expenditures in socialist nations would be higher than in capitalist nations at a similar state of development. Non-Marxists have had little to say on the subject. However, there seems no statistically significant difference in the enrollment rates between the two systems (Pryor 1968). This is true of the two Korean cases. Therefore, the political ideology of communism must be mentioned in relation to North Korean development. Political indoctrination is a core part of the curriculum. The North Korean educational system spends about as much time imparting the ideology of Kim Il Sung as instilling more practical knowledge. Technological adoption is impeded by this climate of ideological dominance. Posters on the walls outside the classrooms call on students to remember the bitterness of prerevolutionary society. The text books are replete with anti-American propaganda. The technical competence of North Korea's labor force and bureaucracy suffers as a result, and it remains inferior to that in the South. The economic planners and top businessmen in South Korea are not only well-educated, many with advanced degrees from foreign universities, but provide extensive training facilities for upgrading the technical skills of a diligent labor force. Big corporations are required to provide training for 15 percent of their employees.

Another important aspect of Confucianism as an ideology is the emphasis placed on effort. Working hard is valued immensely, meaning that the actual process of being industrious is as important as the result. Working hours are long in both Koreas. In 1987, South Korean workers worked longer hours than workers in any other developing country, with both men and women in industry working approximately 52 hours per week. In North Korea work hours per day are 11 for men and 8.5 for women, which would be 66 hours for men and 51 hours for women per week.

The same Confucian value system held by the two Koreas has produced two fundamentally different outlooks toward development. Korea, generally speaking, has historically emphasized the importance of the Confucian belief in scholarship over commerce and material things. The Korean *yangban*, for example, were clearly not commercially minded (Kang 1989, 14). Confucian ideology disdains commercial activities, resulting in the economic stagnation of the Yi dynasty (Lim 985, 33–34). This tradition was easily carried on in North Korea where communism disdained commercial and service activities. People were mobilized not by material incentives but by moral exhortation. In a way, Korean Confucianism was strengthened by communism in North Korea. This particularly explains the lack of development of the service sector and consumer goods in North Korea. In South Korea, firms have recognized this and are trying hard to catch up in the arena of customer service. Pluralistic values help explain the extraordinary commercial bustle, the materialism, and conspicuous consumption of the people in South Korea (Weiner and Huntington 1987, 221–80). Christians are somewhat over represented in the entrepreneurial population in South Korea (Jones and Sakong 1980, 301). This is particularly helped by a Weberian "spirit of capitalism," abetted by aspects of Protestant dogma thought to encourage commercial activities as a means of achieving personal salvation.

The values of Marxism and Leninism in North Korea have brought about radical changes in the nature of society. Loyalty to one's family or lineage has been largely extended to loyalty to the nation as a whole, a shift from an extreme particularism to a limited universalism. Nationalism is expressed through the ideas of *juche*, which stresses national and cultural self-reliance and independence. Yet, the Five Relations of Confucian culture are well retained in communist North Korea. There is no concept of privacy, self-determination, or the rights of the individual. According to Confucianism, what makes people human is not their freedom or individuality, but their acceptance of social roles that integrate them into a preestablished, collective whole, a notion coincident with the collective spirit of communism emphasized in North Korea. Family-based politics, the succession to rule of the leader's son, and the extraordinary veneration of Kim Il Sung are the Confucian legacies.

Income Inequality

The meaning of equality is understood in at least two senses, equality of opportunity and equality of results (Lipset 1977, 278–86). Equality of opportunity is supposedly the classic American meaning of the term. It subsumes the ideal of a competitive system in which there is great social mobility, in which people are supposed to be able to rise according to ability, regardless of social background. Equality of results refers to the old socialist credo "from each according to his ability, to each according to his needs." Although equality of *opportunity* is also emphasized by the communist countries, it is equality of *results* to which a communist country like North Korea is ideally committed. Equality of opportunity can not really exist without equality of result. For the Marxist-Maoist regime, it is impossible to have equality of opportunity if people start out highly unequal. Both of the two dimensions of equality have been supported by socialist countries, and capitalist countries began to accept the significance of the interrelationship to the policy of welfare state.

The equal opportunity model of South Korea did not result in successful development during the early period in the 1940s and 1950s. South Korea's underdevelopment during the early period allowed for political liberty and economic equality in relative terms compared with development in the later period. With the equal opportunity model, corruption early became rampant as an illegitimate means of achieving upward mobility both in the public and the private sectors. What changed the situation in South Korea was the sacrifice of many political an economic liberties, even as equality as an ideology was rigorously pursued during this period.

Large populations in the countryside were transported for the sake of industrialization in urban areas. By world standards, the South Korean economic distribution is relatively equitable, and the overall effect of rapid growth on economic inequality has been not so bad as commonly experienced by many Third World countries (Koo 1987, 375–97). There is also considerable upward mobility and relative equality of opportunity. At the same time however, restrictions on effective political competition by opposition parties were legally implemented by the Yushin Constitution approved in a referendum under martial law. The Yushin Constitution stipulated an indirect election of the President by a virtual rubber-stamp electoral college called the National Conference for Unification. Authoritarian political repression became a major issue as the government followed the equality model.

Although South Korea's growth process has been characterized by a marked degree of distributional equality during the 1960s and 1970s, it has not only been denied to the South Korean people generally, apparently due to political oppression, but also recently has been seriously questioned in the 1980s. Income inequality in South Korea has grown since 1980. South Korean development in the 1980s seems to have brought about more inequality than in the recent past. The excessive growth in service sectors, such as the construction of golf courses and hotels, results in expediting inequality. Most foreign direct investment in the 1980s was pooled in these areas (E.M. Kim 1989, 24–45). It has generated tremendous tensions and conflicts over the past decade and into the 1990s. The working and middle classes have resorted to militant strikes and work stoppages which hinder South Korean development to a significant degree. This is attributable in part to the South Korean people's high aspirations and in part to the rapidity of social change they have experienced. But a more fundamental source of this social tension seems to lie in the nature, not just the magnitude, of social inequality. Whereas social inequality a few decades ago was based on a relatively simple, unstructured distribution of wealth, today it is firmly grounded in antagonistic, contradictory class relations.

In attempting to explain the tension and conflict in South Korean development, it is important to trace the evolution of the working class and its system of low wages over the last three decades, a period in which there have been some profound structural changes. Throughout the 1960s the ranks of the working class were more or less continually augmented by migration from the countryside. Due to the small-holder structure of South Korean agriculture and the underdevelopment of rural industries, industrial workers relied on a large-scale rural exodus (Koo 1990, 673, 675). The speed with which huge numbers of farmers were uprooted and forced to adopt an urban lifestyle was dramatic by historical standards. The proportion of industrial workers increased from 9 percent in 1960 to 30.4 percent in 1987.

In the face of rising expectations, large segments of the South Korean working class have been excluded from any substantial benefits flowing from twenty-five years of rapid growth. The working class did not receive a fair share of the benefits of growth. The powerful bourgeoisie monopolized most of these benefits. Twenty *chaebols* accounted for more than fifty percent of the total South Korean GNP in 1987. The standard of living of the working class seriously declined in the 1980s. The minimum cost of living for a family of five in 1980 was $400 per month, while 56 percent of workers received less than $300. The average household wage per month in 1987 increased slightly to $461, but the minimum household cost of living a month doubled to $596 (EPB 1988). The reduction of inequality among classes will be the most important task in the future of South Korean development. Without a more equal distribution of income, South Korea's development in the 1990s may have negative consequences.

In the capitalist economic development of South Korea, as the Marxists predicted, on-going industrialization produced a large and class-conscious working population possibly feeling deprived of their share of the fruits of development. But, it was not so easy to ignite a proletarian revolution in South Korea, not only because classes in South Korea did not become polarized, but also because the state controlled working-class movements. The South Korean state played a dominant role in organizing industrial workers. By adopting export-oriented industrialization and repressive labor policies, the state has limited labor mobility, and social classes were differentiated in a complex framework. With workers making up 45.8 percent of the South Korean population, there has developed a capitalist class of 1.7 percent and a middle class of 38.5 percent. Various classes have made South Korea more dynamic than North Korea despite the fact that they involve tensions and conflict.

The exclusive existence and the nature of a large middle class in South Korea seem to have a special meaning for sustained development compared with the insignificant numbers of the North Korean middle class. The equality of opportunity model produced a considerable middle class segment, comprising 38.5 percent of the South Korean population. The size of this new middle class has expanded considerably, in both absolute and relative terms. If low-level clerical workers are excluded from the grouping, its size expanded from 8.6 percent of the labor force in 1960 to 21.5 percent in 1985. In a broad definition of all non-manual workers (excluding self-employed professionals), the group is large, 17.7 percent of the total labor force in 1980 and still growing. The role of the new middle class in South Korean development has been remarkable. Capitalist development in South Korea has created a large and differentiated new middle class, made up of upper-level technicians and managers in the private sector, in addition to a range of managerial state employees. The new middle class contributed to technological development and pragmatic economic planning. Their pragmatic and practical policies were ultimately adopted as state policy (Kang 1989, 30).

Critical factors for South Korean development come from within the system. Inequality is a major cause of workers' strikes which hamper rapid growth in South Korea today. Workers' strikes and student demonstrations play a critical role in future economic growth. Income inequality had already led to the severe problems of workers' strikes, curbing exports to half the level of the previous year in 1989 and causing negative economic growth in the first quarter of 1990. Increasingly intense strikes by workers, protests by university students, and the democratic movement initiated by Christian groups are creating parochial radical nationalism. Although tension and conflict maintain this dynamic society, income distribution and workers' strikes are a big burden for future development in South Korea.

The equality of results model of North Korea appeared to have been successful in effecting national development as compared to the South as far as the first ten and fifteen years is concerned. Of course, the North Korean equality model was achieved by sacrificing political and economic liberty to an extreme. That is proved by the fact that while income is evenly distributed throughout the population, the rights to strike, to associate, etc. are banned. It seems that there has not developed any powerful social class to challenge the existing structure of distribution. The new technocrats and some intellectuals are the only visible social classes, but they have shown so far no sign of becoming a challenging class. It was recently reported that criticism of and grievance toward current economic policy have appeared on the public propaganda board. The demands concern political freedom, rather than income equality. Student demonstrations broke out in early 1990 and mining workers' strikes led to the arrest of sixty workers (*Chosun Ilbo*, 23 April 1990).

Income distribution in North Korea is far more equalized than that of South Korea. In this sense, less tension and conflict exist in North Korea than in South Korea. The income level of the majority of North Koreans ranges from the lowest 7 to 50 percent of that of South Korea. The average income of North Korean workers corresponds to the lowest 15 percent of South Korean income. Only the lowest 7 percent of South Koreans at the poverty level fall below the lowest level of North Korean income. While in any objective and measurable sense living conditions in North Korea are far less favorable than in South Korea, relative deprivations are less keenly felt in North Korea. Here the problem is the absolute poverty of all.

The key factor in regard to all such issues—income equality, living standards, personal freedom, and the variety of deprivations people suffer—lies in the realm of expectations, the mainstay of stability. North Korea's low inequality (and political stability, too) is facilitated by low expectations. The strict equality at low level in turn reinforces low expectations. When people have little reason to believe that change will be for the better, or that they can bring it about, they will be quiescent and passive (Hollander 1975, 434). With such a low level of expectations, pseudo-participation encouraged and demanded by the leaders is quite compatible with the traditional passive and fatalistic attitude toward politics and development, which is present in contemporary North Korean society.

At the price of underdevelopment with low expectations, a "paradise on earth" was indeed built in North Korea. North Korea boasts of the three absences in this paradise: no taxes, no crime, and no beggars. This resulted from the fact that all the properties are possessed by the state, not by the people, and that strict equality at a low level of development allows nothing to be stolen and nothing to be given. Some positive aspects of this "paradise" were pointed out by Rinser (1988): the value of money has been minimized in North Korea; there is no unemployment, no alcoholics or drug addicts, and no corruption. Yet, even if they reveal a part of truth, all of these were achieved through the harsh suppression of freedom and consumerism. If the conditions were created with the consent of North Korean people who would accept paradise without consumer goods, it would be fine. But, the real problem is that the people of North Korea are not satisfied with their material life and still want to have television, refrigerators, better clothes, and more comfortable houses. They want to be wealthy, not poor. In this sense, North Korea became a typical totalitarian society, far from a paradise.

The too low level of income in North Korea has hindered advanced development. The low level of average North Korean income cannot support equality at a high level of living. That is, North Korea lacks the material resources and the technological levels that would permit an egalitarian society in which no one had to be inferior to any other because machines, not people, do all the onerous work, in which people can fulfill Marx's dream of people spending part of their time engaged in productive activities and part in leisure or creative intellectual and artistic activity. According to Marx, such a goal can only be achieved in an advanced industrialized society in which material production is enough to support fulfilling activities for all. Without the material base, the so-called equality of North Korea is no more than repression of private consumption.

At such a low average income level, the potential power of North Korea may have suffered the loss of creative minds and innovative ideas. Just as the equality of opportunity model of South Korea has not provided a fair base to start, the equality of result model of North

Korea has failed to offer equal opportunity. Equality of result cannot really exist without equality of opportunity, and vice versa. North Korea excluded private enterprises and private corporations, foreign and domestic. The failure of this policy was not simply that free enterprises were rejected but that North Korea relied so heavily on large scale bureaucracy that virtually all adaptability, innovations, and ability to perform even simple economic tasks become problematic. Maintaining strict equality at the low level is economically inefficient and retards national development. It limits creative efforts, innovative ideas, and finally the capabilities of the human being. In this sense, North Korean communism is not like Marx's, but a pessimistic primitive one based on Rousseau's natural law.

Equality in this sense is not a relative term that can be qualified or which exists in varying degree. Within a given social system, it is an absolute. A man's or woman's sense of equality with other people can exist only when they know they are unchallenged by any predetermined handicap in any area of life. Even the slightest residue of discrimination or prejudice may be enough to eliminate this sense of equality. It can only leave them preoccupied with the residual injustice, for no one savors those freedoms which are also enjoyed by everyone around them. Because of this, progress in the field of civil rights has brought an acceleration of expectations with each new victory. The more that is achieved, the greater looms a preoccupation with what remains to be achieved.

In order to move to greater equality, a society needs more than increased production: it needs freedom for the less privileged to impose their claims on the ruling elites. The first precondition for legitimate equality might be found in the presence or absence of institutionalized opportunities for criticizing, modifying, or altering the political system. Only when such opportunities are available can we begin to assess the degree of support or acceptance any political system enjoys.

North Korean society is faced with crises which come from outside society. Unlike the Marxist assertion that the economy, particularly control over the means of production, determines other institutions in a society such as the class structure, the family, religious institutions, the political order, gender differentiation, the educational system, and even science, North Korean societal developments fits in better with Parsonian functional analysis. Kim Il Sungism and the *Juche* ideology perform the function of pattern maintenance at the apex of the system; it is followed by integration of this value system by the legal and other control sub-systems, next there is goal attainment set by the polity; and lastly there is adaptation being dealt with by the economic and technological sphere. This social system is called "a state-directed form of socialist modernization" by Lane (1976). The values of the system here are socialist, the goals involve change in the direction of modernization, and the instrument of change is the political system. In this system, technological development is highly restricted by the supreme ideology of *juche* and the value of Kim Il Sungism.

The international economic and political situation seems to be a critical factor for North Korean self-reliant national development. There seems little probability of a change of ideological commitment in the North Korean political leadership. The integration fortified with the ideology of *juche*, to a great extent, does not appear to have collapsed in the 1990s. Little serious external economic or cultural interruption is apparent. As the structural-functionalists expect, the major threat to North Korea comes from outside the system, a challenge to the supreme North Korean values of the *juche* ideology. Within Parsons' functional framework, a critical moment or change comes from outside the system. Kim Il Sungism was attacked by the Soviet Union in early 1990, when the Soviet Union demanded liberalization in North Korea and criticized the background of Kim Il Sung's anti-Japanese guerrilla movement and the North's triggering the Korean war (*Chosun Ilbo*, 19 June 1990). There is now the danger of the stoppage of the Soviet Unions' oil supply to North Korea. The international environment of liberal movements in Eastern Europe and the economic stagnation of the Soviet Union will add further pressure for liberalization in future North Korean development. The system propounded in North Korea, based on the Kim cult, could be threatened by the multiplication of contacts with foreigners and an influx of information and ideas from outside the country. In the past, foreign trade was fine and would be encouraged, but only in ways that did not conflict with overriding political requirements.

Domestically, industrialization will inevitably produce a large group of educated middle-income professionals in North Korea who will not be easily mobilized for fanatic ideological struggle. As a consequence of such change in its social constituents, North Korea will likely have a more moderate and rational government that will represent a newly emerging liberal middle class, being adapted to a more practical international environment. In North Korea, a new middle (or upper-middle) class is composed of managers in state enterprises and cooperatives. The change in economic structure has already brought about changes in social structure. North Korea's labor force structure shows that 82 percent of the population belong to either the agricultural (43 percent) or industrial (39 percent) working class, and only 18 percent of the labor force consists of government officials and intellectuals. Since the staffs of agricultural and industrial organizations are governmental officials, the labor force structure in North Korea more or less reveals its class structure. Power seems to be seen as independent of economic reward in North Korean society. Here, power is an important concept to determine the relationship of liberty to equality. North Korea is more egalitarian economically, but much less egalitarian than South Korea in the distribution of power. In North Korea, workers do not have the right to strike, nor have they the right to vote people out of office. Clearly power is more concentrated in North Korea than in South Korea. Analyses seeking to evaluate which system is more egalitarian are necessarily confused by ideologies and abstractions. The concentration of power, and the correlative issue of political oppression, are a serious burden for the future development in North Korea.

Every individual in North Korea is classified into one of fifty-one categories according to his *sungboon*—his family's class background. The elite group at the top of the hierarchy includes anti-Japanese guerrilla fighters and their families; orphans of parents killed in anti-Japanese activities or in the Korean War; and the families of party members, government officials, and military officers. The elite receive preferential treatment in access to food and other consumer goods. Those at the bottom of the ladder include descendants of landlords, capitalists, rich peasants, collaborators with the Japanese, and members of religious groups as well as the families of persons who fled to South Korea. Persons with a good *sungboon* find their entry into the best schools and their rise in the bureaucracy facilitated. Those with a bad *sungboon* have little chance for a good education or a good job. Because family background is passed on from parents to children, stratification seems to be hardening, and opportunities for those at the bottom of the ladder seem to be declining. Class identification has created invidious distinctions, denying individuals equality before the law as well as many civil and political rights.

The collapse of Marxist myths in North Korea, as well as in East Germany, has undermined the defining beliefs of North Korea: for the dedicated Marxist, only the arrival of a socialist economy can liberate humans from such forms of despotism as political dictatorship, the rule of men over women and children, and the tyranny of superstition. This did not take place in North Korea. It led to a regimented society. It is utterly remote from Marx's prediction that the reorganization of society would make it possible to expand mankind's productive capacities to the point of unbounded abundance for consumption. Rather, it proves that in the quest for solutions, moral imperatives acquire an urgency only when they are backed with force, or the threat of force.

The equality model could work out only in the short run, and at the maximum sacrifice of liberty. In more far-reaching terms, the imposition of this model weakens sustained development. Moreover, too low a level of average income proves that sustained development cannot be achieved within the North Korean system because motivation to work declines and low expectations follow. Certain advancements in adult literacy, infant mortality, education, and health care are not necessarily associated with degrees of economic development as demonstrated by both Koreas wherein similar social achievements were achieved at a similar pace regardless of the level of economic development. On the other hand, the development with liberty model may not work at the beginning, because intensive development seems to come together with the high cost of liberty in the short period. Inequality in South Korea, accompanied by an authoritarian structure, created, nevertheless, a large segment of the new and old middle class which contributed to successful development. It is faced with the risk of strikes resulting from the structure of low working-class wages which had been a significant element of South Korean success. However, for sustained development, both high levels of equality and liberty may have to be followed by a government of reconciliation which pursues equal distribution of income at a high level on the basis of voluntary motivation.

In sum, the totalitarian nature of the North Korean regime has impeded the innovation and creative work needed for development. It has resulted in low motivation and low expectations among North Korean workers. In South Korea, the liberal climate has been fostered by political and individual freedom, and produced high expectations and high motivation to work. Confucianism entails similar values in the workplace and ordinary life in both Koreas. Yet, North Korea consciously ignored the positive spirit of Confucianism and stressed the *juche* ideology, which hardly impels the North Korean people toward development. North Korea's spending considerable energy in ideological education also diverts the potential power of North Korean development. In South Korea, a dynamic social structure incorporating both wealth and poverty fosters high expectations and motivation to development. Furthermore, the coexistence of Confucianism, Buddhism, and Christian beliefs contributes to motivation and voluntary desires toward development. Too low a level of income in North Korea reflects a lack of material, technological, and moral resources. Greater levels of economic achievement can only be attained in an advanced industrial society in which material production is great enough to support equal distribution. Without a material base, the apparent equality of North Korea is no more than repression of private consumption. At such a low economic level, the potential power of North Korea to develop is limited by the loss of motivation to increase productivity and by the loss of creative minds and ideas.

References

An, Tai Sung. 1983. *North Korea in Transition: From Dictatorship to Dynasty*. Westport, Conn.: Greenwood Press.

Chosun Ilbo. 1990. Articles on North Korea, 23 April 1990 and 19 June 1990.

Economic Planning Board (EPB). 1988. *Social Indicators in Korea*. Seoul: EPB.

Gregor, A. James 1990. *Land of the Morning Calm: Korean and American Security*. Washington, D.C.: Ethics and Public Policy Center.

Hollander, Paul. 1975. "Comparing socialist systems: Ends and results," Pp 421–36 in Mesa-Lago & Beck (eds.), *Comparative Socialist Systems: Essays on Politics and Economics*. Pittsburgh: UCIS Publications.

Jones, Leroy P. and Il Sakong. 1980. *Government, Business, and Entrepreneurship in Economic Development: The Korean Case*. Cambridge, MA: Harvard University Press.

Kang, T. W. 1989. *Is Korea the Next Japan?: Understanding the Structure, Strategy, and Tactics of America's Next Competitor*. New York: The Free Press.

Kim, Eun Mee. 1989. "Foreign capital in Korea's economic development, 1960–1985." *Studies in Comparative International Development* 24(4):24–45.

Koo, Hagen. 1990. "From farm to factory: Proletarianization in Korea." *American Sociological Review* 55(5):669–81.

_____. 1987. "The interplay of states, social class, and world system in East Asian development: The case of South Korea and Taiwan." in F. Deyo (ed.), *The Political Economy of the New Asian Industrialism*. New York: Cornell University Press.

Lane, David. 1976. *The Socialist Industrial State: Towards a Political Sociology of State Socialism*. Boulder, CO: Westview Press.

Lim, Hyun-Chin. 1985. *Dependent Development in Korea, 1963–1979*. Seoul: Seoul National University Press.

Lipset, Seymour Martin. 1977. "Observations on economic equity and social class." Pp. 278–86 in Irving L. Horowitz (ed.), *Equity, Income, and Policy: Comparative Studies in Three Worlds of Development*. New York: Praeger Publishers.

Park, Chan Wook. 1988. "The 1988 National Assembly election in South Korea: The ruling party's loss of legislative majority." *Journal of Northeast Asian Studies* 7(3):59–76.

Pryor, Frederic L. 1968. *Public Expenditures in Communist and Capitalist Nations*. Homewood, IL: Richard D. Irwin Inc.

Rinser, Louise. 1988. *Bookhan Iyagi*. (Stories on North Korea) Seoul: Hyungsung Press.

Steinberg, David I. 1988. "Sociopolitical factors and Korea's future economic policies." *World Development* 16(1):19–34.

Weiner, Myron and Samuel P. Huntington (eds.) 1987. *Understanding Political Development*. Boston: The Little, Brown and Company.

Zweig, David. 1989. "A Sinologist's observations on North Korea." *Journal of Northeast Asian Studies* 8(3):62–82.

10

Theoretical Implications and
Prospects for the 1990s

Development processes in the two Koreas have been analyzed to
show that capitalist South Korea has outperformed Communist North
Korea during the post liberation period. The size of the capitalist
Korean economy is six times larger than that of Communist Korea, and
the per capita GNP of capitalist Korea is three times larger than that of
Communist Korea. Historically, Communist Korea had earned higher
marks than capitalist Korea for generating per capita economic production until 1975, per capita material production until 1980, and
standard of living until about 1970. In a relatively short period of time
during the early 10 to 15 years of its existence, Communist Korea had
succeeded in transforming a backward agricultural country into a relatively strong industrial state. However, there had been little percep-
tible improvement in living standards, either with respect to housing,
public transportation, or availability of goods in stores. Capitalist Korea, since the 1960s, has been successful in generating high rates of
economic growth, industrializing the economy, and achieving a significantly higher standard of living for its people. Structurally, development in the two Koreas shows striking differences. The proportion
of the Communist Korean industrial production in GNP is more than
double that of capitalist Korea and the proportion of agricultural production in the Communist North's GNP is considerably larger than that
of the capitalist South, while that of the Communist North's service
sector is only one-tenth that of the capitalist South. Trade shows a far
greater contrast: the Communist Korean trade volume is only one-
twentieth of capitalist Korea's. Trade of both South and North Korea
is increasingly dependent on Japan.

The labor force and social structure also show striking differences. The agricultural population in Communist Korea is still a large portion of the work force: 43 percent in 1987 while that in capitalist Korea is 21 percent. As for the service population, which includes the public administrative population, in Communist Korea the share is only 18 percent of the population while it is 50 percent in capitalist Korea. There is apparently a much greater disparity of income distribution in capitalist Korea than in Communist Korea, but the average income level in Communist Korea is very low: it ranges from the lowest seven to fifty-five percent of that of capitalist Korea; the average income of North Korean workers is located in the lowest fifteen percent of South Korean income; and only seven percent of South Korea's people living in poverty fall below the lowest level of North Korean income. As to whether the system is able to meet basic human needs and improve living standards, capitalist South Korea is more successful. Development in urbanization, health care, and education explains in part the higher standard of living in capitalist Korea than in Communist Korea.

The fundamental reason for the uneven development between the two Koreas lies in the different principles of development. The principle of self-reliance characterizes both the successes and failures of North Korean communist development, whereas the principle of imitation characterizes those of South Korean capitalist development. Communist North Korea's conception of development driven only by material production restricts national and human capacities. The principles of both Koreas were considerably affected and shaped by extremist political ideologies, the Korean War, and Korean culture. The ideological principles were pursued through detailed strategies and policies in major fields of society.

Both Korean states have played a significant role not only in the adoption of specific economic plans but also in implementing them rigorously. Nevertheless, the strategies employed by the states produced extraordinarily different results. South Korea practiced state capitalism in which the state owned and operated some key enterprises and financial institutions, allowing for primarily private enterprises, a conglomerated bourgeoisie, and a market economy. The state communism of North Korea achieved fast development by state ownership of the means of production with the principle of self-reliance for its first ten to fifteen years, relying on mass mobilization policies such as socialization of industries and land and collectivization of agriculture. The self-reliance principle impeded further structural development. The capitalist Korean imitation principle is more flexible, pluralistic, and pragmatic than Communist Korean self-reliance, so that capitalist Korea could effectively work within the fluent international capitalist environment by controlling foreign investment and national financial mechanisms. Also, capitalist Korea introduced a mass mobilization movement in the 1970s comparable to that successfully practiced in Communist Korea in the 1950s.

Development in the two Koreas is bound and fostered by structural aspects of the "self-reliance principle" of Communist North Korea, and the "imitation principle" of capitalist South Korea. The self-reliance development in Communist Korea led to the extremely unbalanced growth of heavy industries and to extreme underdevelopment of service industries and trade. Heavy industries require more and more energy and raw materials which cannot be supplied by domestic resources alone. Poor transportation imposed limitations on the supply of materials required by industry. The large labor input into agriculture and the military in Communist Korea is inefficient and an obstacle to further development. Capitalist Korea, on the other hand, has developed in a more balanced way, moving from light industries in the 1960s through heavy industries in the 1970s to technology industries in the 1980s. Capitalist Korea has also taken advantage of foreign capital, technology, and foreign markets, whereas Communist Korea failed to actively use them. The policy of mass mobilization and reliance upon moral incentives was exhausted in fifteen years, while capitalist Korea not only relies on pecuniary incentives, but also imitated the Communist Korean strategy of moral incentives in the 1970s. Heavy defense for Communist Korea is another important reason why the Communist Korean development is lagging behind capitalist Korea. The Communist Korean defense burden is two to six times greater that that of capitalist Korea, and diversion of labor force into military personnel in Communist Korea is three to four times higher than that of capitalist Korea considering the population difference between them.

The problems of democracy, political indoctrination, and income equality have been important sociopolitical reasons for the differences in the economic achievement of the two Koreas. The totalitarian nature of the Communist North Korean regime has impeded the innovation and creative work needed for development. It has resulted in low motivation and low expectations among North Korean workers. In capitalist Korea, the liberal climate in relative terms has fostered political and individual freedom, and produced high expectations and motivation to work. Confucianism which values scholarship and hard work is highly influential in the workplace and ordinary life in both Koreas. Yet, Communist Korea consciously refused the positive spirit of Confucianism and stresses the *juche* ideology. In capitalist Korea, rapid development was achieved through the sacrifices of a large working class whose income was controlled at the lowest level by the state. The dynamic social structure with varying possibilities of wealth and poverty supplies high expectations and motivation to development. Furthermore, the pluralistic values of Confucianism, Buddhism, and Christianity encourage voluntary motivation toward development. Low levels of income in Communist Korea reflect a lack of material, technological, and moral resources. Greater income levels and equality can only be achieved in advanced industrial society in which material production is enough to support high living standards for all. Without a material base, the equality of Communist Korea is no more than repression of private consumption. Within the system of Communist self-reliance, the potential power of North Korea to develop is limited by the loss of motivation to increase productivity and the loss of creative minds and ideas.

In comparing South Korean and North Korean development experiences, it is evident that specific problems currently faced by each state are "complementary," that is, both are each other's best markets. For example, in trade, South Korea could probably become more efficient by importing North Korean fishing and mining products; North Korea could import South Korean capital and technology. Similarly, the resolution of their respective problems lies in each state adopting some of the features of the other's system. In economic structure and labor force, Communist North Korea could probably become more efficient by reducing its agricultural population; capitalist South Korea could do so by relocating some of its wasteful service population.

The two Koreas' experiences have also general implications for Third World development. First of all, Communist self-reliance and mass mobilization measures based on moral incentives tend to be important strategies for a rapid short-term development. They provided both South and North Korea with effective measures helping their dynamic take-offs. Although the policy of mass mobilization leads to a giant step forward for a country at the beginning stage, it is exhausted after a relatively short period. It is suggested that about seven to ten years must be allowed for the effective utilization of the strategy.

For the longer-run term, capitalist measures that rely significantly on Western capital and technology are a more effective strategy for the continued development of the Third World. Despite all the risks of dependence, the large influx of foreign capital and technology worked positively in the two Koreas, even in North Korea for the first few years following the introduction of external capital and technology during the early 1970s. The failure in North Korea resulted rather from the fact that the self-reliant structure of the North Korean economy could not absorb the influx of foreign capital into the system in the long run. It needed to be followed by the expansion of foreign markets and the security of foreign exchanges. In doing so, expansion in foreign export and the support of the state become crucial.

Disciplined and pragmatic guidance of the state sees a necessary condition for Third World development. Controlling all the domestic financial resources, in both Koreas the states exercised immense influence in the process of rapid development. However, the strong state itself does not help development. Communist states exercise far stronger roles in implementing developmental plans than in capitalist countries, but this has not led to successful results. What is needed as a sufficient condition for success are the state's pragmatic guidance of the national economy and trained manpower supporting the leadership. The strong state, to which the success of, say, the NICs is usually credited, has to be examined further by the domestic and foreign policies of development.

The careful allocation of industrial investment, both capital and labor, is crucial in this sense. The heavy-industry strategy of Communist development can achieve somewhat sustained material growth in military weapons, trucks, and tractors, but, the growth of heavy industry needs to be balanced by the growth of light and service industries that support it in one way or another. Lack of development in light industry cannot supply people with necessary consumer goods, which decreases motivation to work. Underdevelopment in social overhead capital, such as communication and transportation, is another obstacle for sustained development. Rapid expansion in foreign trade is required to earn foreign exchange needed for the introduction of foreign capital.

The effect of war and military buildup on the mentality and developmental principle in a nation is significant. Heavy military buildups, do not appear to help economic development. On the contrary, it wastes potential capital and labor that could be invested in economic development. War wastes fruitful wealth and labor. It brings about not only the direct loss of labor, but the indirect one of the outflux of labor force. This is what we called earlier the "division effect" when a significant number of people flee from Communist camps to the capitalist side, causing a serious labor shortage on the Communist side. War also affects the psychology and morale of a people. In the case of Korea, war left a strong feeling of defensiveness in the South and a deep scar of loss and failure in the North. A war could cause a country to stick to a negative inward-oriented strategy of autarky, or it could move on to a more positive outward-oriented policy.

There is a "comparison effect" in the process of development, which is formed by each other's awareness of the alternative Communist and capitalist parts. At the crucial moment of Korean development, each Korea decisively influenced the other: South Korea adopted the North's mass mobilization measure; North Korea introduced the South's measure of relying on foreign capital, and the result was a fatal blow to the North. The comparison effect could be extended to other than capitalist or communist frames of references. Third World countries continuously adopt successful patterns of other developing countries as well as those of the developed. The comparative effect in Third World development beyond the divided situations remains to be further studied.

Finally, income levels and income distribution are important in development. The Communist model of a strictly equal distribution of income at extremely low levels causes low motivation and a consequent drop in productivity. The capitalist model of unequal distribution of income at relatively high levels leads to serve tensions, but high aspirations and increased productivity. It is an option for a country whether to take a capitalist road of rapid development with potential risks of high tension, or to remain in the communist one of underdevelopment with relatively low aspirations and tension. To take both within a unified system remains to be further studied.

Theoretical and Empirical Implications

There are many implications in the two Koreas' experiences for sociological theories of Third World development and for empirical feasibilities. From the viewpoint of dependency theory, it was very difficult for both Koreas to be developed. Korea before division was a Japanese colony for thirty-six years with the extreme forms of dependence which colonial status implies. The colony paid dearly for dependency under Japanese rule. The human and cultural loss from the Japanese colonial rule goes far beyond one's imagination. However, these costs were offset, at least in part, by the development of factories, roads, railroads, and administrative services under colonial power. North Korea benefited from it in its early development during the second half of the 1940s. This suggests that colonialism by itself may not have had so negative an impact as dependency theory indicates.

Cutting economic ties with developed capitalist countries, as dependency theory recommends, is more likely to inhibit than expedite the development of developing countries. To be sure, China and the Soviet Union were not much hurt by a policy of economic self-sufficiency because they had large resource bases, but self-sufficiency is often costly for small countries (Nafziger 1990, 94). North Korea suffered from the strict policy of self-sufficiency. In contrast, South Korea has experienced extremely high rates of economic growth and decreased income inequality since the 1960s (although inequality has grown since 1980) while highly dependent on trade, assistance, and investment from the United States, Japan, and other countries.

Dependence has taken new forms in the last quarter of the twentieth century. Like any late developer, South Korea has perforce relied on technology transfer. Closer examination of this process, however, reveals a determined and largely successful effort to ensure that technology really does get transferred. For example, the manufacture of televisions, VCRs and microwave ovens in South Korea all began with the purchase by Korean firms of Japanese technology, with Japanese firms in each case withholding and retaining a key component. But,

putting their own scientists to work, the Korean firms in each case
developed the "missing" technology themselves, thus forcing the Japanese to cede the patent. Similar patterns are followed in the case of
pharmaceutical business with the USA.

A large debt is obviously risky, but South Korea's debt-service ratio
remains favorably low, and repayments have not so far been a major
problem. Rather, it is North Korea that suffers from a large foreign
debt. It is ironic that the self-reliance model of North Korea is more
vulnerable on dependency issues. South Korea deliberately chose to go
for loans rather than direct foreign investment, in order to keep Korean
hands on the development tiller. That is why South Korea became a
huge debtor country, but it certainly helped rapid and relatively independent development anyhow. Imports have always been reinvested
for export. Trade deficits declined during the last decade, and a final
trade surplus was achieved in 1986. Since then, the debt has decreased.

The solution to these problems is not to withdraw from a world
capitalist system, but rather to generate a more selective policy in
dealing with capitalist countries. Trade, economic aid, capital investments, and technological borrowing from developed countries should
be such that investment is directed into priority industries. South Korean economic growth was achieved with increasing "dependence" on
foreign trade with the U.S. and Japan, but a strong state could manage
to develop in spite of multinational corporations (MNCs), mandating
to local capital. The state has severely limited the entrance of MNCs
the South Korea; only joint ventures with local partners have been
permitted. The state preferred public and commercial loans to direct
investment, which was seriously restricted. The state monopolized
agricultural products, banks, financial institutions, railways, and communications. The state also runs many state industries including defense industries. Half of government revenues came from the public
sector. The state controlled local capital through banking and financial
institutions which were nationalized after the Japanese colonial period.
Discouraging foreign monopoly power, encouraging domestic enterprise, preventing heavy debt burdens, avoiding substantial technological dependence on outsiders, and protecting infant domestic industries
should all be part of this selective policy.

More importantly, the solution largely depends on the policy option
concerning domestic resources. Dependency theory has been inade-

quate in examining national and domestic structures which are more fundamental than the problems of external dependence. The self-reliant model of development needs to concentrate on heavy industry and agriculture rather than light and service industries. This imbalanced allocation of labor force and capital does not help development. It also entails an undue emphasis on motivating workers, or political surveillance of the entire people. Motivations to work decline in such a self-reliant system. These domestic elements which are important aspects of a self-reliant development have not been discussed by dependency theory.

The implication for dependency theory is that the theory is not only inadequate in explaining contemporary Korean development, but has been all but invalidated by the experiences of two Koreas. Regarding economic development, South Korea as well as Taiwan, West Germany, and South Vietnam (in the past) have surpassed their socialist counterparts. Capitalist Third World development is possible even in the situation of dependence on foreign investment, aid, and trade. The state remained strong and protective for national development. Remarkable development was achieved despite many dependency risks. In the light of labor-intensive industries in which South Korea specialized at its take-off stage, modern, capital intensive firms do not seem invariably superior in terms of efficiency and growth potential. Outmoded equipment and technology did not place South Korea at a disadvantage. Even the new technology can be transferred by the dependent countries' investment in research and development and education.

A saving point of dependency theory is that a socialist alternative appears to effect more income-equalization than does capitalist development; income inequality is lower in North Korea than in South Korea. Yet, the level of income in North Korea is far lower than in South Korea. About half of the South Korean population enjoys a higher income than the highest of North Korea; average North Korean income corresponds to the lowest fifteen percent of South Korean income, and only seven percent of the South Korean population falls below the lowest level of North Korean income. Furthermore, the fact that relative inequality in South Korea is low compared with other developing countries, is another strong point indicating that Korean experience seriously weakens dependency theory.

From the perspective of modernization theorist, their prediction turned out to be right. They can point out the South Korean success vis-à-vis North Korean failure as a living proof that capitalism works; that integration into the world market, on the basis of comparative advantage, is the only way forward. However, there are numerous flaws in the explanation. Foreign capital was important, but the role of the South Korean state was equally important in the process of rapid economic growth. And, the state's guidance of the capitalist class and the state's exploitation of large proletarian workers are also among the reasons for the South Korean success that weaken a modernization explanation. The early success of North Korean development cannot be explained by this theory. Radical changes of political and institutional mechanisms are suggested as one of the sources that bring about rapid development in a relatively short period of time.

Moreover, high levels of social development did not create the basis of development as modernization theory posits. Social development has been achieved at the same pace in both South and North Korea regardless of the differences in the level of economic development. Certain social developments such as adult literacy, infant mortality, education, and health care do not appear to lead to economic development, as shown in the two Koreas' developmental processes. Political and institutional changes could be a factor to bring about social improvements in health care and infant mortality. On the other hand, high levels of social development in education and adult literacy could be diverted into the wasteful indoctrination of political ideology.

Bureaucratic-authoritarianism and dependent development theories do not address what they call the "comparison effect," that the two Koreas are mutually stimulated by awareness of each other. Bureaucratic-authoritarianism has explained that a "deeper" level of industrialization accompanies the authoritarian state in Third World development. But, authoritarian transformation could take place not only at the initial stage of this "deeper" level, but also at the stage of economic downturn. Both Koreas had experienced authoritarian transformation in 1972. In South Korea, economic development was on the rise and it needed social stability to attract more international capital when it entered a deeper level of expansive development, which necessitated a more authoritarian state (O'Donnell 1979, 285–318). On the other hand, North Korean economic growth slowed down during the 1960s.

The stagnant economy, driven by mass mobilization, needed revitalization through the introduction of Western capital, which led, in turn, to further authoritarianism and surveillance to prevent popular exposure to the external world.

In addition, Bureaucratic-Authoritarian theory overlooked the so-called "comparison effect" in the authoritarian transformation of the two Korean states. The authoritarian adaptation of both Koreas in 1972 was in part a result of the awareness of each other. North Korea was stimulated by the more rapid economic development of South Korea in the late 1960s, where substantial development was achieved with the help of Western technology and capital. South Korea needed more extensive control in introducing a mass mobilization measure, the New Community Movement, which was stimulated by the nature of early success of North Korean development bases on mass mobilization techniques. South Korea's timely introduction of the mass mobilization measure during the 1970s contributed significantly to its success.

The success of mass mobilization technique is the area that dependent development theory generally overlooked. The theory explains Third World development within the framework of the triple alliance between the state, local capital, and multinationals. Nor does this theory focus on the structure of resource allocation including labor force, military expense, and trade.

The two Koreas' developments are viewed as unique experiences from general theoretical frameworks. It is not sufficient to view the countries' development simply in terms of any one model. All the extant modes of explanation of Korea's development emphasize only a particular aspect of the total process. They may each be valid to some degree, but they do not present an entire picture of the complex nature of Korean development. The exclusionary theories need modification in the light of special historical and sociological circumstances found in the Korean experiences. In this way, the special circumstance of any one nation may help put in perspective current sociological theories about development.

The overall implication of this book for the sociological theories of Third World development is that capitalism works for national development in Third World situations. Communism or socialism could work for income equalization, but certainly not for generating national development in Third World countries. The combined framework of a

Marxist theory of market expansion by the bourgeoisie and resulting
working-class exploitation, and a theory of state domination appears to
provide reasonable explanations for the divergence of the two Koreas'
developments. Unlike dependency theory or dependent development
theory, the primary agent in South Korean development was not the
multinationals, but the domestic bourgeoisie as classical Marxist theory maintained. However, unlike modernization theory, bourgeois entrepreneurship is not the sole motivation. Rather, the state guided the
domestic bourgeoisie affording them sufficient capital and guarantee-
ing a low price of labor. The state even employed mass-mobilization
measures.

In a sense, Marxist explanations could be applied to the communist
development of North Korea. Although national income is equally
distributed "among" North Koreans, there has been growing inequality between "material" production and private consumption. The living standard in North Korea has not increased much since 1970, despite the fact that the state claims the increase of the nation's "material"
production defined by most Communist countries as national development. We had seen this deep-seated problem in the Communist development of Eastern Europe. The real problem here is not just material
deprivation but also relative deprivation between what people produce
and what they really get.

The situation in North Korea is somewhat different from the experience of East European communism. In North Korea, economic development was driven by mobilizing people toward the "battle against
colonialism and imperialism." The experience of colonialism and civil
war legitimizes North Korean regime, and makes the regime last longer
than those of East European countries.

The relevance of the Korean development experience to the Third
World is equivocal because of the two Koreas' highly specific experiences. Although the two Korean models are envied by many developing countries, they do not dare to follow them, because there seem
to be several features which make it hard to imagine the Korean models
being repeated. First, there is the specific geopolitical situation of
South Korea, which led to its receiving large amounts of U.S. aid, on
unrepeatable favorable terms and at a stage in the country's development which has not been duplicated elsewhere (with the marginal

exception of Taiwan). Second, there are the spin-offs from the Korean War, the U.S. military presence, and the Vietnam War. Third, there is the degree of political and social control, which in turn springs partly from the overall situation of confrontation with the North, as well as from the degree of U.S. backing available because of the strategic considerations involved. Finally, a strong state which played an important role is a result of the merging of several authoritarian traditions: Confucianism, the Japanese colonial state, and the authoritarian militarized regime.

The North Korean model, as a total entity, or even purely as an economy, is not a model for the rest of the Third World. Among the specific features which would need to be confronted are: the absence of neocolonialism; no brain drain, at least to a metropolitan country; no external commitments; forcible de-linking from the world economy; the fact that North Korea was the only such state in the socialist camp at a given period and that its economy was susceptible to Soviet-style industrialization. The North Korean regime presents itself and its president, Kim Il Sung, as leaders of the whole of the Third World. Yet there is very little evidence of other Third World states really emulating North Korea. It may have contributed a credible concept, nay even an ideology, of autarkic Stalinism and *juche* as an enormously popular concept on the left wing of the Third World. And, North Korea's defense burden has been so high that no country can adopt it.

South Korean development has been more impressive and feasible than North Korean. The South Korean model of development has been attractive to some envious countries. The "Look East" policy of Malaysia, for example, explicitly states its interest in the South Korean experience. Malaysia's so far unsuccessful experience with its "Look East" tactic limits the possibilities for exporting a South Korean model. The North Korean model has been applied only in a very limited sense. The model can be attractive in certain specific areas, particularly in agriculture and irrigation. In this respect, the North Korean experience is valued by states like Tanzania and Zimbabwe (Halliday 1987, 43). The evidence is that many North Korean aid teams in these fields have done a good job and that their help has been appreciated. Yet, the feasibility of a North Korean development model is far weaker than that of South Korea.

Prospect for the 1990s: Unified Development?

Before the German union recently revealed the difficulties involved in a nation's unification, simple statistics were impressive: as a unified nation, Korea would be the world's twelfth most abundant country in labor force and the world's twentieth wealthiest country in size of the economy; both will be the best markets for each other; the wasteful military defense burdens which combined are the world's fifth largest in military personnel and the thirteenth in military spending, will be diverted to the construction of a powerful economy. The German unification so far shows that a significant portion of the labor force on the Communist side will be faced with unemployment, that most companies fail to survive in the free-market environment, and that the communist camp loses most of their customers (Protzman 1990).

However, unification will be mutually beneficial in the long run. Military tension will be reduced. More importantly, the hatred and conflict caused by the division will be lessened and morale will be restored in the unified land.

Based on the present status of development, there will be a wider gap in the economic situation of the two Koreas in the 1990s. Economic growth in both Koreas will be slower than now, however. At the same time, there will be some progress toward mutual economic exchange between the two, which may be operating as a crucial factor for the breakthrough of mutual development in the next century. All the factors that have influenced and shaped the two Korean developments will continue to affect the future economic situation. All these variables are important for future economic development, because the major change of any one of these variables could interrupt economic growth. Yet, I regard them as peripheral just because I assume they are not going to be changed dramatically within the next decade.

The international political arena in which the two Koreas compete is rapidly moving from a loose bipolar system (U.S. and Japan, vs. China and USSR) to a multipolar system. Both Koreas will have closer relationships with all of the four superpowers in the multipolar system. The balance of the four powers in Northeast Asia will remain without any significant change during the 1990s, because the interest of the four powers are agreed on the present status of the division.

Military build-ups have been one of the major burdens in economic development of both Koreas. North Korea has, in particular, suffered by spending a huge portion of GNP in national defense—over 20% of GNP annually. Given the continued efforts by both sides to obtain increasingly sophisticated weaponry, the prospects for arms control for the next decade look poor. But, North Korea recently reduced defense expenditure from 31.0 percent in 1987 to 12.2 and 12.1 percent from the total government budget in 1988 and 1989, respectively. It is expected that this trend will be continued for the next few years in order to restore the sluggish economy. The major erruption of a civil war into the future Korean economic development is not likely to occur.

The American military presence in South Korea profoundly affects political alignments in both the South and the North. It lightens the military burden of South Korea. It also impedes democratization in the South, and in the North it strengthens xenophobic hard liners centered in the military who are engaged in a growing policy struggle with more moderate, outward-looking elements within the ruling Workers Party. The U.S. military withdrawal from South Korea is an important factor for the future development of both South and North Korea.

The international economic situation in the next decade will become unfavorable for both Koreas. It will affect North Korea more unfavorably than South. For North Korea, the current cold climate from all capitalist countries except Japan will remain without any significant change unless there is a radical shift. South Korea is faced with protectionism. According to some calculations, nearly 40 percent of Korean exports are currently subject to qualitative barriers (Patri 1988, 59). In the past, fortunately, the impact of protection on Korean trade has been more positive than negative, since in a number of important cases foreign protection restrained Korea's competitors more than Korean exports themselves.

It is unlikely that this fortuitous position can be preserved if global protectionism intensifies. Then, economic growth of both Koreas will be slower than now. Both governments are well aware of the difficulty. North Korea announced its Third Seven-Year Plan (1987-93), which envisages annual growth rates of 7.9 percent—a scaling back from past plans, such as the 9.6 percent annual growth targets. Estimates of North Korea's record are about 3 percent at best and almost zero at worst. South Korea also is planning to lower the annual growth targets for the next ten years into the average around 6 percent; GNP growth was around 10 percent in the past two years.

The international liberal situation and its capacity of control will be certainly a critical factor for future North Korean development. Changes of ideological commitment in North Korean political leadership seem unlikely. The way North Korea has developed fits Parsons' functional framework of society. Kim Il Sungism functions as an ultimate value for North Korean society. This does not appear to face collapse within a decade without any serious external cause. Within the Parsons' functional framework, critical moments or changes come from outside the system. An international liberal environment to challenge Kim Il Sungism, rather than domestic elements, will play a critical role in future North Korean development. The recent opening of diplomatic relations between the Soviet Union and South Korea perplexed North Korea in this respect. It will probably push North Korea to approach Japan and the United States more seriously than ever.

Critical factors for South Korean development will come from inside society. Workers' strikes and student demonstrations will play a critical role in future South Korean development. Income inequality already created the severe problems of workers' strikes. In 1989, workers' strikes reduced the export surplus to half of 1988's, and in early 1990 it caused negative economic growth, though it was reversed recently. Increasingly intense protests by university students and the democratic movement by Christian groups are creating radical nationalism. Income distribution and workers' strikes will be a burden of future development.

The dialogue between the two Koreas and mutual economic exchange between the two Koreas will be another critical factor in the economic development of both Koreas in the next ten years. For more than twenty years the two Koreas concentrated exclusively on their confrontation, totally rejected each other's legitimacy as governments, and had no contact whatsoever until they abruptly began to talk to each other in the early 1970s. All the possible "talks" have been suggested and tried from Red Cross talks, to a Prime Minister's meeting, Tripartite talks, Bilateral talks, Parliamentary talks, Olympic talks, and Tripartite Military talks. So far, they have operated less toward making genuine progress toward unification than in attempts to gain advantage in their rivalry. The liberal environment compels North Korea to make substantive progress in the dialogue with South Korea to impress the United States and Japan favorably, to expand foreign trade, and to compete more effectively with South Korea in the international community. As described above, the South and North Korean economies appear to complement each other. South Korea is better in labor-intensive industries such as textiles, clothing, luggage, wigs, etc., and in high technology. North Korea is stronger in agriculture, fishing, mining, and the machine tool industry. Both are excellent world ship-builders.

Although mutual economic exchange will also be a critical factor, the chance that a major breakthrough will occur between the two Koreas within the next ten years is slim, because neither side considers economic exchange as a major issue of unification. North Korea stresses a political solution first, while South Korea maintains a nonpolitical one. A North Korean policy calling for a "Democratic Confederal Republic of Koryo" (DCRK) propose to establish a supragovernment above the current two governments while maintaining the current social and political systems of the two Koreas in the present status. South Korea is trying to establish nonpolitical relations first. Cooperation begins in the area of nonpolitical transactions such as postal exchange, cultural, and academic interchange, free travel, and sports exchange, and then the two Koreas can gradually move toward more political and substantial reconciliations and cooperations between them. Neither suggests the approach of economic exchange first as a major issue.

Given stable condition of the international political balance of forces and domestic military strength, South Korea must face the internal problems of workers' and students' demands in order to ensure further development. On the other hand, North Korea integrated to the greatest extent by the ultimate value of Kim Il Sungism must solve the problem of introducing international capital, including that of Japan and the United States, which in turn may endanger its supreme values. The stagnation of the North Korean economy and the economic difficulties in South Korea caused by international protectionism and rising demands from workers are likely to encourage mutual economic exchange between South and North Korea in the next decade. North Korea will be the primary market of light industries, consumer goods, and construction for South Korea, and South Korea will be the cheap and able source of capital and technology for North Korea. In the next decade, it will establish peaceful coexistence at least, if not full-scale integration. The increase of mutual exchange in the 1990s will be the solid base for the full integration of the Korean nation in the coming century.

References

Nafziger, E. Wayne. 1990. *The Economics of Developing Countries*. 2nd ed. Englewood Cliff, NJ: Prentice Hall.

O'Donnell, Guillermo. 1979. "Tensions in the Bureaucratic-Authoritarian state and the question of democracy." Pp. 285-318 in David Collier (ed.), *The New Authoritarianism in Latin America*. Princeton, N.J.: Princeton University Press.

Petri, Peter A. 1988. "Korea's export niche: Origins and prospects." *World Development*, 16(1):47-63.

Protzman, Ferdinand. 1990. "East Germany's economy far sicker than expected." *New York Times*, 20 September 1990.

Bibliography

Capitalist Development

Alavi, Hamza and Teodor Shanin (eds.). 1982. *Introduction to the Sociology of "Developing Societies."* New York: Monthly Review Press.

Amin, Samir et al. 1982. *Dynamics of Global Crisis.* New York: Monthly Review Press.

_____. 1977. "Self-reliance and the new economic order," *Monthly Review*, 29 (3):1–21.

Bachrach, Peter. 1980. *The Theory of Democratic Elitism: A Critique.* Washington, D.C.: Universal Press of America.

Bendix, Reinhard. 1974. *Nation-Building and Citizenship.* Berkeley: University of California Press.

Berger, Peter L. 1987. *In Search of An East Asian Development Model.* New Brunswick, N.J.: Transaction Publishers.

Boolen, Kenneth A. 1979. "Political democracy and the timing of development." *American Sociological Review* 44:572–87.

_____. 1983. "World system position, dependency, and democracy: the cross-national evidence." *American Sociological Review* 48:468–479.

Boolen, Kenneth A. and Robert W. Jackman. 1985. "Political democracy and the size distribution of incomes." *American Sociological Review* 50:438–457.

Bornschier, V., C. Chase-Dunn and R. Rubinson. 1978. "Cross-national evidence of the effects of foreign investment and aid on economic growth and inequality: a survey of findings and a reanalysis." *American Journal of Sociology*, 84:651:83.

Bradshaw, York W. 1985. "Dependent development in Black Africa: A cross-national study." *American Sociological Review*, 50:195–207.

Brenner, Robert. 1977. "The origins of capitalist development: A critique of neo-Smithiam Marxism," *New Left Review*, 104:25–92.

Buick, Adam and John Crump. 1986. *State Capitalism: The Wages System under New Management.* New York: St. Martin's Press.

Cardoso, Fernando Henrique. 1973. "Associated-dependent development: theoretical and practical implications." Pp. 142–76 in Alfred Stepan (ed.), *Authoritarian Brazil: Origins, Policies, and Future.* New Haven: Yale University Press.

Cardoso, Fernando H. and Enzo Faletto. 1979. *Dependency and Development in Latin America.* Berkeley: University of California Press.

Chase-Dunn, Christopher. 1975. "The effects of international economic dependence on development and inequality." *American Sociological Review* 40:720–39.

Chase-Dunn, Christopher and Richard Rubinson. 1979. "Cycles, trends, and new departures in world-system development." Pp. 276–96 in John Meyer and Michael Hannan (eds.), *National Development and the World System: Educational, Economic, and Political Change, 1950–1970*. Chicago: University of Chicago Press.

Chilcote, Ronald H. and Dale L. Johnson (eds.). 1983. *Theories of Development: Mode of Production or Dependency?* Beverly Hill: Sage Publications.

Chodak, Szymon. 1973. *Societal Development*. New York: Oxford University Press.

Collier, David (ed.). 1979. *The New Authoritarianism in Latin America*. Princeton, NJ: Princeton University Press.

Coutler, Philip O. 1975. *Social Mobilization and Liberal Democracy*. Lexington, MA: Lexington Books.

Cumings, Bruce. 1987. "The origins and development of the northeast Asian political economy: Industrial sectors, product cycles, and political consequences." Pp. 44–83 in F. Deyo (ed.), *The Political Economy of the New Asian Industrialism*. New York: Cornell University Press.

Delacroix, Jacques and Charles Ragin. 1978. "Modernizing institutions, mobilization, and Third World development: a cross-national study." *American Journal of Sociology* 84:123–50.

_____. 1981. "Structural blockage: a cross-national study of economic dependency, state efficacy, and underdevelopment." *American Journal of Sociology* 86:1311–47.

Deyo, Frederic C. (ed.). 1987. *The Political Economy of the New Asian Industrialism*. New York: Cornell University Press.

Dobb, Mourice. 1963. *Studies in the Development of Capitalism*. New York: International.

Donnelly, Jack. 1984. "Human rights and development: complementary or competing concerns?" *World Politics* 36:255–83.

Duvall, Raymond and John Freeman. 1981. "The state and dependent capitalism." *International Studies Quarterly* 25:99–118.

Eisenstadt, S.N. 1966. *Modernization: Protest and Change*. New Jersey: Prentice-Hall, Inc.

Evans, Peter. 1987. "Class, state, and dependence in East Asia: Lessons for Latin Americanists." Pp. 203–226 in F. Deyo (ed.), *The Political Economy of the New Asian Industrialism*. New York: Cornell Univ. Press.

_____. 1979. *Dependent Development: The Alliance of Multinational, State, and Local Capital in Brazil*. Princeton, New Jersey: Princeton University Press.

_____. 1977. "Multinationals, state-owned corporations, and the transformation of imperialism: a Brazilian case study." *Economic Development and Cultural Change* 26:43–64.

Evans, Peter and Michael Timberlake. 1980. "Dependence, Inequality, and the growth of tertiary: a comparative analysis of less developed countries." *American Sociological Review* 45:531–52.

Felix, David. 1965. "Monetarists, structuralists, and import-substituting industrialization: A critical appraisal." *Studies in Comparative International Development*, 1:137–153.

Fidel, Kenneth (ed.). 1975. *Militarism in Developing Countries*. New Brunswick: Transaction Publishers.

Frank, Andre G. 1969. *Latin America: Underdevelopment or Revolution*. New York: Monthly Review Press.

_____. 1973. *On Capitalist Underdevelopment*. New York: Oxford University Press.

_____. 1978. *World Accumulation 1492–1789*. New York: Monthly Review Press.

_____. 1980. *Crisis: In the World Economy*. New York: Holmes & Meier Publishers.

_____. 1981. *Crisis: In the Third World*. New York: Holmes & Meier Publishers.

Gerschenkron, Alexander. 1965. *Economic Backwardness in Historical Perspective*. New York: Frederick A. Praeger.

Huntington, S. P. 1968. *Political Order in Changing Societies*. New Haven: Yale University Press.

_____. 1984. "Will more countries become democratic?" *Political Science Quarterly* 99:193–218.

Huntington, S. P. and Joan M. Nelson. 1976. *No Easy Choice: Political Participation in Developing Countries*. Cambridge, Mass.: Harvard University Press.

Jackman, Robert W. 1975. *Politics and Social Equality: A Comparative Analysis*. New York: Wiley.

_____. 1982. "Dependence on foreign investment and economic growth in the third world." *World Politics* 34:175–96.

Kaufman, Robert R., Harry I. Chernotsky and Daniel S. Geller. 1975. "A preliminary test of the theory of dependency." *Comparative Politics* 7:303–30.

Kourvetaris, George A. and Betty A. Dobratz (eds.). 1977. *World Perspectives in the Sociology of the Military*. New Brunswick: Transaction Publishers.

Krueger, Anne. 1979. *The Development Role of the Foreign Sector and Aid*. Cambridge, MA: Harvard University Press.

Laux, Jeanne Kirk and Maureen Appel Molot. 1988. *State Capitalism: Public Enterprise in Canada*. Ithaca: Cornell University Press.

Lipset, Seymour M. 1960. *Political Man*. Garden City: Anchor Books.

Lipsitz, L. 1967. "Working-class authoritarianism: a re-evaluation." *American Sociological Review* 30:103–109.

Lipson, Leslie M. 1985. "The philosophy of democracy—can its contradictions be reconciled?" *Journal of International Affairs* 38:151–160.

Meier, Gerald M. and Robert E. Baldwin. 1957. *Economic Development: Theory, History, Policy*. New York: Wiley.

Michels, Robert. 1974. *First Lectures in Political Sociology*. New York: Arno Press.

Moore, Barrington. 1966. *Social Origins of Dictatorship and Democracy*. Boston: Beacon Press.

Myrdal, Gunner. 1970. *The Challenge of World Poverty: A World Anti-Poverty Program in Outline*. New York: University of California Press.

Nafzigh, E. Wayne. 1990. *The Economics of Developing Countries*. 2nd ed. Englewood Cliff: Prentice Hall.

Nishimizu, Mieko and John M. Page, Jr. 1987. "Economic policies and productivity change in industry: An international comparison." Mimeo. Washington, D.C.: World Bank.

O'Donnell, Guillermo A. 1973. *Modernization and Bureaucratic-Authoritarianism*. Berkeley: University of California Press.

———. 1979. "Tensions in the bureaucratic-authoritarian state and the question of democracy." Pp. 285–318 in D. Collier (1979), *The New Authoritarianism in Latin America*. New Jersey: Princeton University Press.

Offee, Claus. 1985. *Disorganized Capitalism*. Cambridge, MA: MIT Press.

Olsen, Mancur, Jr. 1963. "Rapid Growth as a Destabilizing Force." *Journal of Economic History* 23:529–52.

Olsen, Marvin E. and Glenn Firebaugh. 1975. "Transforming socioeconomic modernization into national political development." Annual Conference of the American Sociological Association Meeting in San Franciso, CA.

Portes, Alejandro. 1976. "On the sociology of national development: theories and issues." *American Journal of Sociology* 82:55–85.

Powell, Jr., G. Bingham. 1982. *Contemporary Democracies*. Cambridge: Harvard University Press.

Pye, Lucian W. 1966. *Aspects of Political Development*. Boston: Little, Brown and Company.

Roberts, Bryan R. 1979. *Cities of Peasants: the Political Economy of Urbanization in the Third World*. Beverly Hills, CA: Sage Publications.

Schumpeter, Joseph A. 1950. *Capitalism, Socialism, and Democracy*. 3rd edition. New York: Harper & Row, Publishers.

Simpson, M. 1972. "Authoritarianism and education: a comparative approach." *Sociometry* 35:223–234.

Smelser, Neil J. 1973. "Toward a theory of modernization." Pp. 268–84 in Etzioni and Etzioni-Halevy (eds.), *Social Change: Sources, Patterns, and Consequences*. New York: Basic Books.

Smith, Arthur K. 1969. "Socioeconomic development and political democracy." *Midwest Journal of Political Science*, 30:95–125.

Snyder, David and Edward L. Kick. 1979. "Structural position in the world system and economic growth, 1955–1970: multiple-network analysis of transnational interactions." *American Journal of Sociology* 84:1096–1126.

Stepan, Alfred. 1978. *The State and Society*. Princeton, N.J.: Princeton University Press.

Stumpp, Mark, Robert M. Marsh, and Deborah A. Lake. 1978. "The effect of international economic dependence on development: a critique." *American Sociological Review* 43:600–604.

Timberlake, Michael and Kirk Williams. 1984. "Dependence, political exclusion, and government repression: some cross-national evidence." *American Sociological Review* 49:141–46.

Tucker, Robert C. (ed.). 1978. *The Marx-Engels Reader*. 2nd ed. New York: W.W. Norton and Company, Inc.

Wallerstein, Immanuel. 1989. *The Modern World-System III. The Second Era of Great Expansion of the Capitalist World-Economy, 1730–1840s*. New York: Academic Press.

_____. 1984. *The Politics of World-Economy*. New York: Cambridge University Press.

_____. 1983. *Historical Capitalism*. London: Verso Editions.

_____. 1979. *The Capitalist World-Economy*. Cambridge: Cambridge University Press.

_____. 1974. *The Modern World System: Capitalist Agriculture and the Origins of the European World-Economy in the Sixteenth Century*. New York: Academic Press.

Weede, Erich. 1983. "The impact of democracy on economic growth: some evidence from cross-national analysis." *Kyklos* vol.36, no.1:21–39.

Williams, Kirk and Michael Timberlake. 1984. "Structured inequality, conflict, and control: a cross-national test of the threat hypothesis." *Social Forces* 63:414–32.

Zeitlin, M. 1967. "Revolutionary workers and individual liberties." *American Journal of Sociology* 72:619–632.

Socialist Development

Bergmann, Theodor. 1977. *The Development Models of India, the Soviet Union and China*. Amsterdam: Van Gorcum.

Bideleux, Robert. 1985. *Communism and Development*. New York: Methuen & Co.

Bottomore, Tom. 1984. *Sociology and Socialism*. Sussex: Wheatsheaf Books.

Fagen, Richard R., Carmen Diana Deere, and Jose Luis Coraggio (eds.). 1986. *Transition and Development:Problems of Third World Socialism*. New York: Monthly Review Press.

Hollander, Paul. 1983. *The Many Faces of Socialism:Comparative Sociology of Politics*. New Brunswick, N.J.: Transaction Publishers.

_____. 1975. "Comparing socialist systems: Ends and results." Pp. 421–36 in Mesa-Lago and Beck (eds.), *Comparative Socialist Systems: Essays on Politics and Economics*. Pittsburgh: UCIS Publications.

Jameson, Kenneth P. and Charles K. Wilber. 1981. "Socialism and Development:Editor's Introduction," *World Development*, 9(9/10):803–811.

Jeffries, Ian. 1990. *A Guide to the Socialist Economies*. New York: Routledge.

Jones, T. Anthony. 1983. "Models of socialist development," *International Journal of Comparative Sociology*, 24(1/2):86–99.

Kautsky, John H. 1968. *Communism and the Politics of Development*. New York: John Wiley & Sons, Inc.

Lane, David. 1976. *The Socialist Industrial State: Towards a Political Sociology of State Socialism*. Boulder, CO: Westview Press.

Laqueur, Walter. 1989. *Soviet Realities: Culture and Politics from Stalin to Gorbachev*. New Brunswick, N.J.: Transaction Publishers.

Littlejohn, Gary. 1988. "Central planning and market relations in socialist societies," *The Journal of Development Studies*, 24(4):75–101.

Mesa-Lago, Carmelo and Carl Beck (eds.). 1975. *Comparative Socialist Systems: Essays on Politics and Economics*. Pittsburgh: UCIS Publications.

Salfadori, Massimo (ed.). 1968. *Modern Socialism*. New York: Walker and Company.

Schapiro, Leonard B. 1970. *The Communist Party of the Soviet Union*. 2nd ed. New York: Vintage Books.

TIME. 1990. "Slaughter in the Street," by Bruce W. Nelan. 1 January 1990, pp. 34–37.

White, Gorden, Robin Murray and Christine White (eds.). 1983. *Revolutionary Socialist Development in the Third World*. Lexington: The University Press of Kentucky.

White, Stephen, John Gardner and George Schopflin. 1982. *Communist Political Systems: An Introduction*. New York: St. Martin's Press.

Wilczynski, Jozef. 1982. *The Economics of Socialism*. 4th ed. London: George Allen & Unwin.

Wiles, P.J.D. 1962. *The Political Economy of Communism*. Massachusetts: Harvard University Press.

Wiles, P.J.D. (ed.). 1971. *The Prediction of Communist Economic Performance*. London: The Cambridge University Press.

Comparative Development

Badie, Bertrand and Pierre Birnbaum. 1983. *The Sociology of the State*. Trans. by Arthur Goldhammer. Chicago: The University of Chicago Press.

Beling, Willard A. and George O. Totten. 1970. *Developing Nations: Quest for a Model*. New York: Van Nostrand Reinhold Company.

Bergmann, Theodor. 1977. *The Development Models of India, the Soviet Union and China*. Amsterdam: Van Gorcum.

Bergson, Abram. 1978. *Productivity and the Social System: The USSR and the West*. Cambridge: Harvard Univ. Press.

Chilcote, Ronald H. 1984. *Theories of Development and Underdevelopment*. Boulder, CO: Westview Press.

Chirot, Daniel. 1977. *Social Change in the Twentieth Century*. New York: Harcourt Brace Jovanovich, Inc.

Coleman, Kenneth E. and Daniel N. Nelson. 1984. "State Capitalism, State Socialism and Politicization of Workers." The Carl Beck Paper in *Russian and East European Studies*. No. 304. Pittsburgh, PA: Russian and East European Studies Program, University of Pittsburgh.

Ebenstein, William and Edwin Fogelman. 1985. *Today's Isms:Communism, Fascism, Capitalism, Socialism*. Seoul: United Publishing & Promotion Co.

Ehrlich, Eva. 1985. "The size structure of manufacturing establishments and enterprises: an international comparison. *Journal of Comparative Economics* 9:267–295.

Gastil, Raymond D. 1982. *Freedom in the World: Political Rights and Civil Liberties*. New York: Freedom House.

_____. 1985. "The past, present and future of democracy." *Journal of International Affairs* 38:161–179.

_____. 1988. *Freedom in the World, 1987–88*. New York: Freedom House.

Giddens, Anthony. 1987. *Social Theory and Modern Sociology*. Cambridge: Polity Press.

_____. 1984. *The Constitution of Society*. Berkeley: University of California Press.

_____. 1981. *A Contemporary Critique of Historical Materialism*. Berkeley: University of California Press.

_____. 1973. *The Class Structure of the Advanced Societies*. London: Hutchinson & Co.

Giddens, Anthony and David Held (eds.). 1982. *Classes, Power, and Conflict*. Berkeley: University of California Press.

Goldsworthy, David. 1984. "Political power and socio-economic development." *Political Studies* 32:551–569.

Horowitz, Irving Louis. 1982. *Beyond Empire and Revolution*. New York: Oxford University Press.

_____. 1977. "Social Welfare, State Power, and the Limits to Equity." Pp. 1–18 in Irving L. Horowitz (ed.), *Equity, Income, and Policy: Comparative Studies in Three Worlds of Development*. New York: Praeger Publishers.

_____. 1972. *Three Worlds of Development*. New York: Oxford Univ. Press.

Ka, Chin-Ming and Mark Selden. 1986. "Original accumulation, equity and late industrialization: the cases of socialist China and capitalist Taiwan." *World Development* 14: 1293–1310.

Lipset, Seymour Martin. 1977. "Observations on Economic Equity and Social Class." Pp. 278–86 in Irving L. Horowitz (ed.), *Equity, Income, and Policy: Comparative Studies in Three Worlds of Development*. New York: Praeger Publishers.

Matejko, Alexander J. 1986. *Comparative Work Systems: Ideologies and Reality in Eastern Europe*. New York: Praeger Publishers.

_____. 1974. *Social Change and Stratification in Eastern Europe: An Interpretive Analysis of Poland and Her Neighbor*. New York: Praeger Publishers.

Morrison, Christian. 1984. "Income Distribution in East European and Western Countries." *Journal of Comparative Economics* 8:121–138.

Nisbet, Robert A. 1969. *Social Change and History*. New York: Oxford Univ. Press.

Olsen, Marvin E. 1981. "Comparative political sociology." *International Journal of Comparative Sociology*, 22:1–2, 1982.

Pryor, Frederic L. 1968. *Public Expenditures in Communist and Capitalist Nations*. Homewood, IL: Richard D. Irwin Inc.

Ragin, Charles. 1981. "Comparative Sociology and Comparative Method." *International Journal of Comparative Sociology* 22:102–120.

Schumpeter, Joseph A. 1950. *Capitalism, Socialism and Democracy*. 3rd ed. New York: Harper & Row, Publishers.

Shulman, Marshall D. (ed.). 1986. *East-West Tension in the Third World*. New York: W.W. Norton & Company.

Sik, Ota. 1985. "Comparison of the development of productive forces in countries with different economic system. *Korea & World Affairs*, 9:307–319.

Skocpol, Theada (ed.). 1984. *Vision and Method in Historical Sociology*. Cambridge: Cambridge Univ. Press.

Weede, Erich. 1982. "The effects of democracy and socialist strength on the size distribution of income." *International Journal of Comparative Sociology* 23:151–165.

Weiner, Myron and Samuel P. Huntington (eds.). 1987. *Understanding Political Development: An Analytic Study*. Boston: Little, Brown.

Wilczynski, Jozef. 1983. *Industrial Relation in Planned Economies, Market Economies, and the Third World*. New York:St. Martin's Press, Inc.

_____. 1972. *Socialist Economic Development and Reforms*. New York: Praeger Publishers Inc.

Wiles, P.J.D. 1977. *Economic Institutions Compared*. Oxford: Basil Blackwell.

South Korea

Amsden, Alice H. 1989. *Asia's Next Giant: South Korea and Late Industrialization*. New York: Oxford University Press.

Barone, Charles A. 1983. "Dependency, marxist theory, and salvaging the idea of capitalism in South Korea." *Review of Radical Political Economies*, vol.15, no.1:43–67.

Bunge, Frederica M. (ed.). 1982. *South Korea: A Country Study*. Washington, D.C. American University.

Business America. 1983. "Korea:economy set for recovery: U.S. becomes top supplier." by Deborah Lamb and Daniel Duvall. 21 Feb 1983, p.39.

Choi, Jang Jip. 1983. Interest Conflict and Political Control in South Korea: A Study of Labor Unionism Manufacturing Industries. Ph. D. Dissertation in Univ. of Chicago.

Choi, Yearn Hong and Dong Hyun Kim. 1989. "Korea-U.S. trade friction: Content analysis of the Chosun Ilbo, Korea Times, Washington Post, and New York Times," *Korea Observer* 20(4):507–35.

Cole, David C. and Princeton N. Lyman. 1971. *Korean Development: The Interplay of Politics and Economics*. Cambridge, Mass.: Harvard Univ. Press.

Euh, Yoon-Dae and James C. Baker. 1990. *The Korean Banking System and Foreign Influence*. New York: Routledge.

Far Eastern Economic Review. 1988. "Talking about talks" by Mark Clifford. Vol.141. 4 August 1988, Pp. 14–15.

_____. 1988. "Reunification revived" by John McBeth. Vol.141. 14 July 1988. P19.

_____. 1984. "Rising tide of outrage." by Jae-Hoon Shim. Vol. 125. 19 July 1984. Pp.21–23.

_____. 1982. "Eye of Chun's needle." by Jae-Hoon Shim. Vol.118. 17–23 December 1982. P.17.

Frank, Charles R. Jr., Kwang Suk Kim, and Larry Westphal. 1975. *Foreign Trade Regimes and Economic Development: South Korea*. New York: National Bureau of Economic Research.

Hamilton, Clive. 1986. *Capitalist Industrialization in Korea*. Boulder, CO: Westview Press.

Hamilton, Clive and Richard Tanter. 1987. "The antinomies of success in South Korea." *Journal of International Affairs*, 41(1):63–89.

Han, Sungjoo. 1978. "South Korea's participation in the Vietnam conflict: An analysis of the U.S.-Korean alliance," *Orbis*, 21:893–912.

_____. 1974. The Failure of Democracy in South Korea. Berkeley, CA: University of California Press.

Hasan, Parvez. 1976. *Korea: Problems and Issues in a Rapid Growing Economy*. Baltimore: The Johns Hopkins Univ. Press.

Hinton, Harold C. 1983. *Korea under New Leardership: The Fifth Republic*. New York: Praeger.

Jones, Leroy P. and Il Sakong. 1980. *Government, Business, and Entrepreneurship in Economic Development: The Korean Case*. Cambridge, Mass.: Harvard Univ. Press.

Kang, T.W. 1989. *Is Korea the Next Japan?:Understanding the Structure, Strategy, and Tactics of America's Next Competitor*. New York: The Free Press.

Kim, Dae Jung. 1987. *Prison Writings*. Trans. by Sung-Il Choi and David R. McCann. Berkeley: University of California Press.

_____. 1985. *Mass-Participatory Economy: A Democratic Alternative for Korea*. Center for International Affairs: Harvard University.

Kim, Eun Mee. 1989. "Foreign capital in Korea's economic development, 1960–1985," *Studies in Comparative International Development*, 24(4):24–45.

Kim, Kwang Suk and Michael Roemer. 1979. *Growth and Structural Transformation*. Cambridge, Mass.: Harvard University Press.

Kim Kyong-Dong. 1987. "The distinctive features of South Korea's development." Pp. 197–219 in Peter L. Berger, *In Search of An East Asian Development Model*. New Jersey: Transaction Publishers.

_____. 1979. *Man and Society in Korea's Economic Growth: Sociological Studies*. Seoul, Korea: Seoul National University Press.

Kim, Kyong-Dong (ed.) 1987. *Dependency Issues in Korean Development: Comparative Perspectives*. Seoul, Korea: Seoul National University Press.

Kim, Se-Jin. 1971. *The Politics of Military Revolution in Korea*. Chapel Hill, North Carol.: University of North Carolina Press.

Koo, Hagen. 1990. "From farm to factory: Proletarianization in Korea," *American Sociological Review*, 55(5):669–81.

_____. 1987. "The interplay of states, social class, and world system in East Asian development: The case of South Korea and Taiwan." in F. Deyo (1987), *The Political Economy of the New Asian Industrialism*. New York: Cornell University Press.

Korea Development Institute. 1975. *Korea's Economy: Past and Present*. Seoul, Korea: Korea Development Institute.

Kuznets, Paul W. 1977. *Economic Growth and Structure in the Republic of Korea*. New Haven: Yale University Press.

Lau, Lawrence J. (ed.). 1986. *Models of Development: a Comparative Study of Economic Growth in South Korea and Taiwan*. San Francisco: ICS Press.

Lee, Chae-Jin. 1984. "South Korea in 1983: crisis management and political legitimacy." *Asian Survey*, 24:112–21.

_____. 1982. *U.S. Policy toward Japan and Korea: A Changing Influence Relationship*. New York: Praeger.

Lim, Hyun-Chin. 1985. *Dependent Development in Korea, 1963–1979*. Seoul, Korea: Seoul National Univ. Press.

Long, Don. 1979. "Repression and development in the periphery: South Korea," *Bulletin of Concerned Asian Scholars*, 9(20):26–41.

Mason, Edward S. et al. 1980. *The Economic and Social Modernization of the Republic of Korea*. Cambridge, MA: Harvard University Press.

Michell, Tony. 1988. *From a Developing to a Newly Industrialized Country: The Republic of Korea, 1961–82*. Geneva: International Labour Organization Publishers.

Nam, Koon Woo. 1989. *South Korean Politics: The Search for Political Consensus and Stability*. New York: University Press of America.

New York Times. 1988. "Hyundai's bid to move up in class," by John Holusha, 2 November 1988, pp. D1 and D9.

Paige, Glenn D. 1985. *The Korean People's Yearbook 1984–1985*. New York: St. Martin's Press.

Park, Chan Wook. 1988. "The 1988 National Assembly election in South Korea: The ruling party's loss of legislative majority," *Journal of Northeast Asian Studies*, 7(3):59–76.

Petri, Peter A. 1988. "Korea's export niche: Origins and prospects," *World Development*, 16(1):47–63.

Rees, David. 1981. *Crisis and Continuity in South Korea*. London: Institute for the Study of Conflict.

Rhee, Hang-Yul. 1983. "Third world debt and third world industrialization: the case study of Korea, Mexico and Brazil." *Korea and World Affairs*, 7:362:94.

Sanford, Dan C. 1990. *South Korea and the Socialist Countries: The Politics of Trade*. New York: St. Martin's Press.

Steinberg, David I. 1988. "Sociopolitical factors and Korea's future economic policies," *World Development*, 16(1):19–34.

TIME. 1983. "Economy and Business: roaring out of the doldrums." by Charles P. Alexander. 14 November 1983, p.82.

Wade, L.L. and B.S. Kim. 1978. *Economic Development of South Korea: The Political Economic of Success*. New York: Praeger.

North Korea

An, Tai Sung. 1983. *North Korea in Transition: From Dictatorship to Dynasty*.Westport, Conn.: Greenwood Press.

Brandt, Vincent S. R. 1983. "North Korea: anthropological speculation." *Korea and World Affairs* 7:617–28.

Brun, Ellen and Jacques Hersh. 1976. *Socialist Korea: A Case Study in the Strategy of Economic Development*. New York: Monthly Review Press.

Bunge, Frederica M. (ed.). 1981. *North Korea: A Country Study*. Washington, D.C.: Foreign Area Studies, The American University.

Cho, Myung-Hoon. 1989. *Booknyuk Ilgi* (Diary on the trip to the North). Seoul, Korea: Sanha Press.

Chun, Chin O. 1978. *Pyongyang between Peking and Moscow: North Korea's Involvement in the Sino-Soviet Dispute, 1958–1975*. Tuscaloosa, AL: University of Alabama Press.

Chung, Chong-Shik and Gahb-Chol Kim (eds.). 1980. *North Korean Communism: A Comparative Analysis*. Seoul: Research Center for Peace and Unification.

Chung, Joseph Sang-hoon. 1983. "Economic Policy in North Korea." in Scalapino and Kim (eds.), *North Korea Today: Strategic and Domestic Issues*. Berkeley: Institute of East Asian Studies, University of California.

_____. 1974. *The North Korean Economy: Structure and Development*. Stanford, Cal: Hoover Institution Press, Stanford University.

Do, Heung-Ryul. 1988. *"Bookhan sasipnyun"* (Forty years of North Korea: From land reform to the father-son succession). *Shin-Dong-A*, September 1988, pp.256–266.

Economist, The. 1984. "North Korea: Metamorphosis." Vol. 292. 15 September 1984, pp.75–76.

Far Eastern Economic Review. 1988. "Lip service to the Great Leader" by Darryl Gibson, 22 September 1988, p.17.

_____. 1988. "Default on time" by Anthony Rowley. Vol. 141. 14 July 1988, p.81.

_____. 1984. "Pride and paranoia mix in a paradoxical 'paradise.' " by Man Woo Lee. 2 February 1984, pp.25–27.

_____. 1984. "A nimble neutrality keeps Moscow and Peking as allies." by Mike Tharp. Vol. 123. 2 February 1984, pp.28–29.

_____. 1984. "Trying to keep pace with a showcase state." by Hikaru Kerns. Vol.123. 2 February 1984, pp.24–25.

_____. 1984. "Guerilla greybeards keep their grip in Pyongyang." by Jae-Hoon Shim. Vol.123. 2 February 1984, pp.28–29.

_____. 1984. "Pyongyang's military: a state of perpetual alert." by Paul Ensor. Vol.123. 2 February 1984, pp.26–27.

_____. 1984. "The two Kim's dream of peace." Vol.123. 2 February 1984, pp.30–31.

_____. 1982. "Big brother barks: North Korea's proclaimed self-reliance is undercut by detailed evidence published in a Soviet journal," by Ron Richard. 3 December 1982, pp.96–97.

Foreign Language Publishing House. 1977. *The Building of an Independent National Economy in Korea*. Pyongyang, Korea: FLPH.

_____. 1977. *The International Seminar on the Juche Idea*. Pyongyang, Korea: FLPH.

_____. 1975. *Our Party's Policy for the Building of an Independent National Economy*. Pyongyang, Korea: FLPH.

Halliday, Jon. 1983. "The North Korean enigma." Pp.114–154 in White, Murray and White (eds.), *Revolutionary Socialist Development in the Third World*. Lexington: The University Press of Kentucky.

_____. 1981. *"The North Korean model: Gaps and questions."* World Development,9(9/10):

Institute for Unification Affairs. 1989. *Bookhan kyungjae jaryojip* (Collected materials of North Korean economy). Seoul, Korea: Minjok Tongil Publishers.

Japanese Economic and Trade Research Organization. 1990. *The North Korean Economic and Trade Status, 1989*. Tokyo, Japan: JETRO.

Jeffries, Ian. 1990. "Democratic People's Republic of Korea." Pp. 261–270 in Ian Jeffries, *A Guide to the Socialist Economies*. New York: Routledge.

Kang, Thomas Hosuck. 1979. "Changes in the North Korean personality from Confucian to communist." Pp. 61–110 in Jae Kyu Park and Jung Gun Kim (eds.), *The Politics of North Korea*. Seoul, Korea: Kyungnam University Press.

Kihl, Young Whan. 1984. "North Korea in 1983: transforming the hermit kingdom?" *Asian Survey*, 24:100–1.

Kim, Il-pyong J. 1975. *Communist Politics in North Korea*. New York: Praeger.

Kim, Il Sung. 1960. *Selected Works*. Pyongyang, Korea: KWP Press.

Koh, Byung Chul. 1969. *The Foreign Policy of North Korea*. New York: Praeger.

Lee, Chong-sik. 1978. *The Korean Worker's Party: A Short History*. Stanford, Cal: Hoover Institution Press.

Lee, Chong-sik. (Trans. and ed.). 1977. *Materials on Korean Communism, 1945–1947*. Center for Korean Studies, Hawaii: University of Hawaii Press.

Lee, Mun Woong. 1976. *Rural North Korea under Communism: A Study of Sociological Change*. Houston: Rice University Special Studies.

Lee, Pong S. 1982. "The Korean People's Democratic Republic." in Peter Wiles (ed.), *The New Communist Third World*. New York: St. Martin's Press.

_____. 1972. "An Estimate of North Korea's National Income," *Asian Survey* 12 (6):518–526.

Lee, Sang-woo et. al. 1988. *Bookhan sasipnyun* (Forty years of North Korea). Seoul, Korea: Uleue Moonhwa Press.

Nam, Koon Woo. 1974. The North Korean Communist Leadership, 1945–1965: A Study of Factionalism and Political Consolidation. Tuscaloosa, AL: University of Alabama Press.

New York Times. 1979. "North Korea to discuss its debts with Japan." 18 July 1979.

_____. 1979. "North Korea to pay debts." 29 August 1979, p. D2.

New York Times Magazine. 1989. "Great Leader to Dear Leader," by Nicholas D. Kristof. 20 August 1989.

Pang, Hwan Ju. 1988. *Korea Review*. Pyongyang, Korea: FLPH.

Park, Byong-Ho. 1971. "Natural resources and industrial locations in South and North Korea." Pp. 476–513 in Asiatic Research Center in Korea

University, *International Conference on the Problem of Korean Unification, Report*. Seoul: Asiatic Research Center, Korea University.

Park, Jae Kyu and Jung Gun Kim (eds.). 1979. *The Politics of North Korea*. Seoul Korea: Kyungnam University Press.

Park, Jae Kyu, Byung Chul Koh, and Tae-Hwan Kwak (eds.). 1987. *The Foreign Relations of North Korea: New Perspectives*. Boulder, CO: Westview Press.

Perry, John Curtis. 1990. "Dateline North Korea: A communist holdout," *Foreign Policy*, 80:172–91.

Rees, David. 1976. *North Korea: Understanding in Truce*. London: Institute for the Study of Conflict.

Rinser, Louise. 1988. *Bookhan iyagi* (Stories on North Korea). Seoul, Korea: Hyungsung Press.

Scalapino, Robert A. (ed.). 1963. *North Korea Today*. New York: Frederick A. Praeger Publishers.

Scalapino, Robert A. and Jun-Yop Kim (eds.). 1983. *North Korea Today: Strategic and Domestic Issues*. Berkeley: Institute of East Asian Studies, University of California.

Scalapino, Robert A. and Chong-Sik Lee. 1972. *Communism in Korea*, 2 vols. Berkeley: University of California Press.

_____. 1960. "The Origins of the Korean Communist Movement." *The Journal of Asian Studies* 20(1):9–31(Nov. 1960);20(2):149–167(February 1961).

Shin-Dong-A. 1989. *Bookhan, 1945–1988* (North Korea, 1945–1988). Seoul, Korea: Dong-A Ilbo Press.

Suh, Dae-Sook. 1988. *Kim Il Sung: The North Korean Leader*. New York: Columbia University Press.

_____. 1970. *Documents of Korean Communism 1918–1948*. Princeton, N.J.: Princeton University Press.

Wall Street Journal. 1979. "Japan and North Korea agree on repayment of debt by Pyongyang." 28 August 1979.

Yang, Ho-Min et al. 1987. *Bookhan sahoe eui jaeinsik* (Reconsideration on North Korean society). No. 1. Seoul, Korea: Hanul Press.

Yum, Hong-Chul et al. 1987. *Bookhan sahoe eui koojo wa byunhwa* (Structure and change of North Korean society). Seoul, Korea: Kyungnam University Press.

Zweig, David. 1989. "A sinologist's observations on North Korea." *Journal of Northeast Asian Studies*, 8(3):62–82.

Two Koreas

Barnds, William J. (ed.) 1976. *The Two Koreas in East Asian Affairs*. New York: New York University Press.

Beijing Review. 1984. "Korea: relief from the North to the South," by Ren Yun. 27:13 (15 October 1984).

Breidenstein, Gerhard. 1975. "Economic comparison of North and South Korea." *Journal of Contemporary Asia*, 5:165–178.

Bridges, Brian. 1986. *Korea and the West*. New York: Routledge & Kegan Paul.

Chien, Frederick Foo. 1967. *The Opening of Korea: A Study of Chinese Diplomacy 1876–1885*. Hamden, Conn.: The Shoe String Press.

Cho, Soon Sung. 1967. *Korea in World Politics 1940–1950: An Evaluation of American Responsibility*. Berkeley: University of California Press.

Choe, Jae-Hyuon. 1986. "Strategic groups of nationalism in nineteenth-century Korea." Journal of Contemporary Asia, 16(2):223–36.

Chung, Joseph Sanghoon. 1980. "The Economic System." Pp. 274–300 in Kim and Park (1980), *Studies on Korea: A Scholar's Guide*. Honolulu: University Press of Hawaii.

Chung, Joseph Sanghoon (ed.). 1966. *Patterns of Economic Development: Korea*. Kalamazoo, MI: Korea Research and Publications.

Clough, Ralph N. 1987. *Embattled Korea: The Rivalry for International Support*. Boulder, CO: Westview Press.

Cumings, Bruce. 1984. *The Two Koreas*. Foreign Policy Association. No. 269. New York: Headline Series.

_____. 1981. *The Origins of the Korean War:Liberation and the Emergence of Separate Regimes 1945–1947*. Princeton: Princeton University Press.

Economic Planning Board. 1970. *Korea Statistical Yearbook, 1970*. Seoul: EPB, Republic of Korea.

Foster-Carter, Aidan. 1987. "Standing up: The two Korean states and the dependency debate—a bipartisan approach." Pp.229–69 in K.D. Kim (ed.), *Dependency Issues in Korean Development: Comparative Perspectives*. Seoul, Korea: Seoul National University Press.

_____. 1985. "Korea and dependency theory." *Monthly Review*, 37(5):27–34.

Gregor, A. James. 1990. *Land of the Morning Calm: Korea and American Security*. Washington, D.C.: Ethics and Public Policy Center.

Halliday, Jon. 1987. "The economies of North and South Korea." Pp. 19–54 in Sullivan and Foss (1987), *Two Koreas—One Future?* Lanham, MD: University Press of America.

Halliday, Jon and Bruce Cumings. 1988. *Korea:the Unknown War*. New York: Pantheon Books.

Han, Sung-Joo and Robert J. Myers. 1987. *Korea: The Year 2000*. Lanham, MD: University Press of America.

Hatada, Takashi. 1969. *A History of Korea*. Translated by Warren W. Smith and Benjamin H. Hazard. Santa Barbara, CA: ABC-Clio Press.

Henderson, Gregory. 1987. "The politics of Korea." Pp. 95–118 in Sullivan and Foss (eds.), *Two Koreas—One Future?* Lanham, MD: University Press of America.

_____. 1968. *Korea: The Politics of the Vortex*. Cambridge, MA: Harvard University Press.

Kihl, Young Whan. 1984. *Politics and Policies in Divided Korea: Regimes in Contest*. Boulder, CO: Westview Press.

Kim, C. I. Eugene and Han-Kyo Kim. 1967. *Korea and the Politics of Imperialism, 1876–1910*. Berkeley: University of California Press.

Kim, Cae-One. 1981. "Economic interchanges between South and North Korea." *Korea and World Affairs*, 5:77–106.

Kim, Hak-Joon. 1977. *The Unification Policy of South and North Korea, 1948–1976*. Seoul: Seoul National University Press.

Kim, Han-Kyo and Hong Kyoo Park (eds.). 1980. *Studies on Korea: A Scholar's Guide*. Honolulu: University Press of Hawaii.

Kim, Joungwon Alexander. 1975. *Divided Korea: The Politics of Development, 1945–1972*. Cambridge, Mass.: East Asian Research Center, Harvard University.

Kim, Key-Hiuk. 1980. *The Last Phase of the East Asian World Order: Korea, Japan, and the Chinese Empire, 1860–1882*. Berkeley: University of California Press.

Kim, Young C. 1977. *The Future of the Korean Peninsula*. New York: Praeger.

Koh, Byung Chul. 1984. *The Foreign Policy Systems of North and South Korea*. Berkeley: University of California Press.

Kwak, Tae-Hwan, Wayne Patterson and Edward A. Olsen. 1983. *The Two Koreas in World Politics*. Seoul: Institute for Far Eastern Studies, Kyungnam University.

Lee, Byoung-Young. 1980. "Comparison of the economic power between South and North Korea." *Korea and World Affairs*, 4:448–63.

Lee, Hyo-Jae. 1985. "National division and family problems." *Korea Journal*, 25(8):4–18.

Lee, Jeong-Soo. 1985. "The heterogeneity of South and North Korea and methods for its elimination:on the class consciousness policy of North Korea." *Korea and World Affairs*, 9(2):292–306.

Lee, Sang-woo. 1982. *Security and Unification of Korea*. Seoul: Sogang University Press.

National Unification Board. 1988. *A White Paper on South-North Dialogue in Korea*. Seoul: NUB.

_____. 1986. A Comparative Study of South and North Koreann Economies. Seoul: NUB.

_____. 1982. A Comparative Study of South and North Korea. Seoul: National Unification Board.

Polomka, Peter. 1986. *The Two Koreas: Catalyst for Conflict in East Asia?* London: IISS.

Rees, David. 1978. *The Two Koreas in Conflict: A Comparative Study*. London: Institute for the Study of Conflict.

Rosenberg, W. 1975. "Economic comparison of North and South Korea." *Journal of Contemporary Asia*, 5:178–204.

Sullivan, John and Roberta Foss (eds.). 1987. *Two Koreas—One Future?* Lanham, MD: University Press of America.

U.S. Central Intelligence Agency. 1988. *World Factbook, 1988*. Washington, D.C.: U.S. CIA.

———. 1978. *Korea: The Economic Race Between the North and the South* (ER 78–10008). Washington, D.C.: National Foreign Assessment Center, U.S. CIA.

Vining, Jr., Daniel R. 1985. "The Growth of Core Region in the Third World." *Scientific America*, 252:42–44 (April).

Statistical Sources

Bank of Korea. 1989. *Economic Statistics Yearbook, 1989* and various years (1955–1989). Seoul: BOK.

Economic Planning Board. 1989. *Korea Statistical Yearbook, 1989*. Seoul: National Bureau of Statistics, EPB.

———. 1989. *Social Indicators in Korea*. Seoul: EPB.

———. 1989. *Korean Economic Indicators*. Seoul: EPB.

Economist Intelligence Unit. 1989. *Country Profile, 1987–88*. London: EIU.

Europa World Yearbook, The. 1990. *The Europa World Yearbook, 1990* and various years (1984–1990).

Far Eastern Economic Review. 1990. *Asia Yearbook, 1990* and various years (1966–1990). Hong Kong: FEER.

International Institute for Strategic Studies. 1990. *The Military Balance 1989–1990*. London: IISS.

U.S. Arms Control and Disarmament Agency (ACDA). 1988. *World Military Expenditures and Arms Transfers, 1987*. Washington, D.C.: U.S. ACDA.

U.S. Department of State. 1986. *Background Notes:North Korea*, and various years (1984–86).

———. 1987. *Background Notes:South Korea*, and various years (1984–87).

World Bank. 1990. *World Development Report, 1990* and various years (1979–1990). New York: Oxford University Press.

———. 1987. *Korea: Managing the Industrial Transition*. Washington, D.C.: World Bank.

Worldmark. 1984. *Worldmark Encyclopedia of Nations: Asia and Oceania*. New York: Worldmark Press.

Glossary

CHAEBOL. A system of highly centralized family-based industrial and business conglomerates in South Korea. Comparable to *zaibatsu* in Japan

CHOLLIMA WORK TEAM MOVEMENT. Intensive mass campaign to increase economic production in North Korea inaugurated in 1959; began as Chollima Movement, named after the legendary Chinese Flying Horse said to have galloped a phenomenal distance in a single day. Peasants and factory workers were exhorted to excel in the manner of Chollima riders, and exemplary individuals and work teams were awarded special Chollima titles.

CHON. *See* North Korean WON.

CHONMIN. The "despised people" or pariah class of Yi Korea, which included buchers, slaves, jailers, and Buddhist monks and nuns.

CHONGSAN-NI METHOD. A personalized "on-the-spot" management method or spirit reputedly developed by Kim Il Sung in February 1960 during a visit to the Chongsan-ni Cooperative Farm in South Pyongan Province. Also spelled Chongsan-ri. The method has three main components: party and government functionaries must eschew their bureaucratic tendency to only issue orders and directives; they must mingle with the farmers and uncover and solve their problems through comradely guidance; and they should give solid technological guidance to spur efficient and productive achievement.

CHUNGIN. Literally, central mem or middle people. A small class of lowly artisans and technical or administrative officials in Yi Dynasty below the *yangban*, so named because many of them lived in the central district of Seoul.

FIVE RELATIONSHIPS. The Confucian concept of ideal social relationships, formulated by classical Chinese philosophers such as Mencius (372–289 B.C.), which states that there should be affection between father and son, righteousness between ruler and minister, attention to their separate functions between husband and wife, proper order between old and young, and faithfulness between friends.

HWAN. *See* South Korean WON.

JUCHE. The ideology of self-identity, self-reliance, and creativeness, popularized in North Korea since 1955 as an official guideline for independence in politics and foreign policy, self-sustenance in economic endeavors, and self-defense in military preparedness.

JUCHE SASANG. *See* JUCHE.

PYONG. A unit of areas used in both South and North Korea. Approximately six square feet.

SADAE. Literally, "serving the big." Referred to the suzerain-dependent relationship that had characterized the traditional East Asian international system. One of the cardinal rules of the Yi Dynasty's foreign relations in which the submission and loyalty to a strong China was demanded. This had become a mental fixation that discouraged national self-reliance, but later on contributed to a great extent to the formation of the "imitation" principle of the capitalist South Korean development.

SADAECHUII. *See* SADAE.

SAEMAEUL (NEW COMMUNITY) MOVEMENT. A mass mobilization technique started by the government of South Korea in 1971 to improve the environment, living conditions, and incomes of the rural population, with an emphasis on selective investments and village self-help; stimulated by the early success of the technique in North Korea. Since 1974 there has been an urban Saemaeul Movement, which has stressed citizenship and good neighborliness.

SANGMIN. Commoners in Yi Dynasty. The largest segment of traditional Korean society, distinguished from the *yangban*, *chungin*, and *chonmin*.

SIRHAK. Literally, "practical learning." A reform-oriented Confucianism that sought for the ways to develop traditional Korean society into modern one through various policy reforms regarding slavery, distribution of arable land, recruitment of government official, financial and military institutions, and local administration.

SOHAK. Literally, "Western learning" that tried to learn more about Western civilization, particularly, industrial products, know-how, and the social systems of Europe and America; through the mediation of Japan, which achieved a rapid development after the Meiji Restoration in 1868.

SUNGBOON. A family's class background, by which the government of North Korea classifies its people.

TAEAN WORK SYSTEM. A managerial and guidance system or method applied to factories and enterprises in North Korea. Begun in December 1961 by Kim Il Sung while on a visit to the Taean Electrical Appliance Plant, the system adapted the Chongsan-ni Method to industry. Higher level functionaries must assist lower level functionaries and workers in a spirit of close consultation and comradery. Party committees take control of the general management of factories and enterprises and stress both political or ideological work and technological expertise. The system allows for material incentives to production.

THREE REVOLUTIONS. Refers to "ideological, technical, and cultural revolutions" that have been stressed by North Korea since the early 1960s.

THREE REVOLUTION TEAM MOVEMENT. Inaugurated in February 1973 as "a powerful revolutionary method of guidance" for the Three Revolutions. Under this method of the Three Revolution Teams are sent to factories, enterprises, and rural and fishing villages for on-the-spot guidance and problem solving in close consultation with local personnel.

TONGHAK. Or DONGHAK. Literally, "Eastern Learning," and indigenous religious movement founded by Choe Che-U in the early 1860s, which spearheaded a popular, antiforeign rebellion in 1894. Later renamed CHONDOGYO. The Tonghak revolution was the beginning of the Korean nationalist movements that in part incorporated a xenophobic nature. This xenophobic tradition served to a great extent to the JUCHE SASANG, the underlying principles of the Communist North Korean development.

WON. The monetary unit used on South and North Korea, though value differs between them. North Korean *won* is divided into 100 *chon* and multiple exchange rates have been used. Rate for almost all official transactions has been about 1 *won* per US$1: 1.20 *won* from 1961 to 1970, 1.11 *won* in 1971 and 1972; .96 *won* from 1974 to 1977, .93 *won* in 1978, .86 *won* in 1980, .94 *Won* in

1985, and .98 *won* in 1990. Commercial rate for most foreign trade was, per US$1: 2.20 *won* from 1961 to 1966, 2.57 *won* from 1967 to 1970, 2.36 *won* in 1971, 2.66 *won* in 1975, 3.50 *won* from 1976 to 1978, 2.64 *won* in 1979–80, 2.18 *won* in 1985, and 2.18 *won* in 1988. South Korea performed a currency reform in 1961, which converted *hwan* to *won* at the rate of 10 to 1 and returned to a managed, flexible exchange rate. Then, a fixed exchange rate was adopted from December 1974 to January 1980 at US$1 = 484 *won*. After that the Bank of Korea managed a flexible exchange rate, calculating the daily rate with respect to a secret basket of foreign currencies. The rate in 1990 was 690.37 *won*.

YANGBAN. Literally, "two classes," that is, civil and military officials of Yi Dynasty. Refers to the scholar-offical ruling class of traditional Korea, distinguished for its knowledge of neo-Confucianism and its monopoly of high government positions; more broadly, families or lineages decendended from scholar-officials, and scholars who had passed the civil service examinations even though they had not secured an official post.

YUSHIN. Literally, "revitalizing." Referred to the Yushin constitution promulgated by the South Korean government under martial law in October 1972 allowing President Park to serve an unlimited number of six-year terms and exercise extensive power including the right of issuing emergency measures.

ZAIBATSU. A system of highly centralized family-based industrial conglomerates in prewar Japan.

Index

Adenauer, Konrad, 27
Advanced Capitalist Economy (ACE), 38; *see also* capitalism; capitalist economy; market economy
Africa, 7
Agriculture, 35, 39, 48, 57, 62, 70, 73–75, 79, 120, 121, 137–38, 138, 143, 194, 205
Albania, 10
American Military Government (AMG), 108, 110, 112, 113, 115, 131
An Chang Ho, 60, 176
Annam, 32, 53
Anticommunism, 113
Arch of Triumph, 102
Argentina, 47, 166
Arms Control and Disarmament Agency (ACDA), 16, 18, 158, 159, 160, 165, 166
Arms trade, 83; *see also* military trade
Asia, 7; East, 54, 141; Northeast, xi, 48, 54, 206
Autarky, 7, 8, 10, 80, 113, 140, 151, 205; *see also juche*; self-reliance
Authoritarian(ism), 1, 7, 10, 42, 46, 47, 49, 123, 173, 175, 181, 189, 205

Banister, J., 92, 93
Basic Law, 28
Bourgeoisie, 2, 35, 46, 126, 194, 204
Brandt, Willy, 27, 28, 35
Brazil, 44, 45, 47
Brun, E., 5
Buddhism, 33, 102, 177, 190, 196
Bunge, F.M., 5
Bureaucracy, 42, 54–55, 56, 57, 175, 179; in North Korea, 174

Bureaucratic-Authoritarianism (BA), 11, 46–47, 202–3
Burma, 84

Cairo Conference, 61
Cambodia, 32
Canada, 141
Capital. *See* foreign capital
Capitalism, xi, 1, 2, 6, 7, 8, 9, 10–11, 12, 13, 23, 34–35, 36, 38, 42, 43, 47, 113, 114, 124, 130, 169, 202
Capitalist economy, 4, 8, 9, 122, 142, 200; *see also* market economy; world system
Cardoso, F.H., 12, 45
Carter, Jimmy, 161
Catholics, 33
Central Intelligence Agency, 5, 16, 137, 160
Chaju, 60, 134
Chaebol, 118, 126, 182
Chang Myon, 109, 113, 117
Chawi, 134
Chiang Ching-Kuo, 29
Chiang Kai-Shek, 29
Chile, 47
China, xi, 12, 17, 23, 28–31, 48, 53, 54, 58, 80, 91, 107, 111, 112, 121, 128, 129, 131, 146, 147, 151, 152, 153, 160, 166, 167, 199, 206; Communist Party of, 9; North Korea aid from, 120
Ch'ing Dynasty, 29
Chirot, D., 3
Cho Man-Sik, 110, 112
Chollima Movement, 91, 121, 127, 128, 148